AF522072

Hotel, Tourism and Catering Management

HOTEL, TOURISM AND CATERING MANAGEMENT

Ashim Gupta

CENTRUM PRESS
NEW DELHI-110002 (INDIA)

CENTRUM PRESS
H.O.: 4360/4, Ansari Road, Daryaganj,
New Delhi-110002 (India)
Tel: 23278000, 23261597, 23255577, 23286875

B.O.: No. 1015, Ist Main Road, BSK IIIrd Stage,
IIIrd Phase, IIIrd Block, Bengaluru-560085 (INDIA)
Tel: 080-41723429

Email: centrumpress@gmail.com
Visit us at: www.centrumpress.com

Hotel, Tourism and Catering Management

First Edition, 2011

ISBN 978-93-81293-84-3

PRINTED IN INDIA

Printed at Tarun Offset, Delhi

Contents

Preface

Catering is the business of providing food (and often, service) for events. Social caterers are one of the fastest-growing divisions of the hotel industry. This book is a complete conduct to flourishing catering business management. In addition to creating and executing a great menu, successful catering also takes know-how for marketing your business, keeping costs in line, and ensuring the entire operation runs efficiently. Tourism Management will be essential reading for anyone interested in tourism-including tourists-and who want to recognize how the business works, how it makes proceeds and what are the effects of its activities on objectives.

The book examines all the explanation developments now affecting the tourism industry from the impact of technology to the low-cost airlines has transformed the market for leisure travel. "Hotel, Tourism and Catering Management" presents professionals and hopeful caterers detailed recommendation on all the vital business features of the subject for on- and off-premise catering. Updated to meet the needs of this fast-growing industry, the book features material on non-hotel catering operations-such as small business management and running your own catering and Tourism operation. Hope the book is very beneficial to all the readers especially to Hotel Management Students.

Author

1

Basics of Hotel Management

HOTEL BUSINESS ORGANISATIONS CATEGORIES

HOTEL MANAGER

The Hotel manager oversees all of a hotel's daily operations, from staffing to coordinating fresh-cut flowers for the lobby. Many, over time, are given long-term responsibility for negotiating contracts with vendors, negotiating leases with on-site shops, and physically upgrading the hotel. Hotel managers usually relish "the ability to put your own distinctive style on the [hotel] experience." While managing a hotel and giving it your unique flair are wonderful, they come with full responsibility for failure.

"The better you are at what you do, the more responsibilities you are given, the more chances you have to fail," mentioned one hotel manager. When things fall apart, "no one is a hotel manager's friend." Hotel managers can feel great about their positions, create strong relationships with regular customers, and maintain an amicable working environment.

But should the bottom line waver and financial woes occur, the first neck on the chopping block is the hotel manager's. Those in the hotel management industry say that sometimes it seems that you need "to be born on the planet Krypton" to be a good hotel manager because only Superman could juggle the administrative, aesthetic, and financial decisions which constitute daily life on the job. Over 70 per cent of the respondents said that tired was an understatement about how they felt at the end of the day or night. A hotel manager's position as a liaison between the ownership and the staff can be difficult and isolating. But those who can put up with the long hours, the high degree of responsibility, and the variety of tasks emerge with a solid degree of satisfaction and a desire to continue in the profession.

The average tenure of a hotel manager is 6.7 years, though this figure doesn't represent the number of managers who work for two years and those who work for decades. Many work at a variety of hotels, build up their resumes, and then find positions that allow them the freedom to operate their own establishments.Aspiring hotel managers used to begin at the reception desk, as part of the wait staff, or as members of the cleaning staff, then work their way up the ladder. As hotels have become more commercial properties and the duties of hotel managers have expanded, this avenue of advancement has closed off.

Now hotel manager hopefuls go to hotel management school, and those who don't should garner as much practical hotel experience as possible. Each chain or specific hotel puts new employees through their own training programmes, so those applying for jobs should learn all they can about the scope and functioning of the specific hotels where they wish to work. Part of life as a hotel manager can be similar to the life of a doctor, as managers can be called to duty at any time of the day or night.

Hotel managers must handle any and all emergencies, and those who wish to remain in the profession and maintain respect must be quick-thinking and decisive. Candidates should have a good organizational and financial background, excellent communication and interpersonal skills, and strong self-discipline. They should also be extremely detail-oriented; when running a hotel, there is no such thing as an unimportant detail.

The good manager drives himself to improve and upgrade the hotel at every available opportunity.A hotel manager is responsible for the day-to-day management of a hotel and its staff and has commercial accountability for planning, organising and directing all hotel services, including front-of-house, banqueting and housekeeping. In larger hotels, managers often have a specific remit and make up a general management team.

Financial management—preparing budgets and marketing strategies and achieving targets for the business—plays a major role. The manager must strike a balance between customer satisfaction and effective business management, ensuring financial viability, and facilitate a smooth-running customer service, whilst ensuring staff work together as a team.

Typical Work Activities

Typical work activities vary depending on the size and type of hotel, but may include:

- Planning and organising accommodation, catering and other hotel services;
- Promoting and marketing the business;
- Managing budgets and financial plans;
- Maintaining statistical and financial records;
- Achieving profit targets;
- Recruiting, training and monitoring staff;
- Planning work schedules;
- Meeting and greeting customers;
- Dealing with customer complaints and comments;
- Addressing problems and troubleshooting;
- Ensuring events and conferences run smoothly;
- Supervising maintenance, supplies and furnishings;
- Dealing with contractors and suppliers;
- Ensuring security is effective;
- Carrying out inspections of property and services;
- Ensuring compliance with licensing laws, health and safety and other statutory regulations.

The manager of a large hotel may have less contact with guests but will spend time meeting heads of department and planning and monitoring the progress of business strategies. In a smaller establishment, the manager is much more involved in the hands-on day-to-day running of the hotel, which may include carrying out reception duties or serving meals if the need arises. A significant number of hotel managers are self-employed and this can lead to a more general management experience, from greeting guests to managing finances.

How to Become a Hotel Manager

- Ask yourself if you have excellent interpersonal, communication and organizational skills. They are necessary for a successful hotel management career.
- Obtain a college degree in hotel management or restaurant management. Remember that a food services department contributes greatly to the profits of a hotel; a successful restaurant manager can see his or her career advance quickly.
- Take advantage of work-study programmes offered by many colleges so that you will gain solid experience working in hotels.
- Expect to go through a hotel's training programme once you are hired after college. During the first couple of years you will be handling only relatively mundane duties, instead of providing your input on issues such as staffing, hotel decor or conventions.
- Understand that you might be offered a position as a front office manager, a food and beverage manager, a convention services manager, or any of a number of administrative positions after your training period. If you are successful at different managerial positions, your career will benefit in the long run.
- Be aware that a promotion might require you to relocate for a few years if you work for a hotel chain that has properties throughout the country.
- You will need to quickly become proficient with computers because of their widespread use in hotel reservations, billing and overall management operations.
- Consider working for hotels in warm tourist destinations or snowy mountains, depending on your preferred lifestyle.

- Be prepared for long hours, night and weekend work, and the occasional unhappy guest.

Catering managers plan, organise and manage the food and beverage services of organisations and businesses, both inside and outside the hospitality industry, with the aim of achieving good quality at low cost and maintaining high standards of hygiene and customer satisfaction. There is a range of jobs in catering management, along with a number of different routes into the industry. Roles include: managing restaurants, bars and other outlets in hotels, resorts or liners; providing catering services at events; and running catering operations at hospitals, schools and other organisations.

With ongoing growth in the service industry, opportunities in this demanding but rewarding area continue to grow. The role varies according to the size and nature of the establishment: in a small operation, the catering manager has more of a 'hands on' role and will be involved in the day-to-day running of the operation; in contract catering, the catering manager will spend time negotiating with the client organisation, assessing its requirements and ensuring that it is satisfied with the service delivered.

Typical tasks will include:

- Recruiting and training permanent and casual staff;
- Organising, leading and motivating the catering team;
- Planning menus in consultation with chefs;
- Ensuring health and safety regulations are strictly observed;
- Budgeting and establishing financial targets;
- Monitoring the quality of the product and service provided;
- Keeping financial and administrative records;
- Managing the payroll and monitoring spending levels,
- Maintaining stock levels and ordering new supplies as required;
- Interacting with customers if involved with 'front of house' work;
- Liaising with suppliers and clients;
- Negotiating contracts with customers.

In more senior posts, principal tasks will involve:

- Setting and agreeing budgets;
- Monitoring quality standards;
- Overseeing the management of the facilities, for example checking events bookings and the allocation of resources and staff;
- Planning new promotions and initiatives, and contributing to business development;
- Dealing with staffing and client issues, as they arise.

FOOD AND RESTAURANT MANAGER

Fast food restaurant managers are responsible for the provision of standardised food and customer service in outlets based in the high street, motor service areas, stations, airports or multiplexes.Drawing on all the operational functions of a business, the work involves applying financial, marketing and operational know-how, and supervising and training staff.Managers plan, organise, and co-ordinate all resources and activities in a store.

The work involves: setting targets, planning budgets, and controlling stock; recruiting, training and inspiring restaurant teams; creating and driving marketing campaigns; and building bridges with the local community. Ultimately, it is the manager's ideas, initiative and personality that shape the restaurant.

Tasks typically involve:

- Organising the store in terms of products, equipment and people;
- Planning and checking work schedules;
- Carrying out audits to check health safety, food safety and quality of service in the restaurant;
- Making sure the fast-track audit is completed daily to check the safety of equipment and that food is properly cooked, only in-date stock is used, and all other products are discarded;
- Carrying out work outside the restaurant, including 'mystery shopping' at other restaurants within the chain;

- Attending weekly meetings with senior managers;
- Dealing with problems, queries, complaints, staff and customers in the store;
- Monitoring and maintaining high standards of food, service and hygiene;
- Ensuring the company's required standards of customer care are met;
- Administering payrolls;
- Checking and securing cash receipts;
- Budgeting to ensure maximum profitability;
- Achieving set profit and loss targets;
- Maintaining and securing equipment and buildings and all company assets contained within the unit;
- Publicising and marketing restaurants in the locality;
- Motivating restaurant teams;
- Recruiting, selecting and training new staff and fully inducting the restaurant team in accordance with company policy;
- Developing all team members to their fullest potential using the performance management/review system and identifying individual training needs;
- Ensuring the implementation and maintenance of legislation, company standards and procedures;
- Recognising new trends and implementing action plans accordingly;
- Acting as a communication link between senior teams and the restaurant team;
- Leading by example, acting as a role model for the restaurant team.

A successful manager will strike the right balance between creating both a good service for restaurant customers and a fun work environment for members of staff.

CATERING MANAGER

Catering managers plan, organise and manage the food and beverage services of organisations and businesses, both inside and outside the hospitality industry, with the aim of achieving good quality at low cost and maintaining high standards of hygiene and customer satisfaction. There is a range of jobs in catering management, along with a number of different routes into the industry. Roles include: managing restaurants, bars and other outlets in hotels, resorts or liners; providing catering services at events; and running catering operations at hospitals, schools and other organisations. With ongoing growth in the service industry, opportunities in this demanding but rewarding area continue to grow.

Typical Work Activities

The role varies according to the size and nature of the establishment: in a small operation, the catering manager has more of a 'hands on' role and will be involved in the day-to-day running of the operation; in contract catering, the catering manager will spend time negotiating with the client organisation, assessing its requirements and ensuring that it is satisfied with the service delivered.

Typical tasks will include:

- Recruiting and training permanent and casual staff;
- Organising, leading and motivating the catering team;
- Planning menus in consultation with chefs;
- Ensuring health and safety regulations are strictly observed;
- Budgeting and establishing financial targets;
- Monitoring the quality of the product and service provided;
- Keeping financial and administrative records;
- Managing the payroll and monitoring spending levels;
- Maintaining stock levels and ordering new supplies as required;
- Interacting with customers if involved with 'front of house' work;
- Liaising with suppliers and clients;
- Negotiating contracts with customers.

In more senior posts, principal tasks will involve:

- Setting and agreeing budgets;
- Monitoring quality standards;
- Overseeing the management of the facilities, for

example checking events bookings and the allocation of resources and staff;
- Planning new promotions and initiatives, and contributing to business development;
- Dealing with staffing and client issues, as they arise.

HUMAN RESOURCES

Human resources has at least two meanings depending on context. The original usage derives from political economy and economics, where it was traditionally called labour, one of three factors of production. The more common usage within corporations and businesses refers to the individuals within the firm, and to the portion of the firm's organization that deals with hiring, firing, training, and other personnel issues. Modern analysis emphasizes that human beings are not predictable commodity "resources" with definitions totally controlled by contract, but are creative and social beings that make contributions beyond "labour" to a society and to civilization.

The broad term human capital has evolved to contain the complexity of this term, and in macro-economics the term "firm-specific human capital" has evolved to represent the original meaning of term "human resources".Advocating the central role of "human resources" or human capital in enterprises and societies has been a traditional role of socialist parties, who claim that value is primarily created by their activity, and accordingly justify a larger claim of profits or relief from these enterprises or societies.

Critics say this is just a bargaining tactic which grew out of various practices of medieval European guilds into the modern trade union and collective bargaining unit. A contrary view, common to capitalist parties, is that it is the infrastructural capital and intellectual capital owned and fused by "management" that provides most value in financial capital terms.

This likewise justifies a bargaining position and a general view that "human resources" are interchangeable. A significant sign of consensus on this latter point is the ISO 9000 series of standards which requires a "job description" of every participant in a productive enterprise. In general, heavily unionized nations such as France and Germany have adopted and encouraged such descriptions especially within trade unions. One view of this trend is that a strong social consensus on political economy and a good social welfare system facilitates labour mobility and tends to make the entire economy more productive, as labour can move from one enterprise to another with little controversy or difficulty in adapting.

An important controversy regarding labour mobility shows the broader philosophical issue with usage of the phrase "human resources": governments of developing nations often regard developed nations that encourage immigration or "guest workers" as appropriating human capital that is rightfully part of the developing nation and required to further its growth as a civilization. They argue that this appropriation is similar to colonial commodity fiat wherein a colonizing European power would define an arbitrary price for natural resources, extracting which diminished national natural capital.

The debate regarding "human resources" versus human capital thus in many ways echoes the debate regarding natural resources versus natural capital. Over time the United Nations have come to more generally support the developing nations' point of view, and have requested significant offsetting "foreign aid" contributions so that a developing nation losing human capital does not lose the capacity to continue to train new people in trades, professions, and the arts. An extreme version of this view is that historical inequities such as African slavery must be compensated by current developed nations, which benefitted from stolen "human resources" as they were developing.

This is an extremely controversial view, but it echoes the general theme of converting human capital to "human resources" and thus greatly diminishing its value to the host society, *i.e.* "Africa", as it is put to narrow imitative use as "labour" in the using society. In the very narrow context of corporate "human resources", there is a contrasting pull to reflect and require workplace diversity that echoes the diversity of a global customer base. Foreign language and culture skills, ingenuity, humour, and careful listening, are examples of traits that such programmes typically require. It would appear that these evidence a general shift to the human capital point of view, and an acknowledgement that human beings do contribute much more to a productive enterprise than "work": they bring their character, their ethics, their creativity, their social connections, and in some cases even their pets and children, and alter the character of a workplace.

The term corporate culture is used to characterize such processes. The traditional but extremely narrow context of hiring, firing, and job description is considered a 20th century anachronism. Most corporate organizations that compete in the modern global economy have adopted a view of human capital that mirrors the modern consensus.

Some of these, in turn, deprecate the term "human resources" as useless. As the term refers to predictable exploitations of human capital in one context or another, it can still be said to apply to manual labour, mass agriculture, low skill "McJobs" in service industries, military and other work that has clear job descriptions, and which generally do not encourage creative or social contributions. In general the abstractions of macro-economics treat it this way—as it characterizes no mechanisms to represent choice or ingenuity. So one interpretation is that "firm-specific human capital" as defined in macro-economics is the modern and correct definition of "human resources"—and that this is inadequate to represent the contributions of "human resources" in any modern theory of political economy.

In terms of recruitment and selection it is important to consider carrying out a thorough job analysis to determine the level of skills/technical abilities, competencies, flexibility of the employee required etc. At this point it is important to consider both the internal and external factors that can have an impact on the recruitment of employees. The external factors are those out-with the powers of the organization and include issues such as current and future trends of the labour market *e.g.* skills, education level, government investment into industries etc. On the other hand internal influences are easier to control, predict and monitor, for example management styles or even the organizational culture.

In order to know the business environment in which any organization operates, three major trends should be considered:

- *Demographics:* The characteristics of a population/ workforce, for example, age, gender or social class. This type of trend may have an effect in relation to pension offerings, insurance packages etc.
- *Diversity*: The variation within the population/ workplace. Changes in society now mean that a larger proportion of organizations are made up of female employees in comparison to thirty years ago. Also over recent years organizations have become more culturally diverse and have increased the number of working patterns to cope with the changes in both society and the global market. It is important to note here that an organisation must consider the ethic and legal implications of their decisions in relation to the HRM policies they enact to protect employees. Employers have to be acutely aware of the rise in discrimination, unfair dismissal and sexual/racial harassment cases in recent years and the detrimental effects this can have on the employees and the organisation. Anti-discrimination legislation over the past 30 years has provided a foundation for an increasing interest in diversity at work which is "about creating a working culture that seeks respects and values difference."
- *Skills and qualifications*: As industries move from manual to a more managerial professions so does the need for more highly skilled graduates. If the market is 'tight' *i.e.* not enough staff for the jobs, employers will have to compete for employees by offering financial rewards, community investment etc.also the political issues

In regards to how individuals respond to the changes in a labour market the following should be understood:

- *Geographical spread*: How far is the job from the individual? The distance to travel to work should be in line with the pay offered by the organization and the transportation and infrastructure of the area will also be an influencing factor in deciding who will apply for a post.
- *Occupational structure*: The norms and values of the different careers within an organization. Mahoney 1989 developed 3 different types of occupational structure namely craft, organization career and unstructured.
- Generational Difference: Different age categories of employees have certain characteristics, for example their behaviour and their expectations of the organisation.

Recruitment methods are wide and varied, it is important that the job is described correctly and any personal specifications stated. Job recruitment methods can be through job centres, employment agencies/consultants, headhunting, and local/national newspapers. It is important that the correct media is chosen to ensure an appropriate response to the advertised post.

HUMAN RESOURCES WITHIN FIRMS

Though human resources have been part of business and organizations since the first days of agriculture, the modern concept of human resources began in reaction to the efficiency focus of Taylorism in the early 1900s. By 1920, psychologists and employment experts in the United States started the human relations movement, which viewed workers in terms of their psychology and fit with companies, rather than as interchangeable parts.

This movement grew throughout the middle of the 20th century, placing emphasis on how leadership, cohesion, and loyalty played important roles in organizational success. Although this view was increasingly challenged by more quantitatively rigorous and less "soft" management techniques in the 1960s and beyond, human resources had gained a permanent role within the firm. Facing mankind's problems it is opportune to mobilize as many intellectual resources as possible in order to resolve the emerging troubles. The students have to be trained to construct pertinent knowledge together. Students can be trained in constructing knowledge outside the classroom too.

They have to adopt following attitudes:

- Be aware that they are bearing resources
- Be aware that they have to increase their own resources in order to be more attractive inside the community
- Be aware that they can increase their own resources if they communicate
- Be aware that they can increase their own resources if they share their knowledge with other people
- Ability to identify resource from other community members and to make this resource available for all the group
- Ability to search for pertinent resources outside the group
- Ability to connect people looking for proposing resources
- Ability to organize collective thinking in networks

EMPLOYEE ENGAGEMENT

Employee engagement is a concept that is generally viewed in terms of employees feeling a strong emotional bond to the organization that employs them. This is associated with people demonstrating a willingness to recommend the organization to others and commit time and effort to help the organization succeed.

It suggests that people are motivated by intrinsic factors rather than simply focusing on extrinsic factors. The concept has gained popularity as various studies have demonstrated links with productivity. In 1999, The Gallup Organization published research that showed that engaged employees are more productive, more profitable, more customer-focused, safer, and less likely to leave their employer. The review stated that "engagement with employees within a firm has shown to motivate the employee to work beyond personal factors and work more for the success of the firm." Watson Wyatt found that high-commitment organizations out-performed those with low commitment by 47% in the 2000 study and by 200% in the 2002 study.

In a study of professional service firms, the Hay Group found that offices with engaged employees were up to 43% more productive, based on a comparison of revenue generation. Recent research has focused on developing a better understanding of how variables such as quality of work relationships and values of the organization interact and their link to important work outcomes. From the perspective of the employee, "outcomes" range from strong commitment to the isolation of oneself from the organization. The study done by the Gallup Management Journal has shown that only 29 per cent of employees are actively engaged in their jobs. Those "engaged" employees work with passion and feel a strong connection to their company.

Moreover, 54 per cent of employees are not engaged meaning that they go through each workday putting time but no passion into their work. Also, Seventeen per cent of employees are actively disengaged, meaning that they are busy acting out of their own personal unhappiness, which undermines what their engaged co-workers are trying to accomplish. Access to a reliable model enables organizations to conduct validation studies to establish the relationship of employee engagement to productivity/performance and other measures linked to effectiveness.

It is an important principle of occupational psychology that validation studies should be anchored in reliable scales and not simply focus on individual elements in isolation. To understand how high levels of employee engagement affect organizational performance/productivity it is important to have an a priori model that demonstrates how the scales interact. There is also overlap between this concept and those relating to well-being at work and the psychological contract. As employee productivity is clearly connected with employee engagement, creating an environment that encourages employee engagement is considered to be essential in the effective management of human capital.

Employee engagement will be influenced by:

- Employee perceptions of job importance. This study has found that "...an employees attitude towards the job['s importance] and the company had the greatest impact on loyalty and customer service then all other employee factors combined."
- Employee clarity of job expectations. "If expectations are not clear and basic materials and equipment not provided, negative emotions such as boredom or resentment may result, and the employee may then become focused on surviving more then thinking about how he can help the organization succeed."
- Career advancement/improvement opportunities. "Plant supervisors and managers indicated that many plant improvements were being made outside the suggestion system, where employees initiated changes in order to reap the bonuses generated by the subsequent cost savings."
- Regular feedback and dialogue with superiors. "Feedback is the key to giving employees a sense of where they're going, but many organizations are remarkably bad at giving it." "'What I really wanted to hear was 'Thanks. You did a good job.' But all my boss did was hand me a check."
- Quality of working relationships with peers, superiors, and subordinates. "...if employee's relationship with their managers is fractured, then no amount of perks will persuade the employees to perform at top levels. Employee engagement is a direct reflection of how employees feel about their relationship with the boss."
- Perceptions of the ethos and values of the organization. "'Inspiration and values' is the most

important of the six drivers in our Engaged Performance model. Inspirational leadership is the ultimate perk. In its absence, [it] is unlikely to engage employees."

As additional research becomes available, the significance of the various factors will become more evident.

HUMAN INTERACTION MANAGEMENT

Human Interaction Management is the set of principles and patterns for structuring, supporting and controlling human work practices proposed by Keith Harrison-Broninski in his 2005 book "Human Interactions". Current mainstream techniques and tools for work support, whether categorized as Workflow or as Business Process Management deal only with "mechanistic" business processes.

In such business processes, human involvement is limited to key data entry and decision points. Workflow/BPM techniques and tools deal with only the externally-observable aspects of work—tasks, that are visible from outside. HIM extends this to include support for "human-driven" processes focused on human creativity and collaboration.

To achieve this, HIM deals not only with tasks, but also with those aspects of work visible from inside—information, interaction and innovation. In HIM, a business process requiring human knowledge, judgement and experience is divided into Roles, which are then assigned to the appropriate members of an organization via a Human Interaction Management System. A HIMS is also used to manage the work and integrate it with organizational strategy/tactics, via separation into "levels of control".

The main focus of HIM is currently on the integration of organizational objectives with human work practices, in order to implement strategy/tactics and fulfil requirements for compliance. However, HIM has application beyond the improvement of organizational efficiency, since it provides a rich set of patterns for structuring and managing collaborative work that are also finding application in spheres such as social/political negotiation, law enforcement and healthcare.

ACCOUNTING MANAGEMENT

Accounting Management is the practical application of management techniques to control and report on the financial health of the organization. This involves the analysis, planning, implementation, and control of programmes designed to provide financial data reporting for managerial decision making. This includes the maintenance of bank accounts, developing financial statements, cash flow and financial performance analysis. Accounting management is a mandatory knowledge module of any MBA programme.

COST MANAGEMENT

Cost management is the process whereby companies use cost accounting to report or control the various costs of doing business. The term CM is widely used in business today. Unfortunately there is no uniform definition. We use CM to describe the approaches and activities of managers in short run and long run planning and control decisions that increase value for customers and lower costs of products and services. For example, managers make decisions regarding the amount and kind of material being used, changes of plant processes, and changes in product designs. Information from accounting systems helps managers make such decisions, but the information and the accounting systems themselves are not cost management. Cost management has a broad focus. It includes – but is not confined to – the continuous reduction of costs. The planning and control of costs is usually inextricably linked with revenue and profit planning. For instance, to enhance revenues and profits, managers often deliberately incur additional costs for advertising and product modifications. Cost management is not practiced in isolation. It's an integral part of general management strategies and their implementation. Examples include programme that enhance customer satisfaction and quality as well as programmes that promote blockbuster new product development.

CUSTOMER RELATIONSHIP MANAGEMENT

Customer relationship management covers methods and

technologies used by companies to manage their relationships with clients. Information stored on existing customers is analysed and used to this end. Automated CRM processes are often used to generate automatic personalized marketing based on the customer information stored in the system. Customer relationship management is a corporate level strategy, focusing on creating and maintaining relationships with customers.

Several commercial CRM software packages are available which vary in their approach to CRM. However, CRM is not a technology itself, but rather a holistic approach to an organisation's philosophy, placing the emphasis firmly on the customer. CRM governs an organization's philosophy at all levels, including policies and processes, front-of-house customer service, employee training, marketing, systems and information management. CRM systems are integrated end-to-end across marketing, sales, and customer service.

A CRM system should:

- Identify factors important to clients.
- Promote a customer-oriented philosophy
- Adopt customer-based measures
- Develop end-to-end processes to serve customers
- Provide successful customer support
- Handle customer complaints
- Track all aspects of sales
- Create a holistic view of customers' sales and services information

There are three fundamental components in CRM:

- Operational—automation of basic business processes
- Analytical—analysis of customer data and behaviour using business intelligence
- Collaborative—communicating with clients

Operational CRM provides automated support to "front office" business processes. Each interaction with a customer is generally added to a customer's history, and staff can retrieve information on customers from the database as necessary. The Gartner Group operational CRM typically involves three general areas:

- Sales force automation: SFA automates some of a company's critical sales and sales force management tasks, such as forecasting, sales administration, tracking customer preferences and demographics, performance management, lead management, account management, contact management and quote management.
- Customer service and support: CSS automates certain service requests, complaints, product returns and enquiries.
- Enterprise marketing automation: EMA provides information about the business environment, including information on competitors, industry trends, and macroenvironmental variables. EMA applications are used to improve marketing efficiency.

Integrated CRM software is often known as a "front office solution", as it deals directly with customers. Many call centres use CRM software to store customer information. When a call is received, the system displays the associated customer information. During and following the call, the call centre agent dealing with the customer can add further information. Some customer services can be fully automated, such as allowing customers to access their bank account details online or via a WAP phone.

Analytical CRM

Analytical CRM analyses data in an attempt to identify means to enhance a company's relationship with its clients.

The results of an analysis can be used to design targeted marketing campaigns, for example:

- Acquisition: Cross-selling, up-selling
- Retention: Retaining existing customers
- Information: Providing timely and regular information to customers

Other examples of the applications of analyses include:

- Contact optimization
- Evaluating and improving customer satisfaction
- Optimizing sales coverage

- Fraud detection
- Financial forecasts
- Price optimization
- Product development
- Programme evaluation
- Risk assessment and management
- Strategic Marketing
- Operational marketing

Data collection and analysis is viewed as a continuing and iterative process. Ideally, business decisions are refined over time, based on feedback from earlier analyses and decisions. Most analytical CRM projects use a data warehouse to manage data.

Collaborative CRM

Collaborative CRM focuses on the interaction with customers.

Collaborative CRM includes:

- Providing efficient communication with customers across a variety of communications channels
- Providing online services to reduce customer service costs
- Providing access to customer information while interacting with customers

Driven by authors from the Harvard Business School, Collaborative CRM also seems to be the new paradigma to succeed the leading Efficient Consumer Response and Category Management concept in the industry/trade relationship.

In its broadest sense, CRM covers all interaction and business with customers. A good CRM programme allows a business to acquire customers, provide customer services and retain valued customers.

Customer services can be improved by:

- Providing online access to product information and technical assistance around the clock
- Identifying what customers value and devising appropriate service strategies for each customer

- Providing mechanisms for managing and scheduling follow-up sales calls
- Tracking all contacts with a customer
- Identifying potential problems before they occur
- Providing a user-friendly mechanism for registering customer complaints
- Providing a mechanism for handling problems and complaints
- Providing a mechanism for correcting service deficiencies
- Storing customer interests in order to target customers selectively
- Providing mechanisms for managing and scheduling maintenance, repair, and on-going support
- Scalability: the system should be highly scalable, as the volume of data stored in the system grows over time
- Communication channels: CRM can interface with a variety of different channels
- Workflow—a company's business processes need to be represented by the system with the ability to track the individual stages and transfer information between steps
- Assignment—the ability to assign requests, such as service requests, to a person or group.
- Database—the means of storing customer data and histories
- Customer privacy considerations, such as data encryption and legislation.

Improving Customer Relationships

CRM applications often track customer interests and requirements, as well as their buying habits. This information can be used to target customers selectively. Furthermore, the products a customer has purchased can be tracked throughout the product's life cycle, allowing customers to receive information concerning a product or to target customers with information on alternative products once a product begins to be phased out. Repeat purchases rely on customer satisfaction, which in turn comes from a deeper understanding of each customer and their individual needs. CRM is an alternative to the "one size fits all" approach. In industrial markets, the technology can be used to coordinate the conflicting and changing purchase criteria of the sector.

The data gathered as part of CRM raises concerns over customer privacy and enables persuasive sales techniques. However, CRM does not necessarily involve gathering new data, but also includes making better use of customer information gathered as a result of routine customer interaction. The privacy debate generally focuses on the customer information stored in the centralized database itself, and fears over a company's handling of this information.

For example, there is virtually no way a consumer can determine if the company shares private data with third parties. Furthermore, companies may not always accurately declare to the consumer the types of information collected by CRM systems and the specific purposes for which the information is used.

CRM is also important to non-profit organizations, which sometimes use the terms "constituent relationship management", "contact relationship management" or "community relationship management" to describe their information systems for managing donors, volunteers and other supporters.

FINANCIAL MANAGEMENT

New business leaders and managers have to develop at least basic skills in financial management. Expecting others in the organization to manage finances is clearly asking for trouble. Basic skills in financial management start in the critical areas of cash management and bookkeeping, which should be done according to certain financial controls to ensure integrity in the bookkeeping process.

New leaders and managers should soon go on to learn how to generate financial statements and analyse those statements to really understand the financial condition of the business. Financial analysis shows the "reality" of the situation of a business—seen as such, financial management is one of the most important practices in management. This topic will help you understand basic practices in financial management, and build the basic systems and practices needed in a healthy business.

If your small business is a corporation, you would do well to find someone experienced in financial management and encourage them to be your board treasurer. Therefore, it's important to understand the role of the board treasurer. New, more "organic" forms or organizations allow organizations to be more responsive and adaptable in today's rapidly changing world. These forms also cultivate empowerment among employees, much more than the hierarchical, rigidly structured organizations of the past.

Many people assert that as the nature of organizations has changed, so must the nature of management control. Some people go so far as to claim that management shouldn't exercise any form of control whatsoever. They claim that management should exist to support employee's efforts to be fully productive members of organizations and communities—therefore, any form of control is completely counterproductive to management and employees.

Some people even react strongly against the phrase "management control". The word itself can have a negative connotation, *e.g.*, it can sound dominating, coercive and heavy-handed. It seems that writers of management literature now prefer use of the term "coordinating" rather than "controlling". Regardless of the negative connotation of the word "control", it must exist or there is no organization at all. In its most basic form, an organization is two or more people working together to reach a goal.

Whether an organization is highly bureaucratic or changing and self-organizing, the organization must exist for some reason, some purpose, some mission—or it isn't an organization at all. The organization must have some goal. Identifying this goal requires some form of planning, informal or formal. Reaching the goal means identifying some strategies, formal or informal. These strategies are agreed upon by members of the organization through some form of communication, formal or informal. Then members set about to act in accordance with what they agreed to do. They may change their minds, fine. But they need to recognize and acknowledge that they're changing their minds.

This form of ongoing communication to reach a goal, tracking activities towards the goal and then subsequent decisions about what to do is the essence of management coordination. It needs to exist in some manner—formal or informal. The following are rather typical methods of coordination in organizations.

They are used as means to communicate direction and guide behaviours in that direction. The function of the following methods is not to "control", but rather to guide. If, from ongoing communications among management and employees, the direction changes, then fine. The following methods are changed accordingly.

Note that many of the following methods are so common that we often don't think of them as having anything to do with coordination at all. No matter what one calls the following methods—coordination or control—they're important to the success of any organization.

ADMINISTRATIVE CONTROLS

Organizations often use standardized documents to ensure complete and consistent information is gathered. Documents include titles and dates to detect different versions of the document. Computers have revolutionized administrative controls through use of integrated management information systems, project management software, human resource information systems, office automation software, etc. Organizations typically require a wide range of reports, *e.g.*, financial reports, status reports, project reports, etc. to monitor what's being done, by when and how.

Delegation is an approach to get things done, in conjunction with other employees. Delegation is often viewed as a major means of influence and therefore is categorized as an activity in leading. Delegation generally includes assigning responsibility to an employee to complete a task, granting the employee sufficient authority to gain the resources to do the task and letting the employee decide how that task will be carried out. Typically, the person assigning the task shares accountability with the employee for ensuring the task is completed.

Evaluation is carefully collecting and analysing information in order to make decisions. There are many types of evaluations in organizations, for example, evaluation of marketing efforts, evaluation of employee performance, programme evaluations, etc. Evaluations can focus on many aspects of an organization and its processes, for example, its goals and processes, outcomes.

FINANCIAL STATEMENTS

Once the organization has establish goals and associated strategies, funds are set aside for the resources and labour to the accomplish goals and tasks. As the money is spent, statements are changed to reflect what was spent, how it was spent and what it obtained. Review of financial statements is one of the more common methods to monitor the progress of programmes and plans.

The most common financial statements include the balance sheet, income statement and cash flow statement. Financial audits are regularly conducted to ensure that financial management practices follow generally accepted standards, as well. Performance management focuses on the performance of the total organization, including its processes, critical subsystems and employees.

Most of us have some basic impression of employee performance management, including the role of performance reviews. Performance reviews provide an opportunity for supervisors and their employees to regularly communicate about goals, how well those goals should be met, how well the goals are being met and what must be done to continue to meet those goals. The employee is rewarded in some form for meeting performance standards, or embarks on a development plan with the supervisor in order to improve performance. Policies help ensure that behaviours in the workplace conform to federal and state laws, and also to expectations of the organization. Often, policies are applied to specified situations in the form of procedures.

Personnel policies and procedures help ensure that employee laws are followed and minimize the likelihood of costly litigation. A procedure is a step-by-step list of activities required to conduct a certain task. Procedures ensure that routine tasks are carried out in an effective and efficient fashion.

QUALITY CONTROL AND OPERATIONS MANAGEMENT

The concept of quality control has received a great deal of attention over the past twenty years. Many people recognize phrases such as "do it right the first time, "zero defects", "Total Quality Management", etc. Very broadly, quality includes specifying a performance standard, monitoring and measuring results, comparing the results to the standard and then making adjusts as necessary.

Recently, the concept of quality management has expanded to include organization-wide programmes, such as Total Quality Management, ISO9000, Balanced Scorecard, etc. Operations management includes the overall activities involved in developing, producing and distributing products and services.

RISK, SAFETY AND LIABILITIES

For a variety of reasons, organizations are focusing a great deal of attention to activities that minimize risk, avoid liabilities and ensure safety of employees. Several decades ago, it was rare to hear of an organization undertaking contingency planning, disaster recovery planning or critical incident analysis. Now those activities are becoming commonplace.

EVALUATION ACTIVITIES IN ORGANIZATIONS

Evaluation, in the context of management activities, is

carefully collecting information about something in order to make necessary decisions about it. There are a large number and wide variety of evaluations that can occur in businesses, whether for-profit or nonprofit. Evaluation is closely related to performance management which includes identifying measures to indicate results. Evaluation often includes collecting information around these measures to conclude the extent of performance.

ADVERTISING AND PROMOTIONS

Before you learn more about advertising, you should get a basic impression of what advertising is. Advertising is a major "phase" of overall product or service development and management. Advertising is specifically part of the "outbound" marketing activities, or activities geared to communicate to the market, eg, advertising, promotions, public relations, etc. Inbound" marketing activities are geared to communicate from the market, and include, eg, market research about the market.

Although your use of the latest hot marketing and sales strategies may improve the bottom line of your business, you may get into hot "legal waters" if you do not exercise the proper restraints. The boundaries beyond which you do not want to stray lest you run afoul of the laws governing false advertising. Two conflicting principles are involved in advertising law. On the one hand, the First Amendment, which is part of the U.S. Constitution and grants us the right of free speech, protects all forms of communication, including advertising.

On the other hand, the U.S. Constitution gives the federal government the power to regulate interstate commerce. Most state constitutions similarly give state governments the power to regulate commerce conducted solely within that state. In exercising its power over interstate commerce, the Congress has enacted two statutes that have the greatest effect on advertising. These are the Federal Trade Commission Act and the Lanham Act. The FTC Act states that false advertising is a form of unfair and deceptive commerce. The term "false advertising" has been broadly construed. As you might expect, the term includes advertisements that are in fact untrue. However, the term false advertising extends well beyond untrue advertisements. It also includes advertisements that make representations that the advertiser has no reasonable basis to believe, even if the representations turn out to be true. An example would be an advertisement for a photocopier machine which stated that the machine used less toner than any comparable machine.

The advertiser would have committed false advertising if it had no reasonable basis to believe the truth of this claim, even if it turned out to be true. The FTC Act gives the FTC broad authority to regulate advertising. Under this broad mandate, the FTC has issued regulations barring advertisements that could be misleading even if they are true. A famous example involves Anacin, a brand of aspirin. The maker of Anacin ran ads claiming that clinical tests showed that Anacin delivered the same headache relief as the leading pain relief prescription.

The ad did not mention that aspirin itself is the leading pain medicine. The FTC determined that the ad was misleading. The ad implied that Anacin was more effective than aspirin, when in fact, Anacin is really just aspirin. In addition to barring advertisements, the FTC also has the power to order corrective ads. Corrective advertising requires a business to run ads that alert future consumers to certain unfavourable facts about a product not revealed in past advertising campaigns. Another famous example involved Listerine mouthwash.

For years, Listerine was touted as a cold and sore throat remedy. The FTC forced the manufacturer to run ads stating that Listerine would not cure colds or relieve sore throats. Surely, this is not part of a desirable marketing strategy. The FTC has a further power, known as "fencing in." This enables the FTC to bar misleading ads with respect to a particular product and across all of a business's other unrelated product lines. For example a testimonial constituting false advertising regarding product A could lead purchasers to believe that products B and c must also be great. In that case, the FTC could bar use of the ad for products A, B, and C. Only the FTC has the authority to enforce the FTC Act. Private parties, such as consumers or competitors, can bring a legal action regarding false advertising under the Lanham Act.

To establish a violation under the Lanham Act, consumers and competitors must prove the following: (1) the advertiser made false statements of fact about its product; (2) the false advertisements actually deceived or had the capacity to deceive a substantial segment of the target population; (3) the deception was material; (4) the falsely advertised product was sold in interstate commerce; and (5) the party bringing the lawsuit was injured as a result of the deception. Actual loss is not required to show an injury.

All that is needed is a reasonable basis for the belief that the plaintiff is likely to be damaged as a result of the advertising. An example of such damage would include ads that deceive consumers who are the target population of both the advertiser and the plaintiff. The penalties for a Lanham Act violation include the plaintiff's lost profits, the additional profits to the advertiser resulting from the deceptive ad, treble damages, and attorneys' fees.In addition to the FTC Act and the Lanham Act, which are federal statutes, most states, including Illinois, also have laws proscribing false advertising. Illinois is one of many states that has enacted the Uniform Deceptive Trade Practices Act.

Under the Act, a "deceptive trade practice" includes such practices as "palming off," misrepresentation, product disparagement, and bait-and-switch advertising. Palming off occurs when an advertiser creates the impression that its goods or services are those that are furnished by a competitor. For example, this could occur if you set up a hamburger stand that looked like a McDonalds restaurant.

Misrepresentation occurs when an advertiser makes false or misleading claims about its goods or services, as under the FTC Act and the Lanham Act. Product disparagement occurs when an advertiser intentionally makes false or misleading negative remarks about competing goods or services, causing its competitor to lose sales. Bait-and-switch advertising occurs when the advertised goods or services are withdrawn from the market and substitute goods or services are instead offered for sale. The laws regulating false advertising present many traps for the unwary. If you engage a marketing or advertising agent to assist you in your marketing and sales campaign, you might want to get your agent to guarantee that your ads are lawful. Of course, if you are in the business of preparing marketing or advertising campaigns, you might want to get your client to guarantee that the information he or she provides is true.

In either case, when in doubt, you should consult with an attorney. Advertising and promotions is bringing a service to the attention of potential and current customers. Advertising and promotions are best carried out by implementing an advertising and promotions plan. The goals of the plan should depend very much on the overall goals and strategies of the organization, and the results of the marketing analysis, including the positioning statement.

The plan usually includes what target markets you want to reach, what features and benefits you want to convey to them, how you will convey it to them who is responsible to carry the various activities in the plan and how much money is budgeted for this effort. Successful advertising depends very much on knowing the preferred methods and styles of communications of the target markets that you want to reach with your ads. A media plan and calendar can be very useful, which specifies what advertising methods are used and when. For each service, carefully consider: What target markets are you trying to reach with your ads?

What would you like them to think and perceive about your products? How can you get them to think and perceive that? What communications media do they see or prefer the most? Consider TV, radio, newsletters, classifieds, displays/ signs, posters, word of mouth, press releases, direct mail, special events, brochures, neighbourhood newsletters, etc. What media is most practical for you to use in terms of access and affordability? You can often find out a lot about your customers preferences just by conducting some basic market research methods. The following closely related links might be useful in preparation for your planning. Far too often, we think we know what our customers think and want because—well, we just know, that's all. Wrong! Businesses can't be successful if they don't continue to meet the needs of their customers. Period. There should be few activities as important as finding out what your customers want for products and services and finding out what they think of yours.

Fortunately, there are a variety of practical methods that businesses can use to feedback from customers. The methods you choose and how you use them depend on what the type of feedback that you want from customers, for example, to find out their needs in products and services, what they think about your products and services, etc.

Employees

Your employees of usually the people who interact the most with your customers. Ask them about products and services that customers are asking for. Ask employees about what the customers complain about.

Comment Cards

Provide brief, half-page comment cards on which they can answer basic questions such as: Were you satisfied with our services? How could we provide the perfect services? Are there any services you'd like to see that don't exist yet?

COMPETITION

What is your competition selling? Ask people who shop there. Many people don't notice sales or major items in stores. Start coaching those around you to notice what's going on with your competition.

Customers

One of the best ways to find out what customers want is to ask them. Talk to them when they visit your facility or you visit theirs.

Documentation and Records

Notice what customers are buying and not buying from you. If you already know what customers are buying, etc., then is this written down somewhere? It should be so that you don't forget, particularly during times of stress or when trying to train personnel to help you out.

Focus Groups

Focus groups are usually 8-10 people that you gather to get their impressions of a product or service or an idea.

Surveys by Mail

You might hate answering these things, but plenty of people don't—and will fill our surveys especially if they get something in return. Promise them a discount if they return the completed form to your facility.

COMPETITIVE ANALYSIS

Marketing should include competitor analysis. Who are your competitors? What customer needs and preferences are you competing to meet? What are the similarities and differences between their products/services and yours? What are the strengths and weaknesses of each of their products and services? How do their prices compare to yours? How are they doing overall? How do you plan to compete? Offer better quality services? Lower prices? More support? Easier access to services? How are you uniquely suited to compete with them?

Competitive Intelligence for Business Success

Some businesses think it is best to get on with their own plans and ignore the competition. Others become obsessed with tracking the actions of competitors. Many businesses are happy simply to track the competition, copying their moves and reacting to changes.

Competitor analysis has several important roles in strategic planning:

- To help management understand their competitive advantages/disadvantages relative to competitors

- To generate understanding of competitors' past, present future strategies
- To provide an informed basis to develop strategies to achieve competitive advantage in the future
- To help forecast the returns that may be made from future investments

Questions to Ask

What questions should be asked when undertaking competitor analysis?

The following is a useful list to bear in mind:

- Who are our competitors?
- What threats do they pose?
- What is the profile of our competitors?
- What are the objectives of our competitors?
- What strategies are our competitors pursuing and how successful are these strategies?
- What are the strengths and weaknesses of our competitors?
- How are our competitors likely to respond to any changes to the way we do business?

Sources of Information for Competitor Analysis

Davidson describes how the sources of competitor information can be neatly grouped into three categories:

1. *Recorded data:* This is easily available in published form either internally or externally. Good examples include competitor annual reports and product brochures;
2. *Observable data:* This has to be actively sought and often assembled from several sources. A good example is competitor pricing;
3. *Opportunistic data:* To get hold of this kind of data requires a lot of planning and organisation. Much of it is "anecdotal", coming from discussions with suppliers, customers and perhaps, previous management of competitors.

Table Below Lists Possible Sources of Competitor Data Using Davidson's Categorisation.

Recorded Data	Observable Data	Opportunistic Data
Annual report and accounts	Pricing/price lists	Meetings with suppliers
Press releases	Advertising campaigns	Trade shows
Newspaper articles	Promotions	Sales force meetings
Analysts reports	Tenders Seminars/ conferences	
Regulatory reports	Patent applications	Recruiting ex-employees
Government reports		Discussion with shared distributors
Presentations/speeches		Social contacts with competitors

In his excellent book *Even More Offensive Marketing,* Davidson likens the process of gathering competitive data to a jigsaw puzzle. Each individual piece of data does not have much value.

The important skill is to collect as many of the pieces as possible and to assemble them into an overall picture of the competitor. This enables you to identify any missing pieces and to take the necessary steps to collect them.

What Businesses Need to Know about their Competitors

The kinds of competitor information that would help businesses complete some good quality competitor analysis. You can probably think of many more pieces of information about a competitor that would be useful. However, an important challenge in competitor analysis is working out how to obtain competitor information that is reliable, up-to-date and available legally.

What businesses probably already know their competitors
Overall sales and profits
Sales and profits by market
Sales by main brand
Cost structure
Market shares (revenues and volumes)

Organisation structure
Distribution system
Identity/profile of senior management
Advertising strategy and spending
Customer/consumer profile and attitudes
Customer retention levels

What businesses would really like to know about competitors
Sales and profits by product
Relative costs
Customer satisfaction and service levels
Customer retention levels
Distribution costs
New product strategies
Size and quality of customer databases
Advertising effectiveness
Future investment strategy
Contractual terms with key suppliers
Terms of strategic partnerships

COMPETITOR ARRAY

One common and useful technique is constructing a competitor array.

The steps include:

- Define your industry—scope and nature of the industry
- Determine who your competitors are
- Determine who your customers are and what benefits they expect
- Determine what the key success factors are in your industry
- Rank the key success factors by giving each one a weighting—The sum of all the weightings must add up to one.
- Rate each competitor on each of the key success factors—this can best be displayed on a two dimensional matrix—competitors along the top and key success factors down the side.

- Multiply each cell in the matrix by the factor weighting.
- Sum columns for a weighted assessment of the overall strength of each competitor relative to each other.

An example of a competitor array follows:

Key Industry Success Factors	Weighting	Competitor # 1 rating	Competitor #1 weighted	Competitor #2 rating	Competitor #2 weighted
Extensive distribution	.4	6	2.4	3	1.2
Customer focus	.3	4	1.2	5	1.5
Economies of scale	.2	3	.6	3	.6
Product innovation	.1	7	.7	4	.4
Totals	1.0	20	4.9	18	3.7

Based on material presented in "Beat the Competition: How to Use Competitive Intelligence to Develop Winning Business Strategies", Ian Gordon, Basil Blackwell Publishers, Oxford, UK, 1989.

In this example competitor #1 is rated higher than competitor #2 on product innovation ability (7 out of 10, compared to 4 out of 10) and distribution networks (6 out of 10), but competitor #2 is rated higher on customer focus (5 out of 10).

Overall, competitor #1 is rated slightly higher than competitor #2 (20 out of 40 compared to 18 out of 40). When the success factors are weighted according to their importance, competitor #1 gets a far better rating (4.9 compared to 3.7).

COMPETITOR PROFILING

Another common technique is to create detailed profiles on each of your major competitors. These profiles give an in-depth description of the competitor's background, finances, products, markets, facilities, personnel, and strategies. This involves:

- Background

  - Location of offices, plants, and online presences
  - History—key personalities, dates, events, and trends
  - Ownership, corporate governance, and organizational structure
- Financials
  - P-E ratios, dividend policy, and profitability** various financial ratios, liquidity, and cash flow
  - Profit growth profile; method of growth (organic or acquisitive)
- Products
  - Products offered, depth and breadth of product line, and product portfolio balance
  - New products developed, new product success rate, and R&D strengths
  - Brands, strength of brand portfolio, brand loyalty and brand awareness
  - Patents and licenses
  - Quality control conformance
  - Reverse engineering
- Marketing
  - Segments served, market shares, customer base, growth rate, and customer loyalty
  - Promotional mix, promotional budgets, advertising themes, ad agency used, sales force success rate, online promotional strategy
  - Distribution channels used (direct and indirect), exclusivity agreements, alliances, and geographical coverage
  - Pricing, discounts,and allowances
- Facilities
  - Plant capacity, capacity utilization rate, age of plant, plant efficiency, capital investment
  - Location, shipping logistics, and product mix by plant
- Personnel
  - Number of employees, key employees, and skill sets

  - Strength of management, and management style
  - Compensation, benefits, and employee morale and retention rates
- Corporate and marketing strategies
  - Objectives, mission statement, growth plans, acquisitions, and divestitures
  - Marketing strategies

MEDIA SCANNING

We can learn a lot about the competitive environment by scanning our competitors' ads. Changes in a competitor's advertising message can reveal new product offerings, new production processes, a new branding strategy, a new positioning strategy, a new segmentation strategy, line extensions and contractions, problems with previous positions, insights from recent marketing or product research, a new strategic direction, a new source of sustainable competitive advantage, or value migrations within the industry.

It might also indicate a new pricing strategy such as penetration, price discrimination, price skimming, product bundling, joint product pricing, discounts, or loss leaders. It may also indicate a new promotion strategy such as push, pull, balanced, short term sales generation, long term image creation, informational, comparative, affective, reminder, new creative objectives, new unique selling proposition, new creative concepts, appeals, tone, and themes, or a new advertising agency.

It might also indicate a new distribution strategy, new distribution partners, more extensive distribution, more intensive distribution, a change in geographical focus, or exclusive distribution. Little of this intelligence is definitive : additional information is needed before conclusions should be drawn.

A competitor's media strategy reveals budget allocation, segmentation and targeting strategy, and selectivity and focus. From a tactical perspective, it can also be used to help a manager implement his/her own media plan. By knowing the competitor's media buy, media selection, frequency, reach, continuity, schedules, and flights, the manager can arrange his/her own media plan so that they do not coincide. Other sources of corporate intelligence include trade shows, patent filings, mutual customers, annual reports, and trade associations. Some firms hire competitor intelligence professionals to obtain this information.

NEW COMPETITORS

In addition to analysing current competitors, it is necessary to estimate future competitive threats.

The most common sources of new competitors are:

- Companies competing in a related product/market
- Companies using related technologies
- Companies already targeting your prime market segment but with unrelated products
- Companies from other geographical areas and with similar products
- New start-up companies organised by former employees and/or managers of existing companies

The entrance of new competitors is likely when:

- There are high profit margins in the industry
- There is unmet demand (insufficient supply) in the industry
- There are no major barriers to entry
- There is future growth potential
- Competitive rivalry is not intense
- Gaining a competitive advantage over existing firms is feasible

MARKETING

Marketing is a social and managerial function that attempts to create, expand and maintain a collection of customers.

It attempts to deliver demand satisfying output through profitable exchanges:

- Marketing, as suggested by the American Marketing Association, is "an organizational function and a set of processes for creating, communicating and delivering value to customers and for managing customer relationships in ways that benefit the organization and its stakeholders".

- Philip Kotler, in his earlier books, defines marketing as: "human activity directed at satisfying needs and wants through exchange processes". Still another marketing definition, coined by Brian Norris: "The process of repeatedly moving people closer to making a decision to purchase, use, follow, refer, upload, download, obey, reject, conform, become complacent to another person's, society's or organization's value. Simply, if it doesn't facilitate a "sale" then it's not marketing."
- Identifying needs/wants and finding and implimenting solutions that satisfy those needs and wants.
- Add to Kotler's and Norris' definitions, a response from the Chartered Institute of Marketing (CIM). The association's definition claims marketing to be the "management process of anticipating, identifying and satisfying customer requirements profitably". Thus, operative marketing involves the processes of market research, market segmentation, new product development, product life cycle management, pricing, channel management as well as promotion.
- Marketing-"taking actions to define, create, grow, develop, maintain, defend and own markets".
- An approach to business that seeks to identify, anticipate and satisfy customers needs.
- Al Ries and Jack Trout defined marketing as simply "war" between competitors.
- Any activity that connects producers with consumers.
- At a macro level, marketing is the process of raising the standards of living, by identifying the existing problems and unsatisfied needs of people and then satisfying that need with a product/service that delivers value to the customer.

The practice of marketing is almost as old as humanity itself. Whenever a person has an item or is capable of performing a service, and he or she seeks another person who might want that item or service, that person is involved in marketing. A Market was originally simply a gathering place where people with a supply of items or capacity to perform a service could meet with those who might desire the items or services, perhaps at a pre-arranged time. Such meetings embodied all the aspects of today's marketing methods, although in an informal way.

Sellers and buyers sought to understand each other's needs, capacities, and psychology, all with the goal of getting the exchange of items or services to take place. Open air markets throughout the world, with buyers and sellers freely mingling, are today's example of this basic activity. Today's New York Stock Exchange had its humble beginnings as an open air market located at Wall Street in New York City. The rise of Agriculture undoubtedly influenced markets as the earliest means of 'mass production' of an item, namely foodstuffs.

As agriculture allowed one to grow more food than could be eaten by the grower alone, and most food is perishable, there was likely motivation to seek out others who could use the excess food, before it spoiled, in exchange for other items. Prior to the advent of market research, most companies were product-focused, employing teams of salespeople to push their products into or onto the market, regardless of market desire. A market-focused, or customer-focused, organization instead first determines what its potential customers desire, and then builds the product or service.

Marketing theory and practice is justified on the belief that customers use a product/service because they have a need, or because a product/service has a perceived benefit. Two major factors of marketing are the recruitment of new customers (acquisition) and the retention and expansion of relationships with existing customers (base management). Once a marketer has converted the prospective buyer, base management marketing takes over. The process for base management shifts the marketer to building a relationship, nurturing the links, enhancing the benefits that sold the buyer in the first place, and improving the product/service continuously to protect her business from competitive encroachments. Marketing methods are informed by many of the social sciences, particularly psychology, sociology, and economics. Anthropology is also a small, but growing, influence. Market research underpins these activities. Through advertising, it is also related to many of the creative arts. For a marketing plan to be successful, the mix of the four "Ps" must reflect the wants and desires of the consumers in the target market.

Trying to convince a market segment to buy something they don't want is extremely expensive and seldom successful. Marketers depend on marketing research, both formal and informal, to determine what consumers want and what they are willing to pay for. Marketers hope that this process will give them a sustainable competitive advantage. Marketing management is the practical application of this process. The offer is also an important addition to the 4P's theory.

Within most organizations the activities encompassed by the marketing function are led by a Chief Marketing Officer, or an equivalent executive. Most often the CMO position reports to the Chief Executive Officer. The big debate in the marketing discipline is whether marketing is an art or a science. Marketing is a technology or set of technologies. Marketing can be neither an art nor a science because arts and sciences only seek to explain natural phenomena.

The objective of marketing is to manipulate and influence natural phenomena to create practical unnatural outcomes, specifically to manufacture, grow, sustain and defend markets. Marketers use their knowledge of economics, psychology, sociology, anthropology and strategy to arrange and control the external environment to their advantage and lock in profit. To understand what marketing is one must understand that marketing operates on three different levels.

CORPORATE LEVEL MARKETING

Marketing at the corporate levels asks this question as 'What business should we be in and what opportunities should we pursue?' This is marketing before we even have a business, idea or product. This is what is known as entreprenuership. This level of marketing strategy is where the Ted Turners, Bill Gates' and Michael Dells of the world make market changing decisions. This level is also where corporate management of existing companies decide to branch off into new uncharted territories and opportunities.

BUSINESS LEVEL MARKETING

Marketing at the business level asks this question as 'How are we going to compete against the competition?' When Jack Trout says that marketing is 'the war between competitors' and 'the conflict between companies' what he is really doing is defining marketing at the business level. Business level marketing deals with high level strategic marketing concerns. This level deals with long term sustainable advantages and business models.

FUNCTIONAL LEVEL MARKETING

Marketing at the functional level (also known as the operating level) ask this question as 'How do we create and keep customers?' This level deals with marketing tactics and the '4ps' of the marketing mix. This level of marketing defines and develops products, prices them, promotes them and then distributes them in a way that helps a company create and sustain demand for their products.

In popular usage, "marketing" is the promotion of products, especially advertising and branding. However, in professional usage the term has a wider meaning which recognizes that marketing is customer centered.

Products are often developed to meet the desires of groups of customers or even, in some cases, for specific customers. E. Jerome McCarthy divided marketing into four general sets of activities. His typology has become so universally recognized that his four activity sets, the Four Ps, have passed into the language.

The four Ps are:

1. *Product:* The Product management and Product marketing aspects of marketing deal with the

specifications of the actual good or service, and how it relates to the end-user's needs and wants.

2. *Pricing:* This refers to the process of setting a price for a product, including discounts.
3. *Promotion:* This includes advertising, sales promotion, publicity, and personal selling, and refers to the various methods of promoting the product, brand, or company.
4. Placement or distribution refers to how the product gets to the customer; for example, point of sale placement or retailing. This fourth P has also sometimes been called Place, referring to the channel by which a product or service is sold (*e.g.* online vs. retail), which geographic region or industry, to which segment (young adults, families, business people), etc.

These four elements are often referred to as the marketing mix. A marketer can use these variables to craft a marketing plan. The four Ps model is most useful when marketing low value consumer products.

Industrial products, services, high value consumer products require adjustments to this model. Services marketing must account for the unique nature of services. Industrial or B2B marketing must account for the long term contractual agreements that are typical in supply chain transactions. Relationship marketing attempts to do this by looking at marketing from a long term relationship perspective rather than individual transactions.

As a counter to this, Morgan, in Riding the Waves of Change, adds "Perhaps the most significant criticism of the 4 Ps approach, which you should be aware of, is that it unconsciously emphasizes the inside–out view (looking from the company outwards), whereas the essence of marketing should be the outside–in approach".

Even so, having made this important caveat, the 4 Ps offer a memorable and quite workable guide to the major categories of marketing activity, as well as a framework within which these can be used. As well as the standard four Ps (Product, Pricing, Promotion and Place), services marketing calls upon an extra three, totalling seven and known together as the extended marketing mix.

These are:

- *People:* Any person coming into contact with customers can have an impact on overall satisfaction. Whether as part of a supporting service to a product or involved in a total service, people are particularly important because, in the customer's eyes, they are generally inseparable from the total service. As a result of this, they must be appropriately trained, well motivated and the right type of person. Fellow customers are also sometimes referred to under 'people', as they too can affect the customer's service experience, (*e.g.*, at a sporting event).
- *Process:* This is the process(es) involved in providing a service and the behaviour of people, which can be crucial to customer satisfaction.
- *Physical evidence:* Unlike a product, a service cannot be experienced before it is delivered, which makes it intangible. This, therefore, means that potential customers could perceive greater risk when deciding whether or not to use a service. To reduce the feeling of risk, thus improving the chance for success, it is often vital to offer potential customers the chance to see what a service would be like. This is done by providing physical evidence, such as case studies, or testimonials.

As well as the other 7 Packaging has been added to this list by some people. The rationale is that it is very important how the product is presented to the customer, and the packaging is often the first contact that a customer has with a product.

Although some disagree because packaging is seen as a subfield of promotion. "Philosophy" is the potential 8th P of marketing. Products (or services) should reflect the underlying philosophy or ethos of the organization. It should also be clear what the philosophy behind the introduction of the particular product is, as well. In his book, "Meeting Need", Ian Bruce explains this concept as it relates to marketing for charities. It also applies to other products and services

RESOURCES, RELATIONSHIPS, OFFERINGS AND BUSINESS MODELS

Marketing in the past focused mainly on basic concepts like the 4 Ps, and primarily on the psychological and sociological aspects of marketing. Competitive advantage was created by directly appealing to the needs, wants and behaviours of customers, better than the competition. Successful marketing was based on who could create the better brand or the lowest price or the most hype.

Marketing in the future will be based on a more strategic approach to competitive marketing success. Marketers will consciously build and allocate resources, relationships, offerings and business models that other companies find hard to match. Companies with a greater amount of resources than their competitors will have an easier time competing in the marketplace. Resources include: financial (cash and cash reserves), physical (plant and equipment), human (knowledge and skill), legal (trademarks and patents), organizational (structure, competencies, policies), and informational (knowledge of consumers and competitors).

Small companies usually have a harder time competing with larger corporations because of their disadvantage in resource allocation. Success in business, as in life, is based on the relationships you have with people. Marketers must aggressively build relationships with consumers, customers, distributors, partners and even competitors if they want to have success in today's competitive marketplace.

Most companies sell a mix of products and/or services. Today's marketplace is often too competitive for "one-trick ponies". Companies that sell the right mix products and services can have a competitive advantage over companies that sell just one product or service. The concept of product vs. product in competitive marketing is dying. It's slowly becoming business model vs. business model. Business model innovation can make the competition's product superiority irrelevant. Business model innovation allows a marketer to change the game instead of competing on a level playing field.

CUSTOMER FOCUS

Most companies today have a customer orientation (also called customer focus). This implies that the company focuses its activities and products on ever changing consumer demands.

Generally there are tthree ways of doing this: the customer-driven approach, the sense of identifying market changes and the product innovation approach. In the consumer-driven approach, consumer wants are the drivers of all strategic marketing decisions.

No strategy is pursued until it passes the test of consumer research. Every aspect of a market offering, including the nature of the product itself, is driven by the needs of potential consumers. The starting point is always the consumer. The rationale for this approach is that there is no point spending R&D funds developing products that people will not buy. History attests to many products that were commercial failures in spite of being technological breakthroughs.

The next big thing is a concept in marketing that refers to a product or idea that will allow for a high amount of sales for that product and related products. Marketers believe that by finding or creating the next big thing they will spark a cultural revolution that results in this sales increase.

PRODUCT FOCUS

In a product innovation approach, the company pursues product innovation, then tries to develop a market for the product. Product innovation drives the process and marketing research is conducted primarily to ensure that a profitable market segment(s) exists for the innovation. The rationale is that customers may not know what options will be available to them in the future so we should not expect them to tell us what they will buy in the future.

However, marketers can aggressively over pursue product innovation and try to overcapitalize on a niche. When pursuing a product innovation approach, marketers must ensure that they have a varied and multi-tiered approach to product innovation. It is claimed that if Thomas Edison depended on marketing research he would have produced larger candles rather than inventing light bulbs.

Many firms, such as research and development focused companies, successfully focus on product innovation. Many purists doubt whether this is really a form of marketing orientation at all, because of the ex post status of consumer research. Some even question whether it is marketing.

OTHER ASPECTS

- An emerging area of study and practice concerns internal marketing, or how employees are trained and managed to deliver the brand in a way that positively impacts the acquisition and retention of customers (employer branding).
- Diffusion of innovations research explores how and why people adopt new products, services and ideas.
- A relatively new form of marketing uses the Internet and is called internet marketing or more generally e-marketing, affiliate marketing or online marketing. It typically tries to perfect the segmentation strategy used in traditional marketing. It targets its audience more precisely, and is sometimes called personalized marketing or one-to-one marketing.
- With consumers' eroding attention span and willingness to give time to advertising messages, marketers are turning to forms of Permission marketing such as Branded content and Reality marketing.
- The use of herd behaviour in marketing.

Some aspects of marketing, especially promotion, are treated as the subject of criticism. It is especially problematic in classical economic theory, which is based on the assumption that supply and demand are independent.

However, product promotion is an attempt coming from the supply side to influence demand. In this way producer market power is attained as measured by profits that would not be realised under a free market. Then the argument follows that non-free markets are imperfect and lead to production and consumption of suboptimal amounts of the product. Critics acknowledge that marketing has legitimate uses in connecting goods and services to the consumers who want them. Critics also point out that marketing techniques have been used to achieve morally dubious ends by businesses, governments and criminals.

Critics see a systemic social evil inherent in marketing. Marketing is accused of creating ruthless exploitation of both consumers and workers by treating people as commodities whose purpose is to consume. Most marketers believe that marketing, like any other technology, is amoral. It can be used for good or evil purposes, but the technique itself is ethically neutral.

The Observer's survey among 1'206 UK adult consumers in 2001 highlighted some of the stark changes our society has gone through in the last two decades. This raises a question on the effectiveness of the CIM's definition of marketing (anticipating, identifying and satisfying customer needs profitably), mainly in consumer marketing. There are similar concerns in industrial markets, also known as business-to-business or B2B. Core marketing elements such as segmentation, targeting and positioning are still relevant in the modern (or post-modern) world.

However, they are complex topics that need a high level of effort, intelligent thinking as well as resources to be implemented successfully. A definitive statement cannot be made whether the conventional marketing concept is applicable in today's environment. Its relevance is very much situational and depends on many factors such as the product, the segment, time, location, political and economic conditions and the inner workings of a company.

However, some scholars such as Stephen Brown challenge the marketing concept in an extreme language. Their statements, though self-contradicting and sometimes unfair, are relevant. On the one hand Brown makes positive statements about marketing, *e.g.* marketing is endowed with considerable personal charm and has enjoyed more than its fair share of conquests; and indeed, the increasing academic attention that is being devoted to marketing and consumption-related phenomena by non-business disciplines such as sociology, anthropology and history; far from being the second-hand rose of the scholarship, marketing is now something of a fashion leader.

On the other hand, he condemns marketing by saying "marketing has to decide whether to expose its intellectual nakedness or press itself against the searing heat of postmodernism"; and using quotes such as "mid-life crisis"; "in decline; failing; anachronistic; being abandoned; no longer appropriate; in an unprecedented state of crisis; delivered nothing of value; failure; confusion; misunderstanding; occasional inexplicable hitting of the jackpot".

This apparent love-hate relationship is proof in itself that even a sceptic Mr Brown cannot deny the contribution that marketing has made and can make to customer satisfaction and economic value. It has contributed to both customers' and suppliers' quality of life by selecting profitable customer satisfaction as its sole objective. The marketing concept, together with other business disciplines, helped the UK to make the transition from a 19th-century manufacturing economy to a modern model of success in the service industry, creating an economic growth period never seen in UK history before.

It is marketing that has helped create value through customised products, no-questions-asked refund policies, comfortable cars, environmental attention, shopkeepers' smile, and guaranteed delivery dates. Even some government departments address the public not as 'the Queen's subjects' or 'the applicants' any more but as 'customers'. Of course all of the above is done for economic or political gain, for better or worse.

Despite all this achievement, to dismiss marketing as a failure is unfair. Marketing also helps companies avoid unnecessary R&D, operational and sales costs by helping to develop products because customers want them, not for the sake of innovation. Another success is the now commonly implemented value-pricing principle, whereby a product or service is sold for the price the customer is willing to pay, not on a cost-plus basis. This way, both suppliers and customers get a fair deal.

In the context of segmentation, Brown suggests that "the traditional, linear, step-by-step marketing model of analysis, planning, implementation and control no longer seems applicable, appropriate or even pertinent to what is actually happening on the ground". If Mr. Brown had studied "the ground" before making his statement, he would have realised that companies are successful the world over precisely because they implement this model.

They segment their markets, relate their products and services to them, define their value proposition and serve their customers accordingly. Examples are GE, HSBC, PriceWaterhouseCoopers, Smiths Aerospace, BAE Systems, BOC Edwards, Weir Group and BT to name but a few. A brief visit to their websites can make this point clear. Brown also has a constructive suggestion: "I reckon we need more passion in marketing, not less; it is time we banished banishing passion from works of marketing scholarship".

This refers mainly to promotion, which is only one element within the marketing concept. The truth is that marketing today leads the way in segmentation, innovation, pricing, product management, distribution, and last but not least, promotion. After all the contribution as well as further potential, to deny its successes and try to reduce it to only promotion is a great injustice to the marketing profession as well as to academic insight.

Contrary to Brown's suggestion in his final paragraph, we need objectivity, rigour, quantification, models, relationships, paradigm shifts and (some application of) science. Marketing is not full of holes, but a management process that has helped generate wealth and satisfied millions of customers for the most part of the 20th century. It can do even better in the 21st provided practitioners and scholars do not loose faith and focus. Kotler is not dead, but very much alive, and still kicking.

ADVERTISING

Advertising is typically paid communication through a non-personal medium in which the sponsor is identified and the message is controlled. However, it can also include variations, such as publicity, public relations, personal selling, product placement, sponsorship, underwriting, and sales promotion. Major advertisers are typically corporations, but may also include schools, the military, political candidates, advocacy groups, churches, and other organizations that pay to have their message delivered to an audience.

The media through which the message is delivered are varied: they include network and cable TV, radio, magazines, newspapers, the internet, billboards, handmade signs, sky writing, and bumper stickers; the list is almost endless. Strictly speaking, word-of-mouth is not advertising because it is not paid, the message is not controlled, and it is delivered by a personal rather than non-personal medium. Ironically, word-of-mouth communications are often far more effective than advertising campaigns that may have cost many millions of dollars.

"Buzz advertising" is a recent term used to describe an attempt by advertisers to simulate word-of-mouth communications. In ancient times, commercial messages and political campaign displays have been found in the ruins of Pompeii. Egyptians used papyrus to create sales messages and wall posters, while lost-and-found advertising on papyrus was common in Greece and Rome. Wall or rock painting for commercial advertising is another manifestation of an ancient media advertising form, which is present to this day in many parts of Asia, Africa, and South America.

For instance, the tradition of wall painting can be traced back to Indian rock-art paintings that goes back to 4000 BC. As printing developed in the 15th and 16th century, advertising expanded to include handbills. In the 17th century advertisements started to appear in weekly newspapers in England. These early print ads were used mainly to promote books,and newspapers which became increasingly affordable thanks to the printing press, and medicines, which were increasingly sought after as disease ravaged Europe. However, false advertising and so-called "quack" ads became a problem, which ushered in regulation of advertising content. As the economy was expanding during the 19th century, the need for advertising grew at the same pace.

In the United States, classified ads became popular, filling pages of newspapers with small print messages promoting all kinds of goods. The success of this advertising format led to the growth of mail-order advertising such as the Sears Catalog, at one time referred to as the "Farmer's Bible". In 1843 the first advertising agency was established by Volney Palmer in Philadelphia. At first the agencies were just brokers for ad space in newspapers, but it wasn't until N.W. Ayer and Son came along, advertising agencies started to take over responsibility for the content as well.

N.W. Ayer and Son was the first full service Ad Agency. They were also the first agency to start to charge commission on ads. When commercial radio stations began broadcasting in the early 1920's, the programmes were aired without advertising. Many radio stations were established by radio equipment manufacturers and retailers. Programming was provided to sell radio transmitters and receivers. The radio station owners soon realised they could earn more money by selling sponsorship rights to other businesses.

In those days, each show was usually sponsored by a single business, in exchange for a brief mention of the sponsor at the beginning and end of the show. This practice was carried over to televsion in the late 1940's and early 1950's. In the early 1950's, the Dumont television network began the modern trend of selling advertisement time to multiple sponsors. Dumont had trouble finding sponsors for many of their programmes and compensated by selling smaller blocks of advertising time to several businesses.

This eventually became the norm for the commercial television industry in the United States. The 1960s saw advertising transform into a modern, more scientific approach in which creativity was allowed to shine, producing unexpected messages that made advertisements more tempting to consumers' eyes. The Volkswagen ad campaign featuring such headlines as "Think Small" and "Lemon" ushered in the era of modern advertising by promoting a "position" or "unique selling proposition" designed to associate each brand with a specific idea in the reader or viewer's mind.

The late 1980s and early 1990s saw the introduction of cable television and particularly MTV. Pioneering the concept of the music video, MTV ushered in a new type of advertising: the consumer tunes in for the advertisement, rather than it being a byproduct or afterthought. As cable (and later satellite) television became increasingly prevalent, "specialty" channels began to emerge, and eventually entire channels, such as QVC and Home Shopping Network and ShopTV, devoted to advertising merchandise, where again the consumer tuned in for the ads. Marketing through the Internet opened new frontiers for advertisers and led to the "dot-com" boom of the 1990s.

Entire corporations operated solely on advertising revenue, offering everything from coupons to free Internet access. At the turn of the 21st century, the search engine Google revolutionized online advertising by emphasizing contextually relevant, unobtrusive ads intended to help, rather than inundate, users. This has led to a plethora of similar efforts and an increasing trend of interactive advertising. The share of advertising spending relative to total economic output (GDP) has changed little across large changes in media. For example, in the U.S. in 1925, the main advertising media were newspapers, magazines, signs on streetcars, and outdoor posters.

Advertising spending as a share of U.S. GDP was about 2.6% in 1925. By 1998, television and radio had become major advertising media. Nonetheless, advertising spending as a share of GDP was slightly lower—about 2.4%. A recent advertising innovation is "gue-rilla promotions", which involve unusual approaches such as staged encounters in public places, giveaways of products such as cars that are covered with brand messages, and interactive advertising where the viewer can respond to become part of the advertising message. This reflects an increasing trend of interactive and "embedded" ads, such as via product placement, having consumers vote through text messages, and various innovations utilizing social networking sites (*e.g.* Myspace).

PRODUCT ADVERTISING

Certain products use a specific form of advertising known as "Custom publishing". This form of advertising is usually targeted at a specific segment of society, but may also "draw" the attention of others. The same advertising techniques used to promote commercial goods and services can be used to inform, educate and motivate the public about non-commercial issues, such as AIDS, political ideology, energy conservation, religious recruitment, and deforestation. Advertising, in its non-commercial guise, is a powerful educational tool capable of reaching and motivating large audiences.

"Advertising justifies its existence when used in the public interest—it is much too powerful a tool to use solely for commercial purposes."—Attributed to Howard Gossage by David Ogilvy Public service advertising, non-commercial advertising, public interest advertising, cause marketing, and social marketing are different terms for (or aspects of) the use of sophisticated advertising and marketing communications techniques (generally associated with commercial enterprise) on behalf of non-commercial, public interest issues and initiatives.

In the United States, the granting of television and radio licenses by the FCC is contingent upon the station broadcasting a certain amount of public service advertising. To meet these requirements, many broadcast stations in America air the bulk of their required Public Service Announcements during the late night or early morning when the smallest percentage of viewers are watching, leaving more day and prime time commercial slots available for high-paying advertisers. Public service advertising reached its height during World Wars I and II under the direction of several governments. Commercial advertising media can include wall paintings, billboards, street furniture components, printed flyers, radio, cinema and television ads, web banners, web popups, skywriting, bus stop benches, magazines, newspapers, town criers, sides of buses, taxicab doors and roof mounts, musical stage shows, subway platforms and trains, elastic bands on disposable diapers, stickers on apples in supermarkets, the opening part of streaming audio and video, posters, chicken niblets, and the backs of event tickets and supermarket receipts. Any place an "identified" sponsor pays to deliver their message through a medium is advertising.

Covert advertising embedded in other entertainment media is known as product placement. A more recent version of this is advertising in film, by having a main character use an item or other of a definite brand—an example is in the movie Minority Report, where Tom Cruise's character Tom Anderton owns a computer with the Nokia logo clearly written in the top corner, or his watch engraved with the Bulgari logo. Another example of advertising in film is in I, Robot, where main character played by Will Smith mentions his Converse shoes several times, calling them "classics," because the film is set far in the future.

Cadillac chose to advertise in the movie The Matrix Reloaded, which as a result contained many scenes in which Cadillac cars were used. Similarly, product placement for Omega Watches, BMW and Aston-Martin cars are featured in recent James Bond films, most notably, Casino Royale. The TV commercial is generally considered the most effective mass-market advertising format and this is reflected by the high prices TV networks charge for commercial airtime during popular TV events.

The annual Super Bowl football game in the United States is known as much for its commercial advertisements as for the game itself, and the average cost of a single thirty-second TV spot during this game has reached $2.5 million (as of 2006). Virtual advertisements may be inserted into regular television programming through computer graphics. It is typically inserted into otherwise blank backdrops or used to replace local billboards that are not relevant to the remote broadcast audience. More controversially, virtual billboards may be inserted into the background where none existing in real-life. Virtual product placement is also possible. Advertising on the World Wide Web is a recent phenomenon. Prices of Web-based advertising space are dependent on the "relevance" of the surrounding web content and the traffic that the website receives.

E-mail advertising is another recent phenomenon. Unsolicited bulk E-mail advertising is known as "spam". Some companies have proposed to place messages or corporate logos on the side of booster rockets and the International Space Station. Controversy exists on the effectiveness of subliminal advertising and the pervasiveness of mass messages. Unpaid advertising (also called word of mouth advertising), can provide good exposure at minimal cost. Personal recommendations ("bring a friend", "sell it"), spreading buzz, or achieving the feat of equating a brand with a common noun ("Xerox" = "photocopier", "Kleenex" = tissue, and "Vaseline" = petroleum jelly)—these are the pinnacles of any advertising campaign. However, some companies oppose the use of their brand name to label an object.

The most common method for measuring the impact of mass media advertising is the use of the rating point (rp) or the more accurate target rating point (trp). These two measures refer to the percentage of the universe of the existing base of audience members that can be reached by the use of each media outlet in a particular moment in time. The difference between the two is that the rating point refers to the percentage to the entire universe while the target rating point refers to the percentage to a particular segment or target.

This becomes very useful when focusing advertising efforts on a particular group of people:

- For example, think of an advertising campaign targeting a female audience aged 25 to 45. While the overall rating of a TV show might be well over 10 rating points it might very well happen that the same show in the same moment of time is generating only

2.5 trps (being the target: women 25-45). This would mean that while the show has a large universe of viewers it is not necessarily reaching a large universe of women in the ages of 25 to 45 making it a less desirable location to place an ad for an advertiser looking for this particular demographic. Conversely, a TV show with a low overall rating point may be more successful at selling ads when its target rating points are high. In the United States, networks like the WB and FOX have had success with shows based on this premise; the shows had low overall ratings points, but delivered strong target rating points in the desired demographic.

ADVERTISEMENT IMPACT

The impact of advertising has been a matter of considerable debate and many different claims have been made in different contexts. During debates about the banning of cigarette advertising, a common claim from cigarette manufacturers was that cigarette advertising does not encourage people to smoke who would not otherwise. The (eventually successful) opponents of advertising, on the other hand, claim that advertising does in fact increase consumption. Many media sources, the past experience and state of mind of the person subjected to advertising may determine the impact that advertising has.

Children under the age of four may be unable to distinguish advertising from other television programmes, whilst the ability to determine the truthfulness of the message may not be developed until the age of 8. As advertising and marketing efforts become increasingly ubiquitous in modern Western societies, the industry has come under criticism of groups such as AdBusters via culture jamming which criticizes the media and consumerism using advertising's own techniques. The industry is accused of being one of the engines powering a convoluted economic mass production system which promotes consumption. Recognizing the social impact of advertising, Mediawatch-uk, a British special interest group, works to educate consumers about how they can register their concerns with advertisers and regulators. It has developed educational materials for use in schools. The award-winning book, Made You Look How Advertising Works and Why You Should Know, by former Mediawatch (a feminist organisation founded by Ann Simonton not linked to mediawatch-uk) president Shari Graydon, provides context for these issues for young readers.

Public interest groups are increasingly suggesting that access to the mental space targeted by advertisers should be taxed, in that at the present moment that space is being freely taken advantage of by advertisers with no compensation paid to the members of the public who are thus being intruded upon. This kind of tax would be a Pigovian tax in that it would act to reduce what is now increasingly seen as a public nuisance.

Efforts to that end are gathering momentum, with Arkansas and Maine considering bills to implement such taxation. Florida enacted such a tax in 1987 but was forced to repeal it after six months, as a result of a concerted effort by national commercial interests, which withdrew planned conventions, causing major losses to the tourism industry, and cancelled advertising, causing a loss of 12 million dollars to the broadcast industry alone. An extensively documented effect is the control and vetoing of free information by the advertisers.

Any negative information on a company or its products or operations often results in pressures from the company to withdraw such information lines, threatening to cut their ads. This behaviour makes the editors of the media self-censor content that might upset their ad payers. The bigger both companies are, the bigger their relation gets, maximizing control over a single information.

Advertisers may try to minimize information about or from consumer groups, or consumer controlled purchasing initiatives (as joint purchase systems), or consumer controlled quality information systems. Another indirect effect of advertising is to modify the very nature of the communication media where it is shown. Media that get most of their revenues from publicity try to make their medium a good place for communicating ads before anything else. The most clear example is television, where this means trying to make the public stay for a long time and in a mental state that encourages spectators not to switch the channel through the ads. Programmes that are low in mental stimulus and require light concentration and are varied are best for long sitting times.

These make for much easier emotional jumps to ads, which can become more entertaining than regular shows. A simple way to understand the objectives in television programming is to compare contents from channels paid and chosen by the viewer with channels that get their income mainly from advertisements.

There have been increasing efforts to protect the public interest by regulating the content and the reach of advertising. Some examples are the ban on television tobacco advertising imposed in many countries, and the total ban on advertising to children under twelve imposed by the Swedish government in 1991. Though that regulation continues in effect for broadcasts originating within the country, it has been weakened by the European Court of Justice, which has found that Sweden was obliged to accept whatever programming was targeted at it from neighbouring countries or via satellite. In Europe and elsewhere there is a vigourous debate on whether and how much advertising to children should be regulated.

This debate was exacerbated by a report released by the Kaiser Family Foundation in February 2004 which suggested that food advertising targeting children was an important factor in the epidemic of childhood obesity in the United States. In many countries—namely New Zealand, South Africa, Canada, and many European countries—the advertising industry operates a system of self-regulation. Advertisers, advertising agencies and the media agree on a code of advertising standards that they attempt to uphold. The general aim of such codes is to ensure that any advertising is 'legal, decent, honest and truthful'. Some self-regulatory organizations are funded by the industry, but remain independent, with the intent of upholding the standards or codes (like the Advertising Standards Authority in the UK). Naturally, many advertisers view governmental regulation or even self-regulation as intrusion of their freedom of speech or a necessary evil.

Therefore, they employ a wide-variety of linguistic devices to bypass regulatory laws (*e.g.* giving English words in bold and French translations in fine print to deal with the Article 12 of the 1994 Toubon Law limiting the use of English in French advertising). The advertising of controversial products such as cigarettes and condoms is subject to government regulation in many countries. For instance, the tobacco industry is required by law in India and Pakistan to display warnings cautioning consumers about the health hazards of their products.

Linguistic variation is often used by advertising as a creative device to reduce the impact of such requirement. With the dawn of the Internet have come many new advertising opportunities. Popup, Flash, banner, advergaming, and e-mail advertisements (the last often being a form of spam) abound. Each year, greater sums are paid to obtain a commercial spot during the Super Bowl, which is by most measures considered to be the most important football game of the year. Companies attempt to make these commercials sufficiently entertaining that members of the public will actually want to watch them. Another problem is people recording shows on DVRs (ex. TiVo).

These devices allow users to record the programmes for later viewing enabling them to fast forward through commercials. Additionally, as more seasons or "Boxed Sets" come out of Television shows; fewer people are watching their shows on TV. However, the fact that these sets are sold, means that the company will additionally receive profits from the sales of these sets. To counter this effect, many advertisers have opted for product placement on TV shows like Survivor. Particularly since the rise of "entertaining" advertising, some people may like an advert enough that they wish to watch it later or show a friend. In general, the advertising community has not yet made this easy, although some have used the Internet to widely distribute their adverts to anyone wishing to see or hear them. Another significant trend to note for the future of advertising is the growing importance of niche or targeted ads.

Also brought about by the Internet and the theory of The Long Tail, advertisers will have an increasing ability to reach narrow audiences. In the past, the most efficient way to deliver a message was to blanket the largest mass market audience possible. However, usage tracking, customer profiles and the growing popularity of niche content brought about by everything from blogs to social networking sites, provides advertisers with audiences that are smaller but much better defined, leading to ads that are more relevant to viewers and more effective for companies marketing products.

Among others, Comcast Spotlight is one such advertiser employing this method in their video on demand menus. These advertisements are targeted to a specific group and can be viewed by anyone wishing to find out more about a particular business or practice at any time, right from their home. This causes the viewer to become proactive and actually choose what advertisements they want to view.

ADVERTISING CAMPAIGN

An advertising campaign is a series of advertisement messages that share a single idea and theme which make up an integrated marketing communication (IMC). Advertising campaigns appear in different media across a specific time frame. The critical part of making an advertising campaign is determining a campaign theme, as it sets the tone for the individual advertisements and other forms of marketing communications that will be used.

The campaign theme is the central message that will be communicated in the promotional activities. The campaign themes are usually developed with the intention of being used for a substantial period but many of them are short lived due to factors such as being ineffective or market conditions and/ or competition in the marketplace.

COMMUNICATION DESIGN

Communication design is a sub-discipline of design which is concerned with how media intermission such as printed, crafted, electronic media or presentations communicate with people. A communication design approach is more concerned with messages communicated than aesthetics in media.

The distinction between communication design and other applied arts is in the motivation: while the communication design process does involve a certain amount of self-expression and creativity, the goals are often those of the commissioning body rather than the artist's, and the parameters set by the commissioning body are often more constraining.

The term communication design is often used interchangeably with visual communication and more specifically graphic design, but has an alternate broader meaning that includes auditory communications as well as visual. Examples of Communication Design include information architecture, editing, typography, illustration and professional writing skills applied to creative industries.

ENVIRONMENTAL SCANNING

For a company to gain or maintain a sustainable competitive advantage, it must be ever vigilant, watching for changes in the business environment. It must also be agile enough to alter its strategies and plans when the need arises.

There are three ways of scanning the business environment:

- Ad-hoc scanning—Short term, infrequent examinations usually initiated by a crisis
- Regular scanning—Studies done on a regular schedule (say, once a year)
- Continuous scanning—(also called continuous learning)—continuous structured data collection and processing on a broad range of environmental factors

Most commentators feel that in today's turbulent business environment the best scanning method available is continuous scanning. This allows the firm to act quickly, take advantage of opportunities before competitors do, and respond to environmental threats before significant damage is done. Environmental scanning usually refers just to the macroenvironment, but it can also include industry and competitor analysis, consumer analysis, product innovations, and the company's internal environment.

Macroenvironmental scanning involves analysing:

- The Economy
  - GNP or GDP per capital
  - GNP or GDP growth
  - Unemployment rate
  - Inflation rate
  - Consumer and investor confidence
  - Inventory levels
  - Currency exchange rates
  - Merchandise trade balance
  - Financial and political health of trading partners
  - Balance of payments
  - Future trends
- Government
  - Political climate—amount of government activity
  - Political stability and risk
  - Government debt
  - Budget deficit or surplus
  - Corporate and personal tax rates
  - Payroll taxes
  - Import tariffs and quotas
  - Export restrictions
  - Restrictions on international financial flows
- Legal
  - Minimum wage laws
  - Environmental protection laws
  - Worker safety laws
  - Union laws
  - Copyright and patent laws
  - Anti- monopoly laws
  - Sunday closing laws

- Municipal licences
- Laws that favour business investment

- Technology
  - Efficiency of infrastructure, including: roads, ports, airports, rolling stock, hospitals, education, healthcare, communication, etc.
  - Industrial productivity
  - New manufacturing processes
  - New products and services of competitors
  - New products and services of supply chain partners
  - Any new technology that could impact the company
  - Cost and accessibility of electrical power
- Ecology
  - Ecological concerns that affect the firms production processes
  - Ecological concerns that affect customers' buying habits
  - Ecological concerns that affect customers' perception of the company or product
- Socio-Cultural
  - Demographic factors such as:
    - Population size and distribution
    - Age distribution
    - Education levels
    - Income levels
    - Ethnic origins
    - Religious affiliations
  - Attitudes towards:
    - Materialism, capitalism, free enterprise
    - Individualism, role of family, role of government, collectivism
    - Role of church and religion
    - Consumerism
    - Environmentalism
    - Importance of work, pride of accomplishment
  - Cultural structures including:

- Diet and nutrition
- Housing conditions

- Potential Suppliers
  - Labour supply
    - Quantity of labour available
    - Quality of labour available
    - Stability of labour supply
    - Wage expectations
    - Employee turn-over rate
    - Strikes and labour relations
    - Educational facilities
  - Material suppliers
    - Quality, quantity, price, and stability of material inputs
    - Delivery delays
    - Proximity of bulky or heavy material inputs
    - Level of competition among suppliers
  - Service Providers
    - Quantity, quality, price, and stability of service facilitators
    - Special requirements

Scanning these macroenvironmental variables for threats and opportunities requires that each issue be rated on two dimensions. It must be rated on its potential impact on the company, and rated on its likeliness of occurrence. Multiplying the potential impact parameter by the likeliness of occurrence parameter gives us a good indication of its importance to the firm.

SUSTAINABLE COMPETITIVE ADVANTAGE

Competitive advantage (CA) is a position that a firm occupies in its competitive landscape. Michael Porter posits that a competitive advantage, sustainable or not, exists when a company makes economic rents, that is, their earnings exceed their costs, especially including cost of capital. That means that normal competitive pressures are not able to drive down the firm's earnings to the point where they cover all costs and just provide minimum sufficient additional return to keep capital invested. Most forms of competitive advantage cannot be sustained for any length of time because the promise of economic rents drives competitiors to duplicate the competitive advantage held by any one firm. A firm possesses a Sustainable Competitive Advantage when it has value-creating processes and positions that cannot be duplicated or imitated by other firms that lead to the production of above normal rents.

An SCA is different from a competitive advantage (CA) in that it provides a long-term advantage that is not easily replicated. But these above-normal rents can attract new entrants who drive down economic rents. A CA is a position a firm attains that lead to above-normal rents or a superior financial performance. The processes and positions that engender such a position is not necessarily non-duplicable or inimitable. It is possible for some companies to make profits for a time above the cost of capital without sustainable competitive advantage.

A key difference between CA and SCA is that the processes and positions a firm may hold are non-duplicable and inimitable when a firm possesses a SCA. Hence a sustainable competitive advantage is one that can be maintained for a significant amount of time even in the presence of competition. This brings us to the question what is a "significant amount of time".

A CA becomes SCA when all duplication and imitation efforts have ceased and the rival firms have not been able to create the same value that the said firm is creating. Analysis of the factors of profitability is the subject of numerous theories of strategy including the five forces model pioneered by Michael Porter of the Harvard Business School.

In marketing and strategic management, sustainable competitive advantage is an advantage that one firm has relative to competing firms. The source of the advantage can be something the company does that is distinctive and difficult to replicate, also known as a core competency—for example Procter and Gamble's ability to derive superior consumer insights and implement them in managing its brand portfolio.

It can also be an asset such as a brand (*e.g.* Coca Cola) or a patent, such as Viagra. It can also simply be a result of the industry's cost structure—for example, the large fixed costs that tend to create natural monopolies in utility industries.

To be sustainable, the advantage must be:

1. Distinctive, and
2. Proprietary

BUILDING SUSTAINABLE COMPETITIVE ADVANTAGE

There are basically three types of assets that help build an SCA.

These categories are exhaustive and include all of the company's SCAs:

1. Organization and managerial process
   - *Coordination and integration:* Coordination among teams in organization is key to organizational success. Interdepartmental coordination and resource sharing to reach a common goal is fundamental to creating "value". Integrating resources is key to the success of firms. Firms that are able to integrate resources see synergistic effects of resources coming together.
   - *Learning:* Organizational learning is key to the success of a firm. It determines how a firm collects, distributes, interprets and responds to market based information collection and changes in the environment. These changes in the environment could be customer based changes, technological developments, legal and government restrictions. Firms have to develop robust market sensing and spanning capabilities to effectively collect information. Once they collect info they have embed this knowledge in the products they produce.
   - *Reconfiguring and transformation:* The environment for firms is constantly changing and constant reconfiguring and transformation is key to forming SCA. A double loop learning and

transformation is key to producing innovative products. Innovative capacity of a firm determines how it reacts and learns from market information.

2. *Positions:* Market positions are the assets of a company. Most of them are self-explanatory
   - Technological assets
   - Financial assets
   - Reputational assets
   - Structural assets: The structure of a company can determine how it performs. The hierarchy of a company can influence its culture, procedure and routines.
3. Paths
   - *Path dependencies:* At the birth of a company usually accompanied with certain orientations. The progenitor brings certain orientations and attributes that stay with the company for a long time. The path the company takes then determines the development of its competencies.
   - *Technological opportunities:* Technology development at a time can determine how a firm can exploit opportunities to form SCA. Very often we see the advent of several technological factors converging into a capability that forms a SCA. An example would be the rise of companies such as Genentech at the turn of the previous century with the advent of gene mapping, significant developments in target selection and databases of previous studies and gene pools.

STRATEGIC MANAGEMENT

Strategic management is that set of managerial decisions and actions that determines the long-run performance of a corporation. It includes environmental scanning, strategy formulation, strategy implementation and evaluation and control. An organization's strategy must be appropriate for its resources, environmental circumstances, and core objectives. The process involves matching the company's [internal resources (eg IT) and capabilities (eg quality management)] to the external business environment the organization faces.

Strategy formulation involves:

- Doing a situation analysis: both internal and external; both micro-environmental and macro-environmental.
- Concurrent with this assessment, objectives are set. This involves crafting vision statements (long term view of a possible future), mission statements (the role that the organization gives itself in society), overall corporate objectives (both financial and strategic), strategic business unit objectives (both financial and strategic), and tactical objectives.
- These objectives should, in the light of the situation analysis, sugsgest a strategic plan. The plan provides the details of how to achieve these objectives.

This three-step strategy formulation process is sometimes referred to as determining where you are now, determining where you want to go, and then determining how to get there. These three questions are the essence of strategic planning. SWOT Analysis: I/O Economics for the external factors and RBV for the internal factors.

Strategy Implementation involves:

- Allocation of sufficient resources (financial, personnel, time, technology support)
- Establishing a chain of command or some alternative structure (such as cross functional teams)
- Assigning responsibility of specific tasks or processes to specific individuals or groups
- It also involves managing the process. This includes monitoring results, comparing to benchmarks and best practices, evaluating the efficacy and efficiency of the process, controlling for variances, and making adjustments to the process as necessary.
- When implementing specific programmes, this involves acquiring the requisite resources, developing the process, training, process testing, documentation,

and integration with (and/or conversion from) legacy processes.

Strategy formulation and implementation is an on-going, never-ending, integrated process requiring continuous reassessment and reformation. Strategic management is dynamic. It involves a complex pattern of actions and reactions.

It is partially planned and partially unplanned. Strategy is both planned and emergent, dynamic, and interactive. Some people (such as Andy Grove at Intel) feel that there are critical points at which a strategy must take a new direction in order to be in step with a changing business environment. These critical points of change are called strategic inflection points.

TIME SCALES

Strategic management operates on several time scales. Short term strategies involve planning and managing for the present. Long term strategies involve preparing for and preempting the future. Marketing strategist Derek Abell (1993), has suggested that understanding this dual nature of strategic management is the least understood part of the process.

He claims that balancing the temporal aspects of strategic planning requires the use of dual strategies simultaneously. Strategic Management is actually a solid foundation or a framework within which all the functionning managerial operations are bundled together.

This is the highest level corporate activity that sets the terms and goals for a company that it should follow for prosperity. In general terms, there are two main approaches to strategic management which are opposite but complement each other in some ways.

- 'The Industrial Organization Approach'
  - Based on economic theory—deals with issues like competitive rivalry, resource allocation, economies of scale
  - Assumptions—rationality, self discipline behaviour, profit maximization
- The Sociological Approach

- Deals primarily with human interactions
- Assumptions—bounded rationality, satisficing behaviour, profit sub-optimality.

Strategic management techniques can be viewed as bottom-up, top-down, or collaborative processes. In the bottom-up approach, employees submit proposals to their managers who, in turn, funnel the best ideas further up the organization. This is often accomplished by a capital budgeting process. Proposals are assessed using financial criteria such as return on investment or cost-benefit analysis.

The proposals that are approved form the substance of a new strategy, all of which is done without a grand strategic design or a strategic architect. The top-down approach is the most common by far. In it, the CEO, possibly with the assistance of a strategic planning team, decides on the overall direction the company should take.

Some organizations are starting to experiment with collaborative strategic planning techniques that recognize the emergent nature of strategic decisions. In most (large) corporations there are several levels of strategy. Strategic management is the highest in the sense that it is the broadest, applying to all parts of the firm. It gives direction to corporate values, corporate culture, corporate goals, and corporate missions.

Under this broad corporate strategy there are often functional or business unit strategies. Functional strategies include marketing strategies, new product development strategies, human resource strategies, financial strategies, legal strategies, and information technology management strategies. The emphasis is on short and medium term plans and is limited to the domain of each department's functional responsibility.

Each functional department attempts to do its part in meeting overall corporate objectives, and hence to some extent their strategies are derived from broader corporate strategies. Many companies feel that a functional organizational structure is not an efficient way to organize activities so they have reengineered according to processes or strategic business units (called SBUs). A strategic business unit is a semi-autonomous unit within an organization. It is usually responsible for its own budgeting, new product decisions, hiring decisions, and price setting. An SBU is treated as an internal profit centre by corporate headquarters.

Each SBU is responsible for developing its business strategies, strategies that must be in tune with broader corporate strategies. The "lowest" level of strategy is operational strategy. It is very narrow in focus and deals with day-to-day operational activities such as scheduling criteria. It must operate within a budget but is not at liberty to adjust or create that budget. Operational level strategy was encouraged by Peter Drucker in his theory of management by objectives (MBO).

Operational level strategies are informed by business level strategies which, in turn, are informed by corporate level strategies. Business strategy, which refers to the aggregated operational strategies of single business firm or that of an SBU in a diversified corporation refers to the way in which a firm competes in its chosen arenas. Corporate strategy, then, refers to the overarching strategy of the diversified firm. Such corporate strategy answers the questions of "in which businesses should we compete?"

and "how does being in one business add to the competitive advantage of another portfolio firm, as well as the competitive advantage of the corporation as a whole?" Since the turn of the millennium, there has been a tendency in some firms to revert to a simpler strategic structure. This is being driven by information technology.

It is felt that knowledge management systems should be used to share information and create common goals. Strategic divisions are thought to hamper this process. Most recently, this notion of strategy has been captured under the rubric of dynamic strategy, popularized by the strategic management textbook authored by Carpenter and Sanders. This work builds on that of Brown and Eisenhart as well as Christensen and portrays firm strategy, both business and corporate, as necessarily embracing ongoing strategic change, and the seamless integration of strategy formulation and implementation. Such change and implementation are usually built into the strategy through the staging and pacing facets.

Why Strategic Plans Fails

There are many reasons why strategic plans fail, especially:

- Failure to understand the customer
  - Why do they buy
  - Is there a real need for the product
  - Inadequate or incorrect marketing research
- Inability to predict environmental reaction
  - What will competitors do
    a. Fighting brands
    b. Price wars
  - Will government intervene
- Over-estimation of resource competence
  - Can the staff, equipment, and processes handle the new strategy
  - Failure to develop new employee and management skills
- Failure to coordinate
  - Reporting and control relationships not adequate
  - Organizational structure not flexible enough
- Failure to obtain senior management commitment
  - Failure to get management involved right from the start
  - Failure to obtain sufficient company resources to accomplish task
- Failure to obtain employee commitment
  - New strategy not well explained to employees
  - No incentives given to workers to embrace the new strategy
- Under-estimation of time requirements
  - No critical path analysis done
- Failure to follow the plan
  - No follow through after initial planning
  - No tracking of progress against plan

  - No consequences for above
- Failure to manage change
  - Inadequate understanding of the internal resistance to change
  - Lack of vision on the relationships between processes, technology and organization
- Poor communications
  - Insufficient information sharing among stakeholders
  - Exclusion of stakeholders and delegates
- Failure to focus
  - Inability or unwillingness to make choices which are true to the strategic mission (*i.e.* to do fewer things, better), leads to mediocrity, inability to compete

Although a sense of direction is important, it can also stifle creativity, especially if it is rigidly enforced. In an uncertain and ambiguous world, fluidity can be more important than a finely tuned strategic compass.

When a strategy becomes internalized into a corporate culture, it can lead to group think. It can also cause an organization to define itself too narrowly. An example of this is marketing myopia. Most theories of strategic management seem to have a lifespan less than that of the popularity of the latest teen music idol.

Many critics claim that this is because most of them generally do not work. For every theory that gets incorporated into strategic management textbooks there are many that are quickly forgotten. Many theories tend either to be too narrow in focus to build a complete corporate strategy on, or too general and abstract to be applicable to specific situations. The low success rate is further fueled by the management lecture circuit in which hundreds of self-appointed gurus, many without serious academic credentials or substantial expertise, attempt to sell books and explain their "revolutionary" and "groundbreaking" theories to audiences of business executives for a sizable fee. While there are undoubtedly inspirational ideas contained in these seminars, the theories expounded therein have not, for the most part, been subjected to serious study. Some critics take the opposite approach claiming effectively that there are not enough theories, and when they arrive they are too late to help managers make any important decisions.

These commentators remind us that the basic, everyday purpose of strategic management is to match a company's strategy with the business environment that the organization is in. Because the environment is constantly changing, effective strategic management requires a continuous flow of new theories suitable for the new circumstances. The problem with most theories is that they solve yesterday's problems, similar to a business Maginot Line.

Various approaches to solve this problem have emerged, however, including Mintzberg's ideas of 'emergent strategies' and use of ideas from complexity theory in what is often called complexity strategy. Gary Hamel coined the term strategic convergence to explain the limited scope of the strategies being used by rivals in greatly differing circumstances. He lamented that strategies converge more than they should, because the more successful ones get imitated by firms that do not understand that the strategic process involves designing a custom strategy for the specifics of each situation.

2

Understanding the Tourism Management

In this course you will learn about the essential features of tourism industry, definition and meaning of various concepts, how to make travel arrangements, travel management, tourism marketing, tourism in India including emerging dimensions. In this session you will understand the different perspectives on the study of tourism, know the meaning of the term 'tourism', 'visitor tourist', 'excursionist', 'inbound' and 'outbound tourist' and the difference between travel and tourism.

CHANGING FACETS OF TOURISM

From the very inception of life, travel has fascinated man. Travel and tourism have been important social activities of human beings from time immemorial. The urge to explore new places within one's own country or outside and seek a change of environment and experience has been experienced from ancient times. Tourism is one of the world's most rapidly growing industries.

Much of its growth is due to higher disposable incomes, increased leisure time and falling costs of travel. As airports become more enjoyable places to pass through, as travel agency services become increasingly automated, and as tourists find it easier to get information on places they want to visit, tourism grows. The Internet has fuelled the growth of the travel industry by providing on line booking facilities. It has also provided people with the power to explore destinations and cultures from their home personal computers and make informed choices before finalizing travel plans. With its immense information resources, the Internet allows tourists to scrutinise hotels, check weather forecasts, read up on local food and even talk to other tourists around the world about their travel experiences for a chosen destination. This new trend has made the tourism job very challenging.

The holiday makers want a good rate of return on their investment. They are to be lured with value additions and improved customer service. This also put emphasis on the regular flow of manpower with specific skills at the appropriate levels to match and cater to global standards. The success of the hospitality industry comes from provision of quality rooms, food, service and ambience. There is no doubt that fitness has increasingly become a larger part of everyone's life. And business and leisure travellers alike look to maintain their fitness goals while away from home.

Awareness should be created about the environment and education. A collective effort and co-operation with powerful networking are the need of the hour. People should be acting as the watchdogs of the society as far as environmental issues are concerned. Eco-tourists are a growing community and tourism promotions have to adopt such eco-practices which could fit this growing community. Another growing trend in the tourism scene is the Incentive Market and the scope of the destination to attract conferences and convention traffic.

Here the prospects are better for those destinations where state of the art infrastructure has been developed along with a safe and clean image. Tourism today is much more than just developing products. It is more about quality, insightful thinking and ability to have global information about technology, partners, contacts and responding quickly to global and regional trends.

The fundamental task before tourism promotion is to facilitate integration of the various components in the tourism trade as active participants in the nation's social and cultural life. There is a long road ahead. All must work towards a society where people can work and participate as equal partners. Tourism should be a vehicle for international cooperation and understanding of the various civilizations and a harbinger of peace. From the foregoing we can see how fast the face of tourism is changing and how challenging the job of travel agencies is now. There is therefore a need for proper training of the personnel working in the industry through thorough and a detailed study of the subject A unified approach to the subject is also needed since at present people from different fields have been studying tourism from different perspectives.

DIFFERENT PERSPECTIVES ON THE STUDY OF TOURISM

GEOGRAPHICAL PERSPECTIVE

Geographical Perspective—from a geographer's perspective the main concern of tourism is to look into aspects like the geographical location of a place, the climate, the landscape, the environment, the physical planning and the changes in these emerging from provisioning of tourism facilities and amenities. A geographer feels that it is the climate, landscape or physical attributes which draw the tourist to a destination, for example; if a person from Delhi goes to Shimla in the summer he does so because of the cooler climate which he cannot get in Delhi

SOCIOLOGICAL PERSPECTIVE

From a sociologist's perspective Tourism is a social activity; it is about interaction between different communities—hosts and guests—and encounter between different cultures. This approach studies social classes, habits and customs of both hosts and guests in terms of tourism behaviour of individuals or groups of people and the impact of tourism on society.

HISTORICAL PERSPECTIVE

An historian's perspective tourism is a study of the factors instrumental in the initiation of tourism to a particular destination, the order of happenings leading to tourism development, the reasons for happening of the occurrences in that order, beneficiaries of the tourist activity and an untimely and premature identification of negative effects. For example we all know that a lot of tourists visit Taj Mahal in Agra but a historian would be interested in studying the factors that bring the tourist there, *e.g.* the architecture, the story behind the monument, or something else that draws them there.

MANAGERIAL PERSPECTIVE

The management perspective tourism is an industry, and therefore needs managerial skills in order to be properly managed. As the industry grows we see continuous changes in various organisations and services linked with the industry, the tourism products and so on so this approach concentrates on management activities such as planning, research, pricing, marketing, control etc. as vital to the operation of a tourist establishment.

ECONOMIC PERSPECTIVE

From an economist's perspective tourism is a major source of foreign exchange earnings, a generator of personal and corporate incomes, a creator of employment and a contributor to government earnings. It is a dominant global activity surpassing even trade in oil and manufactured goods. Economists study the effects of tourism industry on the economy. This is a two way process.

THE IMPORTANCE OF MANAGERIAL AND ECONOMIC PERSPECTIVES OF TOURISM

Now due to higher disposable incomes, increased leisure time and falling cost of travel, the Tourism industry has shown a very high growth and since tourism is a service industry it comprises of a number of tangible and intangible components. The tangible elements include transport systems—air, rail, road, water and now, space; hospitality services—accommodation, food and beverage, tours, souvenirs; and related services such as banking, insurance and safety and security. The intangible elements include: rest and relaxation, culture, escape, adventure, new and different experiences. As there are number of bodies involved the need arises for a management of services related to this industry and so the study of Tourism acquires a great practical necessity and usefulness. Tourism industry is very fast growing and this industry involves activities and interests of Transport Undertakings, Owners of Tourist Sites and Attractions, Various tourist Service Providers at the tourist destinations and Central and Local Government, etc.

Each of these serves both the resident population and the tourists and their management must reconcile the needs of tourists with the needs of the resident population. So it becomes important to study tourism from the perspective of Management, since the management of various bodies in this industry is invaded.

TOURISM IN INDIA—DEFINITION AND MEANING

Tourism is the largest service industry in India, with a contribution of 6.23% to the national GDP and 8.78% of the total employment in India. India witnesses more than 5 million annual foreign tourist arrivals and 562 million domestic tourism visits. The tourism industry in India generated about US$100 billion in 2008 and that is expected to increase to US$275.5 billion by 2018 at a 9.4% annual growth rate. The Ministry of Tourism is the nodal agency for the development and promotion of tourism in India and maintains the "Incredible India" campaign.

World Travel and Tourism Council, India will be a tourism hotspot from 2009–2018, having the highest 10-year growth potential. The Travel and Tourism Competitiveness Report 2007 ranked tourism in India 6th in terms of price competitiveness and 39th in terms of safety and security. Despite short- and medium-term setbacks, such as shortage of hotel rooms, tourism revenues are expected to surge by 42% from 2007 to 2017. India has a growing medical tourism sector. The 2010 Commonwealth Games in Delhi are expected to significantly boost tourism in India.

TOURISM BY STATE

Andhra Pradesh

Andhra Pradesh has a rich cultural heritage and a variety of tourist attractions. The state of Andhra Pradesh comprises scenic hills, forests, beaches and temples. Also known as The City of Nizams and The City of Pearls, Hyderabad is today one of the most developed cities in the country and a modern hub of information technology, ITES, and biotechnology. Hyderabad is known for its rich history, culture and architecture representing its unique character as a meeting point for North and South India, and also its multilingual culture. Andhra Pradesh is the home of many religious pilgrim centres. Tirupati, the abode of Lord Venkateswara, is the richest and most visited religious centre in the world. Srisailam, the abode of Sri Mallikarjuna, is one of twelve Jyothirlingalu in India, Amaravati's Siva temple is one of the Pancharamams, and Yadagirigutta, the abode of an avatara of Vishnu, Sri Lakshmi Narasimha.

The Ramappa temple and Thousand Pillars temple in Warangal are famous for some fine temple carvings. The state has numerous Buddhist centres at Amaravati, Nagarjuna Konda, Bhattiprolu, Ghantasala, Nelakondapalli, Dhulikatta, Bavikonda, Thotlakonda, Shalihundam, Pavuralakonda, Sankaram, Phanigiri and Kolanpaka.

The golden beaches at Visakhapatnam, the one-million-year old limestone caves at Borra, picturesque Araku Valley, hill resorts of Horsley Hills, river Godavari racing through a narrow gorge at Papi Kondalu, waterfalls at Ettipotala, Kuntala and rich bio-diversity at Talakona, are some of the natural attractions of the state. Visakhapatnam is home to many tourist attactions such as the INS Karasura Submarine museum, Yarada Beach, Araku Valley, VUDA Park, Indira Gandhi Zoological Gardens.

The weather in Andhra Pradesh is mostly tropical and the best time to visit is in November through to January. The monsoon season commences in June and ends in September, so travel would not be advisable during this period. Also worth visiting, the only Indian Buddhism Based Theme Park and Resorts on the Vijayawada—Guntur Highway—Agrigold Haailand.

Arunachal Pradesh

Arunachal Pradesh attracts tourists from many parts of the world. Tourist attractions include Tawang, a beautiful town famous for its Buddhist monastery, Ziro, famous for cultural festivals, the Namdapha tiger project in Changlang district and Sela lake near Bomdila with its bamboo bridges overhanging the river. Religious places of interest include Malinithan in Lekhabali, Rukhmininagar near Roing and Parshuram Kund in Lohit district. Rafting and trekking are common activities. A visitor's permit from the tourism department is required. Places like Tuting have wonderful, undiscovered scenic beauty.

Assam

Assam is the central state in the North-East Region of India and serves as the gateway to the rest of the Seven Sister States. Assam boasts of famous wildlife preserves–the Kaziranga National Park, which is home to the Great Indian One-Horned Rhinoceros and the Manas National Park, the largest river island Majuli, historic Sivasagar, famous for the ancient monuments of Ahom Kingdom, the city of eternal romance, Tezpur and tea-estates dating back to time of British Raj. The weather is mostly sub-tropical.

Assam experiences the Indian monsoon and has one of the highest forest densities in India. The winter months are the best time to visit. Assam has a rich cultural heritage going back to the Ahom Kingdom, which governed the region for many centuries before the British occupation.

Other notable features include the Brahmaputra River, the mystery of the bird suicides in Jatinga, numerous temples including Kamakhya of Tantric sect. 'Gurdwara Sri Guru Tegh Bahadur also known as Damdama Sahib at Dhubri '. This famous Gurudwara is situated in the heart of the Dhubri Town on the bank of the mighty Brahmaputra river in far north-east

India. Guru Nanak the first Sikh Guru visited this place in 1505 and met Srimanta Sankardeva as the Guru travelled from Dhaka to Assam, ruins of palaces, etc. Guwahati, the capital city of Assam, boasts many bazaars, temples, and wildlife sanctuaries.

Bihar

Bihar is one of the oldest continuously inhabited places in the world with history of 3000 years. The rich culture and heritage of Bihar is evident from the innumerable ancient monuments that are dotted all over this state in eastern India. This is the Place of Aryabhata, Great Ashoka, Chanakya and many more.

Attractions:

- *Patna*: The capital of Bihar, famous for its rich history and royal architecture. Golghar and Budha Smriti Park are famous lanmarks.
- *Gaya*: Known for Bodh Gaya the place at which Gautam Buddha attained enlightenment.Attraction for Buddhists across the globe.
- *Barauni*: Petrochemical work for national level
- *Muzaffarpur*: Famous for its education.
- *Kesariya*: World's largest Buddhist Stupa located here.
- *Nalanda*: World's oldest university remains here.
- *Sasaram*: Tomb of Sher Shah Suri, the great Emperor of Mughal age who defeated Humayun.
- *Sonpur*: The Sonepur Cattle Fair or Sonepur Mela,it is the biggest cattle fair of Asia and stretches on from fifteen days to one month.
- *Takht Sri Patna Sahib*: One of the famous Sikh pilgrimage known for the birth place of Sikh's Tenth Guru Sri Guru Gobind Singh Sahib.

Bihar is one of the most sacred places of various religions such as Hinduism, Buddhism, Jainism, Sikhism and Islam. Famous Attraction includes Mahabodhi Temple, a Buddhist shrine and UNESCO World Heritage Site is also situated in Bihar, Barabar Caves the oldest rockcut caves in India, Khuda Bakhsh Oriental Library the Oldest Library of India.

Delhi

Delhi is the capital city of India. A fine blend of old and new, ancient and modern, Delhi is a melting pot of cultures, religions. Delhi has been the capital of numerous empires that ruled India, making it rich in history. The rulers left behind their trademark architectural styles. Delhi currently has many renowned historic monuments and landmarks such as the Tughlaqabad fort, Qutub Minar, Purana Quila, Lodhi Gardens, Jama Masjid, Humayun's tomb, Red Fort, and Safdarjung's Tomb. Modern monuments include Jantar Mantar, India Gate, Rashtrapati Bhavan, Laxminarayan Temple, Lotus temple and Akshardham Temple.

New Delhi is famous for its British colonial architecture, wide roads, and tree-lined boulevards. Delhi is home to numerous political landmarks, national museums, Islamic shrines, Hindu temples, green parks, and trendy malls.

Goa

Goa is one of the most famous tourist destinations in India. A former colony of Portugal, Goa is famous for its excellent beaches, Portuguese churches, Hindu temples, and wildlife sanctuaries. The Basilica of Bom Jesus, Mangueshi Temple, Dudhsagar Falls, and Shantadurga are famous attractions in Goa. Recently a Wax Museum has also opened in Old Goa housing a number of wax personalities of Indian history, culture and heritage. The Goa Carnival is a world famous event, with colourful masks and floats, drums and reverberating music, and dance performances. The celebrations run three days culminating in a carnival parade on fat Tuesday.

Himachal Pradesh

Himachal Pradesh is famous for its Himalayan landscapes and popular hill-stations. Many outdoor activities such as rock climbing, mountain biking, paragliding, ice-skating, and heli-skiing are popular tourist attractions in Himachal Pradesh. Shimla, the state capital, is very popular among tourists. The Kalka-Shimla Railway is a Mountain railway which is a UNESCO World Heritage Site. Shimla is also a famous skiing attraction in India. Other popular hill stations include Manali and Kasauli. Dharamshala, home of the Dalai Lama, is known for its Tibetan monasteries and Buddhist temples. Many trekking expeditions also begin here.

Jammu and Kashmir

Jammu and Kashmir is the northernmost state of India. Jammu is noted for its scenic landscape, ancient temples, Hindu shrines, castles, gardens and forts. The Hindu holy shrines of Amarnath in kashmir attracts about.4 million Hindu devotees every year. Vaishno Devi alsoattract tens of thousands of Hindu devotees every year. Jammu's historic monuments feature a unique blend of Islamic and Hindu architecture styles.

Tourism forms an integral part of the Kashmiri economy. Often dubbed "Paradise on Earth", Kashmir's mountainous landscape has attracted tourists for centuries. Notable places are Dal Lake, Srinagar Phalagam, Gulmarg, Yeusmarg and Mughal Gardens etc. Kashmir's natural landscape has made it one of the popular destinations for adventure tourism in South Asia.Marked by four distinct seasons,Ski enthusiasts can enjoy the exotic himalayan powder during winters.

7000000 tourists arrived in kashmir in the months of April,May and June alone In recent years, Ladakh has emerged as a major hub for adventure tourism. This part of Greater Himalaya called "moon on earth" comprising of naked peaks and deep gorges was once known for the silk route to High Asia from the subcontinent. Leh is also a growing tourist spot.

Karnataka

Karnataka has been ranked as fourth most popular destination for tourism among states of India. It has the second highest number of protected monuments in India, at 507. Kannada dynasties like Kadambas, Western Gangas, Chalukyas, Rashtrakutas, Hoysalas and Vijayanagaras, ruled Karnataka particularly North Karnataka. They built great monuments to Buddhism, Jainism, Shaivism. The monuments are still present at Badami, Aihole, Pattadakal, Hampi,

Lakshmeshwar, Sudi, Hooli, Mahadeva Temple, Dambal, Lakkundi, Gadag, Hangal, Halasi, Galaganatha, Chaudayyadanapura, Banavasi, Belur, Halebidu, Shravanabelagola, Sannati and many more. Notable Islamic monuments are present at Bijapur, Bidar, Gulbarga, Raichur and other part of the state.

Gol Gumbaz at Bijapur, has the second largest pre-modern dome in the world after the Byzantine Hagia Sophia. Karnataka has two World heritage sites, at Hampi and Pattadakal, both are in North Karnataka. Karnataka is famous for its waterfalls. Jog falls of Shimoga District is one of the highest waterfalls in Asia. This state has 21 wildlife sanctuaries and five National parks and is home to more than 500 species of birds. Karnataka has many beaches at Karwar, Gokarna, Murdeshwara, Surathkal. Karnataka is a rock climbers paradise. Yana in Uttara Kannada, Fort in Chitradurga, Ramnagara near Bangalore district, Shivagange in Tumkur district and tekal in Kolar district are a rock climbers heaven.

Kerala

Kerala is a state on the tropical Malabar Coast of southwestern India. Nicknamed as one of the "10 paradises of the world" by National Geographic, Kerala is famous especially for its ecotourism initiatives. Its unique culture and traditions, coupled with its varied demography, has made it one of the most popular tourist destinations in India. Growing at a rate of 13.31%, the tourism industry significantly contributes to the state's economy. Kerala is known for its tropical backwaters and pristine beaches such as Kovalam.

Madhya Pradesh

Madhya Pradesh is called the "Heart of India" because of its location in the centre of the country. It has been home to the cultural heritage of Hinduism, Islam, Buddhism, Sikhism, Jainism. Innumerable monuments, exquisitely carved temples, stupas, forts and palaces are dotted all over the State. The temples of Khajuraho are world-famous for their erotic sculptures, and are a UNESCO World Heritage Site. Gwalior is famous for its forts, the Tomb of Rani Lakshmibai, and the Palace of Tansen. Madhya Pradesh is also known as Tiger State because of the tiger population. Famous national parks like Kanha, Bandhavgadh, Shivpuri, Sanjay, Pench are located in MP. Spectacular mountain ranges, meandering rivers and miles and miles of dense forests offering a unique and exciting panorama of wildlife in sylvan surroundings.

Maharashtra

Maharashtra is the second most visited state in India by foreign tourists, with more than 2 million foreign tourists arrivals annually. Maharashtra boasts of a large number of popular and revered religious venues that are heavily frequented by locals as well as out-of-state visitors. Ajanta Caves, Ellora Caves and Chhatrapati Shivaji Terminus are the three UNESCO World Heritage sites in Maharashtra and are highly responsible for the development of Tourism in the state. Mumbai is the most cosmopolitan city in India, and a great place to experience modern India.

Mumbai famous for Bollywood, the world's largest film industry. In addition, Mumbai is famous for its clubs, shopping, and upscale gastronomy. The city is known for its architecture, from the ancient Elephanta Caves, to the Islamic Haji Ali Mosque, to the colonial architecture of Bombay High Court and Chhatrapati Shivaji Terminus. Maharashtra also has numerous adventure tourism destinations, including paragliding, rock climbing, canoeing, kayaking, snorkeling, and scuba diving in places like Kolad, Tarkarli, Koyna, Manor. aharashtra also has several pristine national parks and reserves, some of the best ones are Tadoba with excellent accommodation and safari experiences besides little known by amazing wildlife destinations like Koyna, Nagzira, Melghat, Dajipur, Radhanagari and of course the only national park within metropolic city limits in the world—Sanjay Gandhi National Park.

The Bibi Ka Maqbara at Aurangabad the Mahalakshmi temple at Kolhapur, the cities of Nashik, Trimbak famous for religious importance and the city of Pune the seat of the

Maratha Empire and the fantastic Ganesh Chaturthi celebrations together contribute for the Tourism sector of Mahrashtra.

Manipur

Manipur as the name suggest is a land of jewels. Its rich culture excels in every aspects as in martial arts, dance, theater and sculpture. The charm of the place is the greenery with the moderate climate making it a tourists' heaven.

The beautiful and seasonal Shirui Lily at Ukhrul, Sangai and the floating islands at Loktak Lake are few of the rare things found in Manipur. Polo, which can be called a royal game, also originated from Manipur.

Some of the main tourist attractions are:

- Imphal
- Churachandpur
- Keibul Lamjao National Park
- War cemeteries
- Loktak Lake
- Shree Govindajee Temple
- Moreh

Meghalaya

Meghalaya has some of the thickest surviving forests in the country and therefore constitutes one of the most important ecotourism circuits in the country today. The Meghalayan subtropical forests support a vast variety of flora and fauna. Meghalaya has 2 National Parks and 3 Wildlife Sanctuaries. Meghalaya also offers many adventure tourism opportunities in the form of mountaineering, rock climbing, trekking and hiking, water sports etc.

The state offers several trekking routes some of which also afford and opportunity to encounter some rare animals such as the slow loris, assorted deer and bear. The Umiam Lake has a water sports complex with facilities such as rowboats, paddleboats, sailing boats, cruise-boats, water-scooters and speedboats. Cherrapunjee is one of the most popular tourist spots in North East of India. It lies to the south of the capital

Shillong. The town is very well known and needs little publicity. A rather scenic, 50 kilometer long road, connects Cherrapunjee with Shillong. The popular waterfalls in the state are the Elephant Falls, Shadthum Falls, Weinia falls, Bishop Falls, Nohkalikai Falls, Langshiang Falls and Sweet Falls. The hot springs at Jakrem near Mawsynram are believed to have curative and medicinal properties.

Orissa

Orissa has been a preferred destination from ancient days for people who have an interest in spirituality, religion, culture, art and natural beauty. Ancient and medieval architecture, pristine sea beaches, the classical and ethnic dance forms and a variety of festivals. Orissa has kept the religion of Buddhism alive. Rock-edicts that have challenged time stand huge and over-powering by the banks of the river Daya.

The torch of Buddhism is still ablaze in the sublime triangle at Udayagiri, Lalitagiri and Ratnagiri, on the banks of river Birupa. Precious fragments of a glorious past come alive in the shape of stupas, rock-cut caves, rock-edicts, excavated monasteries, viharas, chaityas and sacred relics in caskets and the Rock-edicts of Ashoka. Orissa is also famous for its well-preserved Hindu Temples, especially the Konark Sun Temple and The Leaning Temple of Huma.

Orissa is the home for various tribal communities who have contributed uniquely to the multicultural and multilingual character of the state. Their handicrafts, different dance forms, jungle products and their unique life style blended with their healing practices have got world wide attention. The Sitalsasthi Carnival is a must see for everyone who wants to see a glimpse of the art and culture of Odisha at one place.

Puducherry

The Union Territory of Puducherry comprises four coastal regions *viz*- Puducherry, Karaikal, Mahe and Yanam. Puducherry is the Capital of this Union Territory and one of the most popular tourist destinations in South India.

Puducherry has been described by National Geographic as "a glowing highlight of subcontinental sojourn". The city has many beautiful colonial buildings, churches, temples, and statues, which, combined with the systematic town planning and the well planned French style avenues, still preserve much of the colonial ambience.

Punjab

The state of Punjab is renowned for its cuisine, culture and history. Punjab has a vast public transportation and communication network. Some of the main cities in Punjab are Amritsar, Chandigarh, and Ludhiana.

Punjab also has a rich religious history incorporating Sikhism and Hinduism. Tourism in Punjab is principally suited for the tourists interested in culture, ancient civilization, spirituality and epic history.

Some of the villages in Punjab are also a must see for the person who wants to see the true Punjab, with their beautiful traditional Indian homes, farms and temples, this is a must see for any visitor that goes to Punjab. India-Pakistan border at Wagha is also a popular tourist attraction.

Rajasthan

Rajasthan, literally meaning "Land of the Kings", is one of the most attractive tourist destinations in Northern India. The vast sand dunes of the Thar Desert attract millions of tourists from around the globe every year.

Attractions:

- *Jaipur*: The capital of Rajasthan, famous for its rich history and royal architecture and motidungari lord ganesha temple.
- *Jodhpur*: Fortress-city at the edge of the Thar Desert, famous for its blue homes and architecture.
- *Udaipur*: Known as the "Venice" of India.
- *Jaisalmer*: Famous for its golden fortress.
- *Barmer*: Barmer and surrounding areas offer perfect picture of typical Rajasthani villages.
- *Bikaner*: Famous for its medieval history as a trade route outpost.

- *Mount Abu*: Is the highest peak in the Aravalli Range of Rajasthan.
- *Pushkar*: It has the first and one of the very Brahma temples in the world.
- *Keoladeo Bird Sanctuary*: A UNESCO world heritage site
- *Nathdwara*: This town near Udaipur hosts the famous temple of Shrinathji.
- *Ranthambore*: Situated near Sawai Madhopur, this town has one of the largest and most famous national parks in India.

Sikkim

Originally known as Suk-Heem, which in the local language means "peaceful home", Sikkim was an independent kingdom till the year 1974, when it became a part of the Republic of India. The capital of Sikkim is Gangtok, located approximately 105 kilometers from New Jalpaiguri, the nearest railway station to Sikkim. Although, an airport is under construction at Dekiling in East Sikkim, the nearest airport to Sikkim would be Bagdogra.

Sikkim is considered as the land of Orchids and mystic cultures and colourful traditions. Sikkim is well known among trekkers and adventure lovers, as West Sikkim has a lot to give them. Places near Sikkim include Darjeeling also known as the Queen of hills and Kalimpong. Darjeeling, other than its world famous "Darjeeling tea" is also famous for its refined "Prep schools" founded during the British Raj. Kalimpong is also famous for its flora cultivation and is home to many internationally known Nurseries.

Tamil Nadu

Tamil Nadu is the top state in attracting the maximum number of foreign tourists in India. Tamil Nadu. Marina Beach, Carnatic music, Bharata Natyam dance and country's largest Shopping locality. This city is also famous for Medical tourism and houses Asia's largest hospital. Archaeological sites with civilization dating back to 3800 years are found in Tamil Nadu. With more than 34000 temples this state also holds the credit of having maximum number of UNESCO heritage sites in India which includes Great Living Chola Temples and Mahabalipuram. Country's largest temple srirangam and Pichavaram the world's Second largest Mangrove forest are located in this state. Tamilnadu has some great temples like Madurai Meenakshi Amman Temple, Tanjore Brihadeeswarar Temple, Srirangam Ranganathaswamy Temple and all the mentioned temples has world class architecture that really mesmerize everyone. Kanyakumari is the southernmost tip of India provides sceneic view of sunset and sunshine over the Indian ocean.Hill stations like Yercaud, Kodaikanal, Ooty, Valparai, Yelagiri are widely visited. Velankanni Church and Nagoor Dharga are visited by people of all religion.Water Falls and Wildlife sanctuaries are located across the state.

Uttarakhand

Uttarakhand, the 27th state of the Republic of India, is called "the abode of the Gods". It contains glaciers, snow-clad mountains, valley of flowers, skiing slopes and dense forests, and many shrines and places of pilgrimage. Char-dhams, the four most sacred and revered Hindu temples: Badrinath, Kedarnath, Gangotri and Yamunotri are nestled in the Himalayas. Haridwar which means Gateway to God is the only place on the plains.

It holds the watershed for Gangetic River System spanning 300 km from Satluj in the west to Kali river in the east. Nanda Devi is the second highest peak in India after Kanchenjunga. Dunagiri, Neelkanth, Chaukhamba, Panchachuli, Trisul are other peaks above 23000 Ft. It is considered the abode of Devtas, Yakashyas, Kinners, Fairies and Sages. It boasts of some old hill-stations developed during British era like Mussoorie, Almora and Nainital.

Uttar Pradesh

Situated in the northern part of India, Uttar Pradesh is important with its wealth of monuments and religious fervour. Geographically, Uttar Pradesh is very diverse, with Himalayan foothills in the extreme north and the Gangetic Plain in the centre. It is also home of India's most visited site, the Taj Mahal, and Hinduism's holiest city, Varanasi. The most populous state of the Indian Union also has a rich cultural heritage, and at the heart of North India, Uttar Pradesh has much to offer. Places of interest include Varanasi, Agra, Kanpur, Lucknow, Mathura, Jhansi, Prayag, Sarnath, Ayodhya, Dudhwa National Park and Fatehpur Sikri.

West Bengal

Kolkata, one of the many cities in the state of West Bengal has been nicknamed the City of Palaces. This comes from the numerous palatial mansions built all over the city. Unlike many north Indian cities, whose construction stresses minimalism, the layout of much of the architectural variety in Kolkata owes its origins to European styles and tastes imported by the British and, to a much lesser extent, the Portuguese and French. The buildings were designed and inspired by the tastes of the English gentleman around and the aspiring Bengali Babu. Today, many of these structures are in various stages of decay. Some of the major buildings of this period are well maintained and several buildings have been declared as heritage structures.

From historical point of view, the story of West Bengal begins from Gour and Pandua situated close to the present district town of Malda. The twin medieval cities had been sacked at least once by changing powers in the 15th century. However, ruins from the period still remain, and several architectural specimens still retain the glory and shin of those times. The Hindu architecture of Bishnupur in terracotta and laterite sandstone are renowned world over. Towards the British colonial period came the architecture of Murshidabad and Coochbehar.

NATURE TOURISM

India has geographical diversity, which resulted in varieties of nature tourism.

- Water falls in Western Ghats including Jog falls.
- Western Ghats

- Hill Stations
- Wildlife reserves
- Deserts

Wildlife in India

India is home to several well known large mammals including the Asian Elephant, Bengal Tiger, Asiatic Lion, Leopard and Indian Rhinoceros, often engrained culturally and religiously often being associated with deities. Other well known large Indian mammals include ungulates such as the domestic Asian Water buffalo, wild Asian Water buffalo, Nilgai, Gaur and several species of deer and antelope.

Some members of the dog family such as the Indian Wolf, Bengal Fox, Golden Jackal and the Dhole or Wild Dogs are also widely distributed. It is also home to the Striped Hyaena, Macaques, Langurs and Mongoose species. India also has a large variety of protected wildlife. The country's protected forest consists of 75 National parks of India and 421 Sanctuaries, of which 19 fall under the purview of Project Tiger.

Its climatic and geographic diversity makes it the home of over 350 mammals and 1200 bird species, many of which are unique to the subcontinent. Some well known national wildlife sanctuaries include Bharatpur, Corbett, Kanha, Kaziranga, Periyar, Ranthambore, Manas and Sariska. The world's largest mangrove forest Sundarbans is located in southern West Bengal. The Kaziranga National Park,Manas National Park, Sundarbans and Keoladeo National Park is UNESCO World Heritage Site.

Hill Stations

Several hill stations served as summer capitals of Indian provinces, princely states, or, in the case of Shimla, of British India itself. Since Indian Independence, the role of these hill stations as summer capitals has largely ended, but many hill stations remain popular summer resorts.

Most famous hill stations are:

- Mount Abu, Rajasthan

- Pachmarhi, Madhya Pradesh—It is also known as The Queen of Satpura.
- Araku, Andhra Pradesh
- Gulmarg, Srinagar and Ladakh in Jammu and Kashmir
- Darjeeling in West Bengal
- Munnar in Kerala
- Ooty, Yercaud and Kodaikanal in Tamil Nadu
- Shillong in Meghalaya
- Shimla, Kullu in Himachal Pradesh
- Nainital in Uttarakhand
- Gangtok in Sikkim
- Mussoorie in Uttarakhand
- Manali in Himachal Pradesh
- Tawang in Arunachal Pradesh
- Mahabaleshwar in Maharashtra
- Haflong in Assam

In addition to the bustling hill stations and summer capitals of yore, there are several serene and peaceful nature retreats and places of interest to visit for a nature lover.

These range from the stunning moonscapes of Leh and Ladhak, to small, exclusive nature retreats such as Dunagiri, Binsar, Mukteshwar in the Himalayas, to rolling vistas of Western Ghats to numerous private retreats in the rolling hills of Kerala.

Beaches

India offers a wide range of tropical beaches with silver/ golden sand to coral beaches of Lakshadweep. States like Kerala and Goa have exploited the potential of beaches to the fullest. However, there are a lot many unexploited beaches in the states of Andhra Pradesh, Gujarat, Maharastra, Tamil Nadu and Karnataka. These states have very high potential to be develop them as future destinations for prospective tourists. Some of the famous tourist beaches are:

- Beaches of Vizag, Andhra Pradesh
- Beaches of Puri, Orissa
- Beaches of Digha, West Bengal

- Beaches of Goa
- Kovalam Beach, Kerala
- Marina Beach, Chennai
- City Beach, Puducherry
- Beaches of Mahabalipuram
- Beaches in Mumbai
- Beaches of Diu
- Beaches of Midnapore, West Bengal
- Beaches of Andaman and Nicobar Islands
- Beaches of Lakshadweep Islands

Adventure Tourism

- River rafting and kayaking in Himalayas
- Mountain climbing in Himalayas
- Rock climbing in Madhya Pradesh
- Skiing in Gulmarg or Auli
- Boat racing in Bhopal
- Paragliding in Maharashtra

DIFFERENCES BETWEEN TRAVEL AND TOURISM

Though the words Travel and Tourism are synonymised and used interchangeably but Tourism is a wider concept and encompasses a lot more than travel alone. Travel implies journeys undertaken from one place to another for any purpose including journeys to work and as a part of employment, as a part of leisure and to take up residence; whereas Tourism includes the journey to a destination and also the stay at a destination outside one's usual place of residence and the activities undertaken for leisure and recreation.

All tourism includes some travel, but not all travel is tourism.A person may often travel for a wide variety of purposes of which tourism is only one. However if properly handled, a part of the travel for non tourism purposes can be motivated into travel for tourism as an additional purpose. For example a person on a journey as a part of employment to a place with one or more tourist attractions –like a spot of scenic beauty or historical significance, a pilgrimage, a lake, etc. can be induced to spare some time and money for a short visit and or stay for tourism purposes alone.In this sense every traveller is a 'potential' tourist and is upto the managers of the industry to tap this 'potential' and convert the traveller into an 'actual' tourist.

Some of the characteristics that distinguish tourism:

- Temporary, to distinguish it from the permanent travel of the tramp and nomad
- Voluntary, to distinguish it from the forced travel of the exile and refugee
- Round up, to distinguish it from the one-way journey of the migrant
- Relatively long, to distinguish it from the recurrent trips of the holiday house owner

DEFINITIONS

The term Tourist is believed to have been derived from the Latin word 'TORNUS' which means a tool, a circle or a turner's wheel.

In the sense of the word of the origin, tourist is a person who undertakes a circular trip, *i.e.*, ultimately comes back to the place from where he sets about his journey.

Based on the various definitions of a Tourist here are some of the characteristics of a Tourist:

- He takes up his journey of his own free will.
- He takes up the journey primarily in search of enjoyment.
- The money spent on the visit is the money derived from home, not money earned in the places of visit.
- He finally returns to his original starting point.

We now proceed to discuss the definition of Tourist as given by WTO.But since WTO considers a tourist a type of a Visitor. As suggested, first discuss the definition of a Visitor. The WTO in a conference held in 1963 introduced the term 'Visitor'.

A Visitor is defined as 'Any person visiting a country other than that in which he has his usual place of residence for any reason other than being interested in an occupation remunerated from within the country visited.

The term includes two types of visitors:

- *Tourist*: Tourist is a temporary visitor staying for a period of at least 24 hours in the country visited and the purpose of whose journey can be classified under one of the following heads:
  - Leisure
  - Business, family, mission, meeting.
  - *As per the WTO's definition following persons are to be regarded as tourists*:
    a. Persons travelling for pleasure, for domestic reasons, for health etc.
    b. Persons travelling for meetings or in representative capacity of any kind
    c. Persons travelling for business purposes.
    d. Persons arriving in the course of sea cruises, even when they stay for less than 24 hours in respect of this category of persons the condition of usual place of residence is waived off.
  - *However persons belonging to the following categories are not considered as tourists*:
    a. Persons arriving with or without a contract to take up an occupation or engage in any business activity in that country.
    b. Residents in a frontier zone and persons domiciled in one country and working in an adjoining country.
    c. Students and young persons in boarding establishments of schools/colleges.
    d. Travellers passing through a country without stopping, even if the journey takes more than 24 hours.
- *Excursionist*: Excursionist is a temporary visitor staying for a period of less than 24hours in the country visited..

The drawback of the definition of a Visitor as per WTO is that it does not talk about the Visits made within the country. For these purposes a distinction is drawn between a Domestic and an International Visitor.

DOMESTIC VISITOR

A person who travels within the country he is residing in, outside the place of his usual environment for a period not exceeding 12 months.

INTERNATIONAL VISITOR

A person who travels to a country other than the one in which he has his usual residence for a period not exceeding 12 months. After we have discussed the definition of a visitor, tourist, and excursionist as per WTO and made a distinction between a Domestic and an International Visitor, we now come to definitions used in India for the purpose of collecting tourism statistics.

3

Catering Management: An Introduction

INTRODUCTION

Hospitality is probably the most diverse but specialized industry in the world. It is certainly one of the largest, employing millions of people in a bewildering array of jobs around the globe.

Sectors range from the glamourous five-star resort to the less fashionable, but arguably more specialised, institutional areas such as hospitals, industrial outfits, schools and colleges. Yet of these many different sectors, catering has to be the most challenging. Whatever the size of the catering operation, the variety of opportunities available is endless. "The sky is the limit with catering".

CATERING INDUSTRY

The food service industry encompasses those places, institutions and companies that provide meals eaten away from home. This industry includes restaurants, schools and hospital cafeterias, catering operations, and many other formats, including 'on-premises' and 'off-premises' caterings. Catering is a multifaceted segment of the food service industry. There is a niche for all types of catering businesses within the segment of catering.

The food service industry is divided into three general classifications: commercial segment, noncommercial segment, and military segment. Catering management may be defined as the task of planning, organizing, controlling a n d executing. Each activity influences the preparation and delivery of food, beverage, and related services at a competitive, yet profitable price. These activities work together to meet and exceed the customer's perception of value for his money.

CATERING SEGMENTS

Catering management is executed in many diverse ways within each of the four segments. The first, commercial segment, traditionally considered the profit generating operation, includes the independent caterer, the restaurant caterer, and the home-based caterer. The food service catering industry is segmented.

The non-commercial segment, or the 'not-forprofit' operations, consists of the following types of catering activities: business/industry accounts, school, college and university catering, health care facilities, recreational food service catering, social organizations and transportation food service catering. The military segment encompasses all catering activities involved in association with the armed forces and/ or diplomatic events.

KINDS OF CATERING

There are two main types of catering on-premises and offpremises catering that may be a concern to a large and small caterer. On-premise catering for any function—banquet, reception, or event—that is held on the physical premises of the establishment or facility that is organizing/sponsoring the function.

On-premise catering differs from off-premise catering, whereby the function takes place in a remote location, such as a client's home, a park, an art gallery, or even a parking lot, and the staff, food, and decor must be transported to that location.

Off-premise catering often involves producing food at a central kitchen, with delivery to and service provided at the client's location. Part or all of the production of food may be executed or finished at the location of the event. Catering can also be classified as social catering and corporate catering. Social catering includes such events as weddings, bar and mitzwahs, high school reunions, birthday parties, and charity events.

Business catering includes such events as association conventions and meetings, civic meetings, corporate sales or stockholder meetings, recognition banquets, product launches, educational training sessions, seller-buyer meets, service awards banquets, and entertaining in hospitality suites.

ON-PREMISE CATERING

All of the required functions and services that the caterers execute are done exclusively at their own facility. For instance, a caterer within a hotel or banquet hall will prepare and cater all of the requirements without taking any service or food outside the facility. Many restaurants have specialized rooms on-premise to cater to the private-party niche.

A restaurant may have a layout strategically designed with three separate dining rooms attached to a centralized commercial food production kitchen. These separate dining rooms are available at the same time to support the restaurant's operation and for reservation and overflow seating.

In addition, any of the three dining rooms may be contracted out for private-event celebrations and may require their own specialized service and menu options. Other examples of on-premise catering include hospital catering, school, University/college catering.

OFF-PREMISE CATERING

Off-premise catering is serving food at a location away from the caterer's food production facility. One example of a food production facility is a freestanding commissary, which is a kitchen facility used exclusively for the preparation of foods to be served at other locations.

Other examples of production facilities include, but are not limited to, hotel, restaurant, and club kitchens. In most cases there is no existing kitchen facility at the location where the food is served. Caterers provide single-event foodservice, but not all caterers are created equal. They generally fall into one of three categories:

Party Food Caterers

Party food caterers supply only the food for an event. They drop off cold foods and leave any last-minute preparation, plus service and cleanup, to others.

Hot Buffet Caterers

Hot buffet caterers provide hot foods that are delivered from their commissaries in insulated containers. They sometimes provide serving personnel at an additional charge.

Full-Service Caterers

Full-service caterers not only provide food, but frequently cook it to order on-site. They also provide service personnel at the event, plus all the necessary food-related equipment-china, glassware, flatware, cutleries, tables and chairs, tents, and so forth.

They can arrange for other services, like décor and music, as well. In short, a full-service caterer can plan and execute an entire event, not just the food for it.

TYPES OF CATERING ESTABLISHMENTS

Various catering establishments are categorised by the nature of the demands they meet. The following are some of the catering establishements.

RESTAURANT

A restaurant is an establishment that serves the customers with prepared food and beverages to order, to be consumed on the premises. The term covers a multiplicity of venues and a diversity of styles of cuisine.

Restaurants are sometimes also a feature of a larger complex, typically a hotel, where the dining amenities are provided for the convenience of the residents and for the hotel to maximize their potential revenue. Such restaurants are often open to non-residents also.

TRANSPORT CATERING

The provision of food and beverages to passengers, before, during and after a journey on trains, aircraft and ships and in buses or private vehicles is termed as transport catering. These services may also be utilised by the general public, who are in the vicinity of a transport catering unit. The major forms of modern day transport catering are airline-catering, railways catering, ship catering and surface catering in coaches or buses which operate on long distance routes.

Airline Catering

Catering to airline passengers on board the air craft, as well as at restaurants situated at airport terminals is termed as airline catering. Modern airports have a variety of food and beverage outlets to cater to the increasing number of air passengers. Catering to passengers en route i s normally contracted out to a flight catering unit of a reputed hotel or to a catering contractor or to the catering unit operated by the airline itself as an independent entity.

Railway Catering

Catering to railway passengers both during the journey as well as during halts at different railway stations is called railway catering. Travelling by train for long distances can be very tiring; hence a constant supply of a variety of refreshment choices helps to make the journey less tedious. On-board meal services are also provided on long distance trains.

Ship Catering

Ship catering is catering to cargo crew and passenger ship passengers. Ships have kitchens and restaurants on board. The quality of service and facilities offered depends on the class of the ship and the price the passengers are willing to pay. There are cruises to suit every pocket. They range from room service and cocktail bars to speciality dining restaurants.

Surface Catering

Catering to passengers traveling by surface transport such

as buses and private vehicles is called surface catering. These eating establishments are normally located around a bus terminus or on highways. They may be either government run restaurants, or privately owned establishments. Of late there has been a growing popularity of Punjabi style eateries called dhabas on the highways.

OUTDOOR CATERING

This catering includes the provision of food and drink away from home base and suppliers. The venue is left to the peoples' choice. Hotels, restaurants and catering contractors meet this growing demand. The type of food and set up depends entirely on the price agreed upon. Outdoor catering includes catering for functions such as marriages, parties and conventions.

RETAIL STORE CATERING

Some retail stores, apart from carrying on their primary activity of retailing their own wares, provide catering as an additional facility. This type of catering evolved when large departmental stores wished to provide food and beverages to their customers as a part of their retailing concept.

It is inconvenient and time consuming for customers to take a break from shopping, to have some refreshments at a different location. Thus arouse the need for some sort of a dining facility in the retail store itself. This style of catering is becoming more popular and varied nowadays.

CLUB CATERING

Club catering refers to the provision of food and beverages to a restricted member clientele. Some examples of clubs for people with similar interests are turf clubs, golf clubs, cricket clubs etc.

The service and food in these clubs tend to be of a fairly good standard and are economically priced. Night clubs are usually situated in large cities that have an affluent urban population. They offer entertainment with good food and expensive drinks.

WELFARE CATERING

The provision of food and beverages to people to fulfil a social obligation, determined by a recognised authority, is known as welfare catering. This grew out of the welfare state concept, prevalent in western countries. It includes catering in hospitals, schools, colleges, the armed forces and prisons.

INDUSTRIAL CATERING

The provision of food and beverages to 'people at work,' in industries and factories at highly subsidised rates is called industrial catering. It is based on the assumption that better fed employees at concessional rates are happy and more productive.

Catering for a large workforce may be undertaken by the management itself, or may be contracted out to professional caterers. Depending on the choice of the menu suggested by the management, catering contractors undertake to feed the workforce for a fixed period of time at a predetermined price.

LEISURE-LINKED CATERING

This type of catering refers to the provision of food and beverages to people engaged in 'rest and recreation' activities. This includes sale of food and beverages through different stalls and kiosks at exhibitions, theme parks, galleries and theatres. The increase in the availability of leisure time and a large disposable income for leisure activities has made it a very profitable form of catering.

RELATIONSHIP BETWEEN CATERING INDUSTRY AND ALL OTHER INDUSTRIES

Food is the sustainer of life regardless of whether they belong to animal kingdom or plant kingdom. All living beings consume food as they come in nature. Subsequently they may convert the raw natural food into usable form on their own. This transformation never involves the art and science of coking, which is a speciality of human beings alone. Importance of food for the human beings is amply, accurately and appropriately stated in the following age old sayings:

"hungry man is an angry man" and "even the army marches on stomach" where stomach implies food Employment of largest number of people in the world in general terms and in commercial terms is in food preparation and servicing. Roughly half the world population is actively engaged in the art and science of food production and then alone comes reproduction.

Food production, simply stated, is the transformation of raw food material into palatable, appetizing and easily palatable tasty food. Unlike all other living organisms, man has to "buy" food by paying money. Where does the money come from? It comes only from industries. Any industry in the world has the primary objective of making money. Money so generated by the industrial activity is shared between the employer and the employee, however disproportionate it may be. Money so shared is used to take care of the three important objectives: food, clothing and residence.

Whatever left after meeting these primary objectives may go towards acquiring wealth. Food is the very basis of existence or survival. To buy food, man needs money. The money comes or must come from industries, all of which have the primary objective of making money and share with those who help generate it. Since the raw food needs to be transformed into palatable food fit for consumption which is achieved, as already stated, through general cooking or commercial cooking.

Therefore, there is no industry in the world which is not directly or indirectly, one way or the other, related to the food industry. Commercial food industry or the catering industry is the only industry that provides food, at a price, away from home. Various types of catering services available would include general or speciality services such as transport catering, welfare catering, industrial catering, etc.

CATERING AND CUSTOMER

CATERING TO DIVERGENT

It sounds rather crass, but when they die, in the next 10-

15 years, all of their money-some $10 trillion dollars-is going to another group of people, most of whom don't like banks. They would rather go to Fidelity, play the market, not having lived through a downturn. One of the challenges as we go forward is how the banking industry is going to transform itself, move from the current group who provides the bulk of our earnings, to a second group who will assume society's wealth, and who does not realty like us.

Who likes banks? Those 55 years and older plus those who have lower incomes and less education, according to a 1997 ABA survey-valued customers, but not a group we can solely survive on. Also customer satisfaction is slipping somewhat for banks.

You need to know when you should allocate resources from the group giving you the bulk of your earnings now, to the group that does not like you. You will also get a boost from the federal government's change to electronic benefits transfer on January 1, 1999. Most states will have an EBT environment by the end of 1998.

The people who now get a Social Security check will have to become accustomed to an electronic transaction, and that's in your favour. A lot of the back-office work, you can change through electronic transactions. EBT will provide a large infusion of the infrastructure required for electronic commerce, by increasing the number of point-of-sale terminals.

The ABA asked the Federal Reserve and the Treasury to review the regulations surrounding transaction accounts, because the existing regulations are all in the realm of paper-based accounts. We would really like to get rid of the periodic statement under Regulation E because a purely electronic account will not have any outstanding items so you don't realty need a statement.

Banks will have to do some new things, though-electronic benefits transactions on automated teller machines, and maybe statements on demand. What can you do today on the Internet? You can do consumer education; you can have interactive advertising; you can distribute forms and applications; you can provide account information. You can do some internal transactions, some bill payment and, perhaps, some electronic commerce for the more daring. Electronic commerce, a broader term than electronic banking, better describes what ultimately we might want to do. What customers want today is not necessarily what they are going to want next year. You have to continually reassess.

Reliability on Tomorrow's Systems

Today, most of you keep your real stuff on a mainframe, a rather secure system. On the Internet, how are you going to let people like me hack around in your computer? You are going to be doing the same kinds of things on the Internet that you do today to render service and security to your customers. You will have a lot of the same, concerns. You could have a saboteur on the inside.

You could have a huge virus or software that fails. The new one is the hackers, but then you've got people who forge checks, too; they just attack in a different way. Whatever system you have must be reliable, sound, and secure. What kinds of things will give you these qualities? Well, you have technical standards; you have best practices, and the regulators providing guidance to the industry.

You are going to a much more efficient system and you should have greater margins as you implement it, but meanwhile, many larger institutions have proprietary systems that work very well. Probably nobody here has had a customer question, in the past 50 years, whether her check is going to clear. You are coming off of that kind of reliability. Bankers have systems that, perhaps, can be expanded to an Internet environment.

Determining who has the best products to help you is part of creating a plan. You want, perhaps, to start small, with, say, electronic bill payment, see how secure it is, how your customers accept it, and then go forward. You may lose money, but you are going to do it because your customers want it. There are threats to banks' dominance of the payments system, one of the biggest of which is the post office. You may say that will never happen because it is not an insured depository, but I would submit, for example, that the largest financial institution in Japan is the post office. Financial modernization, after 30 years, seems finally to be coming. Companies with unlimited capital, such as, say, General Electric Corp., will be able to compete very effectively, not for the little old ladies' $50,000 CDs but for their kids' money.

That's why ABA is very concerned. With direct deposit, a customer need never walk into a branch. A customer in Alaska can directly deposit funds into a bank in Alabama and write checks or use his debit card all day long in Alaska. All across the country, community bankers are saying to themselves "Aha!

Maybe I have an opportunity here." This stuff is coming. How are you going to respond? You are concerned about how your customers perceive you. Are you stodgy-as one of ABA's new industry ads shows -or are you out there on roller-blades? Now, you have to be concerned about customer perception beyond the community where you do business.

The Growth of Service Activities

Service sector economics now constitutes a major branch of economic studies although it is a field which no more than a decade ago was variously referred to as the 'poor relation' and the 'Cinderella of academics and politicians alike'.

The explanation of the interest recently evinced in the economics of the service sector is to be found in the extent to which service industries have expanded relative to other economic activities. Whilst the tendency for the tertiary sector to grow in comparison to primary and secondary activities has been identified and commented on for many decades special factors, such as the potential for services to generate new jobs, have helped thrust the sector to the forefront of economic analysis in the last few years.

The relative growth of services in the British economy since 1971, quantified on the basis of official statistics, could well stand as on outline of events in most developed economies during this period. Between 1971 and 1986 the output of the service sector increased by 2.5 per cent a year, or more than twice the rate, 1.1 per cent, achieved by other economic activities. Within the sector commercial services-distribution, catering, financial, business, recreational and personal services-expanded faster than other services, 3.1 per cent compared with 1.7 per cent a year, whilst specific commercial services grew very rapidly indeed-banking and business services by as much as 5.1 per cent per annum.

As a result, by 1985, service activities in Britain accounted for three-fifths of GDP and commercial services themselves were responsible for a third of total output. The importance of service activities is no less when judged by labour force size. On the basis of both numbers of employees, and by numbers of employees plus the self-employed, by 1985· services accounted for 66 per cent of Britain's labour force compared with 53 per cent in 1971. Commercial services alone provided jobs for 37 per cent of all employees in 1985.

The Need for New Measures

At a time when the bases, compilation, accuracy and usefulness of a range of official economic statistics have come under close scrutiny, the measurement of service outputs has not escaped attention. Recently there has been some shift away from a simple acknowledgement that service output measures may be subject to a degree of unreliability towards an apprehension that any errors they contain might lead to a downward bias in the measure of service output, and therefore, GDP growth rates.

It has in fact been suggested that output increases in services may have been underestimated in recent years by as much as 2-1/2 per cent a year implying that annual growth of GDP itself should have been substantially higher. For both conceptual and practical reasons the outputs of many service activities are notoriously difficult to quantify both absolutely and in terms of change over time.

Yet because of their size and growth it is especially important that a reasonable degree of accuracy must attach to service output measures which should reflect current best practice given the data and resources available. If this is not the case then, because of the weight of service activities in the total economy, the accuracy of the registred change in GDP and national productivity, the relative contribution to growth of service and non-service activities, the pattern of structural change within the service sector and the policies to which these various phenomena have given rise, must all be called in question. This assembles some of the principal results which have emerged from a study of alternative output measures for British service industries.

The study reviews the methods currently used by the CSO to measure real output changes in specified services and seeks to devise, develop and implement new measures for these activities. For this purpose an empirical approach has been adopted. Whilst basic conceptual considerations are taken fully into account in that the alternative measures which are compiled can be integrated into the national accounting framework, it is felt that the theoretical complexities associated with service output measurement have received due attention elsewhere whilst very little has been done at the practical level.

When compiling new service output measures the two principal uses for which they are employed must be borne in mind. The original raison d'etre for measuring service sector output is for use, in conjunction with output indicators for industrial activities, to yield a measure of real growth in total GDP. This is the primary role for which the CSO devises and compiles output measures for service sector activities. Increasingly, however, as the weight of services in the economy has grown service output indicators are now used extensively, in conjunction with labour force and other relevant economic series, for the analysis of long-term developments in individual service industries.

Their employment in the latter context accentuates the requirement that they fulfill minimum reliability criteria: it is possible that offsetting errors in individual service industry output measures may modulate their impact on the reliability of overall GDP measurement but this does not apply when attention is focused on the analysis of developments in a specific service industry. The results obtained in the present exercise suggest that official measures of GDP growth may well have been marginally understated as a result of the methods used to track service output changes. Even more significantly, perhaps, the alternative measures which have been compiled portray patterns of development for some individual commercial service industries which are very different from those yielded by official output measures.

When considering alternative output measures attention has been directed first at the strengths and weaknesses of official practice as a prelude to an attempt to improve the rationale and reliability of the resulting output indicators. However in some cases it is necessary to regard the new measure simply as an alternative to the official index: an alternative with a different, rather than superior, base and/or derived from quite separate data sources.

Another feature of the search for alternative indicators is that it has been conducted with an eye to the improved reliability of service output measurement in the future. To some extent this means that data series which are available only for recent years have been drawn upon. Nevertheless a major objective of the study has been to assess the extent to which the official picture of past service sector developments is changed if alternative output measures are used.

The alternative measures have therefore been carried backwards in some cases to 1971, in others to 1973 and for a large number to 1978, using 1985 as the base year. There are three reasons for the latter choice. First data limitations mean that all series cannot be uniformly taken back to a common early date so that a recent year must be adopted as the base. Secondly at the time when the research was initiated 1985 was the latest year for which data-whether values, 'quantities' or 'weights'-were generally available.

Thirdly, the CSO was then in the process of re-basing its output indicators using 1985 GDP weights. The new output measures draw much more extensively on unofficial data sources than do those compiled by the CSO. Broadly such sources can be divided into two types: those which yield data series covering an industry-wide set of activities; and those which contain data relating to individual service industry organisations and firms. Typically the assistance of the latter was enlisted to provide weights with which industry-wide quantity series for different kinds of output can be combined to produce a single output measure for the service sector in question. It is to the credit of the CSO that there has been a continuous attempt to modify service output measures in the light of methodological developments and the emergence of alternative data sources.

Whilst this has had the desired result of improving the reliability of service output measurement inevitably it also introduces inconsistencies and breaks in the time series where-either on practical or other grounds-the new methods have not been carried back to earlier years. A feature of the new measures postulated below is that every effort has been made to ensure temporal consistency in the series which they yield. It has not proved possible to devote to 'quality' aspects of service output the attention they properly merit.

In part this reflects the fact that the incorporation of quality changes in output measures may be even more difficult in services than in goods-producing industries where frequently its assessment is equally neglected. This in turn is due to the consideration that the quality of a given service varies greatly and in many cases is highly subjective. Nevertheless the results do have implications for this aspect of service output measurement, especially in the case of the catering trades. Were quality aspects taken into account more fully, further consideration would need to be given to the relative merits of measures based on deflated value series and service output units.

Coverage of the Measures

The search for alternative output measures has been restricted to the commercial service industries, essentially distribution, catering, financial, business and personal services, foı which suggests that output has risen especially rapidly. Within this group of commercial services the CSO distinguishes for output measurement purposes as many as 37 service industries, output changes in which are currently assessed by a total of 114 indicators. These services accounted for some 30 per cent of total GDP in 1985 and about a third of people employed in Great Britain. Given the vast range of service activities which must be covered by official output measures it is natural that the CSO makes use of readily available, relevant, series to yield the required indicators, series which themselves are normally official in the sense that they are compiled by other government departments.

Since the quest for new measures has entailed a search for and detailed examination of, alternative data, involving the identification, location and perusal of non-official sources and also the co-operation of individual firms and organisations it proved necessary to regard the full range of commercial service activities as no more than a frame from which individual service industries could be selected for intensive analysis.

When choosing industries from this list for which alternative measures of output change are identified and implemented, several criteria have been applied. A principal consideration has been to direct efforts to services where, on the face of it, current practice appears to be weak. At one end of the scale this principle tends to divert attention away from activities such as retailing, where the measures are generally regarded as being relatively sound, towards such services as advertising where the official output indicator is based on an employment series.

Secondly some priority was given to activities for which at first blush-sometimes deceptive-alternative measures appeared feasible. Thirdly an attempt has been made to cover the larger service industries such as banking and insurance, and ceteris paribus, attention was focused on service activities which, a priori, are thought to be rapidly expanding, a criterion which points to the inclusion of, especially, financial and business services. Since a systematic attempt has been made to base alternative output measures on numbers of service units produced, such service industries as estate agents, stockbroking and legal services where official output measurement is already founded on numbers of service units-of property transfers, transactions, and court proceedings-have not been considered as candidates for alternative measures. The service industries for which new measures were ultimately compiled fall neatly into three groups.

First, there are ten selected financial and business services: banking, building societies, finance leasing, hire-purchase, insurance, accountants, architects, advertising, computer services and construction plant hire. Secondly eight recreational services have been covered: broadcasting, theatres, libraries, museums, professional sports, participatory sports, local authority leisure centres and betting and gaming. Thirdly, the five catering trades-restaurants, public houses, clubs, catering contractors and hotels-have also been included.

Alternative Output Measures

Continuous CSO action to modify and improve service output measures means that they have developed from year to year in an essentially ad hoc manner with considerable diversity in their conceptual underpinning. Output measures for the commercial service sector rely heavily on deflated value and employment indicators and whilst output measurement for some service activities is based on counting numbers of service units, such practice applies to only a fraction of the output of the commercial service sector.

In fact it has emerged that the use of this type of measure can be extended to a considerable number of commercial services and an attempt has therefore been made to generalise and implement this approach, especially in the case of the financial and recreational services. This method can be summarised as the compilation of [sigma]poqo where q represents the industry's output quantities of the industry's output prices and 0 and 1 refer to the years compared.

This is 'the traditional [measure] used for multi-product industries wherein an index of production is constructed from a weighted sum of various outputs produced by the industry'. Such a deflated value approach to output measurement will yield the required result-as measured by the traditional direct method based on weighted quantities-only if the deflator, the price index, relates specifically to the products or services in question. This condition is not fulfilled in the case of many service output measures where for practical reasons some form of general price index is used.

It is partly to remedy this weakness in service output measurement that, wherever possible, alternative measures have been based in this exercise on the traditional direct methodology using numbers of service output units. A fundamental requirement for the use of this 'traditional' or 'direct' approach is that, for purposes of practical measurement, the outputs of the industry or service in question should be relatively homogeneous.

No economic activity yields a single, identical, product or service so that in practice it is sufficient if the bulk of an industry's activity is represented by a limited range of output types. It is their supposed inability to fulfill this criterion which has discouraged the application of the traditional, direct, measurement methodology to service activities.

Generally it has been assumed that there exists, virtually, an infinite variety and range of outputs in the case of most, especially financial, services: that no two life insurances, mortgages, bank accounts, and the output activities associated with them, are the same. It is argued that this view is based largely on a misconception, associated with what, for want of a better term, we shall call the 'digit illusion', and that in fact many service industries-including betting and gaming-fulfil the basic criterion for the application of the traditional, direct measurement methodology in that the bulk of their output is accounted for by a limited range of essentially homogeneous activities.

For the impression of enormous diversity in the output of most financial services derives from the fact that the values associated with a specific activity-the sums assured by a life company, sizes of mortgages provided by a building society, the amounts loaned under hire-purchase agreements by a finance house, the values of cheques cleared by a commercial bank, the car insurance premiums charged by an insurer etc- do have an infinitely large range. It has been assumed in the search for new output measures that such differences can be essentially ignored. In the case of mortgages, for example, the output associated with writing 500,000 pounds sterling in a deed is, with some relatively minor qualifications, little different from that associated with inscribing 50,000 pounds sterling or even 5,000 pounds sterling; differences in the numbers of digits required in this and other financial instruments-cheques, insurance policies, hire-purchase agreements, betting slips-have relatively little bearing on the amount of output involved.

In brief for a given type of financial activity it is normally legitimate, when measuring output, to ignore the 'digit illusion'. This has the effect of rendering homogeneous a wide range of financial activities, making them amenable, in principle, to the traditional direct, measurement methodology. It means, by way of illustration, that output changes for the life insurance industry can be based on changes in numbers of policies. It must be stressed however that a distinction must be drawn, and numbers counted, for each major type of service/activity provided by the service industry in question where value added per service unit varies significantly between activity types.

This means, for instance, in the case of the life insurance industry, that numbers of policies must be counted separately for ordinary life insurance, industrial life, annuities and personal pensions. It also means that attention needs to be drawn to a feature of this approach which is peculiar to financial service industries: the distinction between stocks and flows. Clearly, the resources devoted to, and therefore the amount of output associated with, the annual 'maintenance' of pre-existing mortgage will be substantially less than required when initiating a new mortgage.

In principle, and where practical, it is as important therefore to draw a distinction when measuring output between numbers of existing mortgages issued in a given year and the numbers of existing mortgages as it is to count separately the numbers of, say, different kinds of policy issued by life insurance companies. Indeed the same distinction needs to be drawn in the case of life insurance-between new policies and policies in force-and in principle at any rate in many other financial service industries: between new and existing contracts for hire-purchase and finance leases for instance.

The practicability of extending the traditional measurement methodology to commercial services thus hinges, in the case of each activity, on the availability of two kinds of data: industry-wide series of numbers of each type of principal product, the series q; and appropriate weights with which these various product series can be combined to yield an aggregate output measure for the service industry in question. To a degree inadequacies in the measurement of service output changes simply reflect the relative lack of interest with which they were regarded in the past and a consequent failure to devote sufficient resources to the collection of basic output data.

Also, it is to some extent, due to the 'insubstantiality' of most services, the fact that they 'pass away' in the moment of production, that a systematic effort has not been made to base their output measurement to a much larger extent on numbers of service units produced. In fact regardless of whether or not a service has any kind of physical embodiment, in the vast majority of cases there exists a physical record or token that a particular service has been performed. The outputs of all kinds of commercial service industries are very well 'documented'-by the ticket required for entrance to Wimbledon, the bill for a meal, the contract which records the finance leasing of a fleet of aircraft-in a form which in principle allows the numbers of each type of service to be recorded.

In this sense, and at this level, the output of service activities is registered at least as well as the products of industrial pursuits. The nig universal existence, at the 'grass roots' level, of this detailed record of service sector outputs, to an ever increasing extent in computerised form, augurs well for the future extension and development of the kind of direct output measurement advocated here. This comprehensive data base has not yet been properly exploited to yield aggregate series of the numbers of each type of service produced on an industry-wide basis. However research and enquiry have revealed that representative bodies of various kinds at the industry level-especially trade associations-have come to regard the compilation of aggregate numbers of each kind of service produced, using these data bases, as one of their primary tasks, and such sources have been widely drawn upon. That they may not be based on series for numbers of service units which are fully comprehensive for the industry in question should not be regarded as a major weakness of the alternative output measures.

Usually only the major 'products' are counted and in this respect the circumstances are no different from those which exist when the method is applied to industrial activities. For both industrial and service activities so measured the implicit assumption is the same: that real changes in the non-covered outputs parallel the aggregate change measured for the covered operations. Unfortunately, with few exceptions, service industry organisations, do not collect, process or publish, the kind of data which are needed to obtain the 'weights' required for aggregating these various output series into a single measure for the industry in question. In these circumstances it has proved necessary to have recourse inter alia to the goodwill of individual firms in order to derive suitable weights which must be accepted as typical for the service industry in which they operate.

Wherever possible alternative measures have been derived from an application of the traditional, direct methodology based on numbers of service output units. However even when allowance is made for the 'digit illusion' some service industries-such as architecture and accountancy-remain in that class where output units are, in essence, infinitely variable in nature. In these cases an attempt has nevertheless been made to upgrade the output measure, usually by identifying and compiling a more appropriate price deflator. This presents the results of the search for new output measures for the selected commercial activities. Initially the new output series are presented separately for the three major service complexes-financial and business services, recreational services and the catering trades-which have been covered and compared with the official measures. The part concludes with a consideration of the implications of the results for future developments in the measurement of service output.

Financial and Business Services

In 1985 the ten financial and business services for which new output measures have been compiled contributed, in total, about 35 pound sterling billion to GDP and employed approximately a million people. In the case of banking, the largest of the services in this sector, it proved possible to base the new measure wholly on numbers of service units-numbers of accounts, clearings, cash and credit card transactions. This contrasts with official practice in which indicators derived from deflated series for deposits and loans, as well as employment, carry the bulk of the weight.

In life insurance, also, numbers of policies of various types, distinguishing between new policies and policies in force, replace the official series comprising deflated consumer expenditure. Similarly the new building society measure is founded wholly on numbers of service units-shareholders, existing borrowers and new loans-instead of, as is the case with the official measure, a combination of deflated liabilities, employment and numbers of advances. For general insurance, a measure reflecting broadly the stock of insurable assets has been substituted for the official indicator based on deflated premiums.

In the case of two services, architects and advertising, a deflated value series places officla measures based on employment. The primary feature of the new measures used for accountants, computer services and hire-purchase, is the use of deflators which have been specially constructed to reflect more closely than those officially employed developments in the activities in question. The official practice for both construction plant hire and finance leasing has been to base indicators on output developments in user industries.

Instead of this approach the new measures are derived from gross output in the case of construction plant hire and the value of assets newly leased and of the stock of leased assets in the case of finance leasing, each deflated by price indices specifically compiled for the activities in question. The new measures for the covered financial and business services are set alongside the official indicators.

The basic date series from which these were derived are such that not all of them cover the full span of years, 1971 to 1986, so that it is convenient to combine them into three groups: five industries-building societies, hire-purchase, insurance, advertising and construction plant hire-for which growth rates are available for the whole period 1971-86; six industries where the information is shown for 1973-86; and all ten covered financial services, architects, finance leasing and computer services-for which alternative and official growth rates can be compared for the period 1978-86.

In the case of the first group, for which measures extend over the full period 1971-86, whilst there are some very significant differences between alternative and official growth rates-for building societies the former is appreciably higher than the latter whilst the opposite is true for hire-purchase-the arithmetic average growth rate for all five services, at 4.1 per cent per annum, is identical for both alternative and official measures. The same generalisation applies to the group of six industries over the period 1973-86: for hire-purchase, advertising, construction plant hire and banking the two measures yield quite different results but these contrasts offset each other so that the average alternative growth rate is identical with the average official growth rate.

Results for the group of ten industries, relating to the period 1978-86, paint a very similar picture; of individual industry diversity but overall similarity. In this case only for building societies, insurance, advertising and accountants do alternative and official methods yield rates of output change that are at all akin. Yet, overall, the average alternative growth rate, 7.4 per cent per annum, is not much greater than the 7.0 per cent registered officially. The official measure for finance leasing is constructed to minimise distortion in GDP measurement whilst the alternative measure has been compiled in such a way as to enhance the reliability of the industry's growth indicator *per se*. If this service industry is left out of account, the average alternative growth rate, at 6.6 per cent, is below the average official rate, 7.6 per cent.

This set of results contains a further point of interest. Whilst, as pointed out, there are substantial differences in the case of most industries between the alternative and official measures, the inter-industry growth patterns are remarkably similar whether gauged by alternative or official indicators: again leaving out finance leasing the correlation coefficient for the remaining nine pairs of, alternative and official, growth rates is +0.95. Although comparisons of unweighted average growth rates can be quite instructive more attention should be focused on differences between alternative and official measures revealed by weighted aggregate indices of the kind. These output indices, derived from the alternative and official measures for individual industries and relating to the same groups of industries and periods specified have been obtained from an aggregation procedure which is based on 1985 contributions to GDP.

The results contained are summarised in the form of average annual rates of growth that also contains growth rates obtained from weights derived from 1980 industry contributions to GDP and 1985 industry employment levels, to test the sensitivity of the results to alternative weighting systems. In the case of the five industries for which there is full coverage over the period 1971 to 1986 the alternative growth rate is 4.4 per cent and the official one 4.8 per cent on the basis of 1985 GDP weights.

A discrepancy of no more than a tenth between the two versions is also suggested by 1980 GDP weights. This group of five industries accounted for only 20 per cent of the contribution to GDP and an estimated 27 per cent of employment of all financial and business services in 1985. In contrast the group of six was responsible for 56 per cent of output and an estimated 42 per cent of employment and the group of ten for as much as 74 per cent of output and 56 per cent of employment. Greater significance should therefore be attached to the results obtained for these latter two groups. All three weighting systems show that for the group of six industries, over the years 1973 to 1986, the official measure understated growth by about a fifth when compared with the aggregate alternative measure; much the same picture emerges for the group of ten industries during the period 1978 to 1986 where, on the basis of both 1985 and 1980 GDP weights, the official measure, compared with the alternative, under estimates growth by about a fifth.

When considering this disparity two industries merit special attention: banking which is by some way the largest of the ten industries; and finance leasing on account of the fundamental difference in the methods underlying the alternative and official measures. In fact if banking-with alternative and official growth rates of respectively 8.2 and 6.5 per cent per annum for the period 1978 to 1986-is left out of account the picture hardly changes at all: the alternative aggregate growth rate for the remaining nine industries over the period 1978 to 1986 emerges as 8.0 per cent per annum compared with an official growth rate of 6.0 per cent.

This is in sharp contrast to the effect of excluding finance leasing. In this case the alternative growth measure for the nine remaining industries falls to 7.5 per cent whilst the official measure rises to 7.2 per cent so that most of the differential disappears.

Recreational Services

In 1985, recreational services, SIC class 97, contributed almost 6 billion pounds sterling to GDP and provided employment for 430,000 people. Apart from cinemas, for which the official output indicator is based on numbers of attendances, the measures used by the CSO rely for the most part on deflated series of turnover or consumers' expenditure on the service in question. In the case of local authority libraries, however, employment-based indicators are used. In the search for alternative measures it has proved possible, for these services, to base the new indicators largely on numbers of service units. Thus the output index for 'group' 974, broadcasting and theatres, reflects changes in numbers of radio and television hours transmitted and of attendances at theatres etc, whilst that for libraries and museums has been founded on numbers of books issued and numbers of visitors. The new measures for sport, 'group' 979, an activity that accounts for almost half of the output of recreational services, has been derived from a variety of indicators which reflect, inter alia, changes in numbers of attendances at paying spectator sports, sports hours transmitted by television and radio, membership of participatory sports clubs and measures which trace changes in numbers of betting slips and football coupons.

Only in the case of local authority leisure facilities was recourse made to conventional deflated value series. The output series set out for cinemas and for authors and artists are those used officially: that for cinemas being already based on numbers of service units whilst no alternative measure could be readily identified for 'group' 976. For comparison with the overall official measure for recreational services the five component output measures have been combined into a single output index using weights based on 1985 contributions to GDP. The official measure suggests that the output of this service industry complex grew, between 1973 and 1988, at an average annual rate of 2.9 per cent; the alternative points to a significantly slower rate of increase of 2.0 per cent.

One factor which may go some way towards explaining this discrepancy is that whilst in principle the alternative measure includes local authority libraries and leisure facilities throughout the period, the official indicator embraces these activities only since their transfer to class 97 of the 1980 SIC. Yet it can be seen that even in recent years the official measure has registered a significantly higher rate of growth for this industry than that shown by the alternative measure.

THE CATERING TRADES

In 1985 the catering trades' contribution to GDP totalled 7-1/2 pounds sterling billion and the industry employed more than a million people. Output measures for these trades are summarised, in terms of average annual growth rates. In the early years of the period covered the official indicator was based on turnover data supplied by a voluntary panel of catering organisations deflated by price indices specific to each of the catering trades.

From the beginning of the 1980s the official measure has been derived from changes in the margins of the individual catering trades as recorded in the DTI's annual catering trades' enquiry, again deflated by specific price indices. Although in principle it should be possible to measure output in the catering trades on the basis of numbers of service units-hotel bed occupancy, numbers of bar transactions etc-attempts to use this approach proved, for practical reasons, to be fruitless. Therefore to test the sensitivity of the official measure alternative output series were constructed using the price indices officially compiled but applying them throughout to turnover data yielded by the catering trades inquiries, interpolating results for early years where no such inquiries were conducted.

It is clear that these alternative measures alter the picture quite significantly for some trades. Whilst for restaurants, clubs and catering contractors changes in output are not greatly different whether measured on the official or alternative bases, sharply contrasting developments emerge for public houses and the hotel trade: the substantial growth recorded for public houses by the official measure virtually disappears with the alternative, whilst the opposite occurs in the case of hotels. These quite significant modifications to the subsectoral picture, in effect, cancel out: on both official and alternative methods catering output increased over this period by about 1 per cent a year.

The reliability of catering output changes cannot, however, be allowed to rest there. For when these changes are compared with labour force developments there would seem to have been substantial long-term declines in labour productivity: taking the official output measure in conjunction with changes in the number of employees in catering, labour productivity appears to have fallen by as much as 1.7 per cent a year between 1971 and 1986. To help determine whether these results reflect real developments in this service industry or whether they arose from statistical series which are sufficiently unreliable as to produce a misleading picture of events, alternative, more sophisticated, full-time equivalent labour force series have been constructed.

Since both part-time working and self-employment are important features of the catering trades' labour force, allowance for developments in both these aspects has been made in the FTE series shown. Whilst the introduction of FTE labour force series improves the productivity picture there nevertheless remains an apparently substantial fall in catering productivity: an annual average decline of 1.7 per cent a year using numbers of employees is modified to a deterioration of 1.2 per cent on an FTE basis. Of the individual trades only catering contractors emerge with enhanced FTE productivity, displaying an improvement of 1.7 per cent a year.

The other four trades register deteriorations: restaurants by 2.1 per cent a year, public houses 0.1 per cent, clubs 3.6 per cent and hotels 1.2 per cent. It is theoretically feasible, on the basis of most formulations of the production function, that in certain circumstances output in any economic activity might increase over the long term at a rate below that registered for labour inputs.

This could arise in particular if there were a fall in capital intensity but such a development does not appear to have been a feature of catering during this period. A measure compiled for the industry suggests that between 1971 and 1986 the stock of equipment grew at an annual average rate of 3.6 per cent a year which, in conjunction with an annual rise of 2.3 per cent in the FTE labour force, points to a 1.4 per cent annual increase in capital intensity.

In these circumstances it is difficult to accept that either the official or alternative output measures presented adequately reflect output growth in the catering trades. A probable explanation of this deficiency is that the measures fail to take sufficient account of developments, in some general sense, in the quality of catering output, be it a reflection of changes in the range of services offered, the milieu in which they are provided, the nature of the food and drink supplied or the standards of customer service. It is relevant that following comparatively little change in its size during the 1950s and 1960s the catering industry's labour force has grown substantially over the last two decades, especially during the early 1970s.

These developments have generally been explained by contrasts in the nature of the labour market between, on the one hand, the earlier decades and on the other the 1970s and 1980s. The earlier prevalence of full employment meant that because catering work was notoriously unattractive and ill-paid the industry was able to adjust its labour force towards its basic manning requirements. This kind of effect was reinforced by the impact of the selective employment tax which led to a significant fall in catering employment when it was implemented during the later years of the 1960s and a rapid increase in the early years of the 1970s after its abandonment. This thesis is also supported by case studies of the impact on the industry of technological innovations.

A recent survey of organisations operating in the catering trades revealed that rather than causing redundancies 'the time saved by new technology and improved productivity was being used wherever possible to enhance customer service'. A stagnant productivity performance in catering is equally difficult to reconcile with the rapid growth of both take-away food facilities and self-catering accommodation. In the event it has been decided to use labour inputs, to be precise the FTE measure shown, as a surrogate output measure for this industry.

It is felt that whilst far from ideal it provides a less unsatisfactory output measure, over the period in question. On this basis an annual average growth rate of 2.3 per cent emerges for catering output, hardly an unreasonable achievement for what is largely a leisure industry during a period when GDP increased, on average, by 1.7 per cent a year. Furthermore when applied to the individual catering trades this labour force based method yields results, for changes in real output over these years, which are intuitively much more plausible than those derived from either the official or alternative methods. It suggests that between 1971 and 1986 output in all five trades increased substantially: in restaurants by 2.4 per cent a year, in public houses by 2.5 per cent, in clubs by 3.1 per cent, in catering contractors by 2.8 per cent and in hotels by 1.6 per cent.

Measure for All Covered Services

The alternative output measures compiled for financial services, recreational services and the catering trades are combined and compared with their official counterparts. Group 1, for which the series relate to the full period 1971-86, comprises five financial services and the catering trades. Group 2 covering the period 1973-86 includes in addition banking and recreational services. Whilst group 3, for which the output indicators are available for the period 1978-86, embraces all the service industries for which alternative measures have been compiled.

These aggregate output indices, both official and alternative, are derived from those presented in the relevant tables using as weights the 1985 contribution of each activity to GDP. The results are summarised in the form of average annual rates of change. To check the sensitivity of these final results alternative and official measures of growth are also compared using as weights the services' 1985 employment levels and 1980 contributions to GDP.

The picture which emerges is one in which the alternative measure consistently points towards a higher growth rate than that indicated by its corresponding official index. Moreover the size of the differential varies comparatively little regardless of the group, period or weighting system to which attention is directed. If most attention is attached-in view of the size of their coverage-to the results for groups 2 and 3, it appears that compared with the alternative methods the official indicators have understated growth by between 13 and 18 per cent. Given that in most cases the alternative measurement methods differ radically from those officially employed it is perhaps remarkable that, overall, the discrepancy should be no greater than this. To what extent, as it stands, would the official measure of GDP growth be changed if the alternative measure is substituted for the official indicator? The answer is: very little. Basing this adjustment on the alternative/official differential revealed for group 2 the annual average GDP growth rate for 1973-86 is unchanged at 1.3 per cent per annum, and using the group 3 results the annual growth rate for 1978-86 rises from 1.6 per cent to 1.7 per cent. If the disparity between official and alternative growth rates depicted held for the commercial services excluded from this exercise then the official GDP growth rate of 1.3 per cent registered for the period 1973-86 is boosted to 1.5 per cent per annum and the GDP growth rate of 1.6 per cent for the years 1978-86 is raised to 1.9 per cent a year.

There are good reasons for supposing that these upward revisions to the GDP growth rate will understate rather than overstate the actual shortfall. In the first place output measures which lean towards numbers of service units will to some extent be biased downwards compared with those derived from deflated sales or turnover values because the data sources in question tend to cover any new services in the latter but not the former.

Secondly whilst official output measures which rely on employment series usually incorporate some productivity improvement, this has not been applied to the FTE based measure compiled for catering so that it may well underestimate actual output growth in this activity. Thirdly salary indices which have been used as surrogate price deflators in the case of accountancy and computer services will tend to overestimate actual output price increases-and therefore bias downwards the resulting output measure-since no allowance is made for the impact on unit labour costs of any productivity improvements in these services. While the implications for GDP measurement of the substitution of alternative aggregate service output indicators may not be unduly significant it is clear that they are more substantial for the commercial service sector as a whole. They are even more significant for individual service complexes. Although the new measure for financial and business services differs relatively little from the official measure, especially if account is taken of the contrasting conceptual treatment of finance leasing in the respective approaches, the alternative obtained for recreational services points to a significantly lower growth rate and that compiled for catering is about twice the official growth rate. Contrasts between alternative and official measures are even more pronounced for individual service industries.

Service Output Measurement

Substitution of the new output measures for those officially compiled would have made little difference to GDP growth rates in recent years. In effect discrepancies which emerged between alternative and official output measures for individual service industries have tended to offset each other. There is no guarantee that this condition would hold in the future and for this reason alone the search for alternative, improved, measures of service output change should be pursued. In contrast significantly large differences between alternative and official output measures have emerged for particular services and these have very important implications for the analysis of economic developments in individual service industries.

The validity of the economic analyses to which these activities are now widely subjected depends crucially on the accuracy of the output and productivity measures that are employed to map their development over time. For this reason, especially, new and improved service output measures are required.

The research which lies behind the results is that new service output measures can be further developed both extensively and intensively. Whilst the service industries examined were chosen as systematically as possible on the basis of specific criteria, only limitations imposed by time and resources prevented other service activities being subjected to a similar kind of scrutiny. Moreover in many of those service industries which have been surveyed scope for further measurement improvements remain. In this connection attention needs to be drawn to the results obtained for building societies and the catering trades. In the case of the former serious doubts attach to the alternative measure which, although it yields a growth rate higher than the official one, nevertheless implies, as it stands, a long-term fall in labour productivity in this service industry. Also it is clear that the search for improved catering output measures needs to be continued: the labour force indicator adopted for the purpose of this exercise must be regarded as no more than a stop-gap strategem though on the basis of existing statistical sources there is at present little immediate prospect of new measures being based on numbers of service output units.

None the less the data deficiencies are essentially practical, not conceptual, in nature and with appropriate statistical arrangements could no doubt be remedied eventually: already there is some experience of collecting data relating to hotel room utilisation which some time in the future might form the basis of a service unit-based measure. Generally there seems to exist a large reservoir of data relating to both output indicators and weights, collected by a variety of service industry organisations, which lies outside the purview of official sources.

It is difficult to avoid the impression that the current exercise has barely scratched the surface of this fund of material and that, in particular, much is available at the firm level which has yet to be systematically collated in a way that it can be used to measure developments for whole industries. Certainly it is clear that within the firms in question most service outputs are documented in detail, increasingly in computerised records, so that alternative measures based on numbers of output units should become progressively more practicable. There appear to be two basic options for tapping into this kind of data base. One would comprise an official periodic survey of each of the main service industries in which, as in the case of some industrial censuses, questionnaires would seek information about numbers and values of those output units which are best measured for each service. The inquiries into the distributive, catering and service trades periodically conducted by the Business Statistics Office might be developed in this direction.

The alternative is to adopt the approach followed, in the main, in this exercise and base new output measures on the information which is collected by trade associations and other industry organisations. This option is less attractive than the systematic collection of the requisite data, on a comprehensive and consistent basis, by means of an official census.

IMPORTANCE AND USAGE OF DRESS CODES

A survey was conducted to investigate the nature and use of employee dress codes of organizations that market professional services. The study sample consisted of personnel administrators employed in selected service organizations that are members of the American Society of Personnel Administrators; the total sample included 1000 administrators. The analysis of responses revealed that dress is important in marketing services and that compliance to a dress code is a criterion for employee performance evaluation.

While most administrators agreed that dress is a significant factor in their companies' success, few organizations had formal written dress codes; dress codes are most often communicated orally. Traditions in the professions, the expectations of customers, Chief Executive Officers of the organizations, and past experiences were the factors that dominate the development of dress codes. On the question of dress code requirements for male vs. female employees, the study revealed that more service organizations specify dress for males than for females.

For traditional business attire, comparing the dress codes of the different service organizations revealed several significant relationships. In recent years much emphasis has been placed on the importance of dress and appearance for professional success. Often organizations make an effort to manage dress and appearance so as to communicate to the client/customer in the most effective manner. Such controls have traditionally been manifested in policies called "dress codes." The responsibility for the administration of dress codes has conventionally been treated as a personal function. "Proper" business dress has long been a part of the norms of professional services practitioners such as bankers, accountants, stock brokers and management consultants. However, it is interesting to note that in the marketing literature there is little attention devoted to dress as it relates to the marketing of professional services.

This is particularly interesting when one considers the growth of professional service industries as a part of the U.S. economy and the broadscale increases in attention focused on services marketing by practitioners and academicians. The marketing literature does, however, address the issue of personal appearance as it relates to the personal sales interview.

It is well documented from a behavioural standpoint that dress has a significant impact upon perception and image formation as a part of the interpersonal communication process. Peak discovered that when personality traits are correlated with clothing styles, persons who wear conservative clothing are perceived as being more intelligent, mature, generous, sincere, trustful, understanding and dependable than those wearing more "daring" styles. Premeaux and Mondy, dress establishes a level of respect and authority. This is often necessary to get the work done.

In a study on occupation and grooming it was found that less positive characteristics are attributed to those who were groomed "poorly" than to those well groomed. There is an essential difference between the professional salesperson and the professional service practitioner which underlies the justification of this study.

Sales personnel are designated as the "front-line" customer contact persons for an organization which markets goods. Management, as well as salespersons themselves, are not only aware of the role of personal appearance and dress in interpersonal communication, but have employed the resources necessary to incorporate dress codes into promotion and marketing strategies. On the other hand, it is argued that professional service practitioners see themselves as "doers" rather than, sellers". Therefore, it is felt by some that these employees do not focus the necessary attention on those behavioural factors important in selling or marketing as would designated marketing personnel.

As Denny states: One of the fundamental misconceptions many accountants have about marketing is that...someone else can bring in the new clients and then they can take over and do the work. Unfortunately they are wrong...It takes an accountant to sell accounting services. The literature dealing with services marketing ends support to the premise that the dress behaviour of employees could be a salient attribute of the buyer when involved in the purchase process of a professional service.

Two commonly cited characteristics of services, intangibility and inseparability, give credence to this postulate. Because services are intangible in nature, perceptual and communication problems exist during the exchange process which make the true quality of the service difficult to evaluate and distinguish. Pricing and valuation problems result, leading the buyer to feel uncertainty.

With complex technical services such as legal, financial or consulting research, the problem is magnified because of the lack of knowledge of the buyer. It can be argued that because the buyer cannot see the true quality of the service for evaluation that he might use surrogate criteria such as the behaviour of the practitioner, the physical appearance of the facility or other tangible cues. Dress behaviour, then, can become a tangible evaluative criteria for the buyer, regardless of the relationship dress has to the skills of the practitioner or quality of the service performed.

Another theoretical argument offered which distinguishes services from goods is that of inseparability. Often production and consumption of services cannot be separated temporally or spatially. Consequently, personal contact exists between the producer and consumer, allowing the buyer to have the perceptual exposure necessary to observe behavioural and physical characteristics of the seller. The premise set forth as the rationale for this study is that through their behaviour, each practitioner in a service organization which has customer/client contact plays a role in marketing that organization's service. Since dress is an important aspect of that behaviour which plays a role in the communication process during this interaction, dress behaviour can be a salient factor in the exchange process.

If this premise is accepted, and dress is perceived to be important in marketing of professional services, then the question of management or control of employee dress arises. One would assume that organizations would make an effort to manage appearance so as to communicate to the client/customer in the most effective manner.

The purposes of this study were to identify the nature and extent of usage of dress codes among selected service organizations and to determine the importance of dress in the marketing of professional services as reflected in the attitudes and opinions of personnel administrators and in the policies of their organizations. The study sample consisted of personnel administrators employed in selected service organizations that are members of the American Society of Personnel Administrators; the total sample included 1000 administrators. The study involved a questionnaire designed to secure information about the perceived importance of dress codes among selected service organizations.

Questions concerned the importance of employee appearance for service organizations, the factors used in developing dress codes, the requirements of dress codes, the effect of dress codes on employee performance evaluations, and the dress code requirements for male and female employees. Questionnaires were returned by 304 personnel administrators, a 30.4 per cent return. Data was analysed using frequency distributions, and cid-squares were computed to determine statistical significance. The number of respondents from various types of service industries which were used in this study: Type of Service Organization Number in Sample

Management/Marketing Consultants 51 Health Care and Human Services 47 Hotel/Restaurant/Entertainment 40 Financial 39 Employment Agencies 39 Other 35 Engineering and/or Computer Services 30 Legal 13- Total 304 The personnel administrators responding to the questionnaire clearly indicated that appearance of professional employees was a significant factor when a potential client or customer evaluated their company's services. Most of the respondents indicated that personal appearance was a "very important" factor in this evaluation process.

Of the 304 responding personnel administrators, 73% indicated that a dress code, either formally or informally communicated, had been established for their service organizations. Among those respondents whose organizations employed any type of dress code, 67% noted that individual employee compliance to the code was a criterion for employee performance evaluation. Eighty-five per cent of the respondents indicated that compliance to a dress code was either absolutely necessary or very important when employers underwent performance evaluation.

The employment of an established dress code varied little by type of services, ranging from 66 per cent for management consultants to 83 per cent for employment placement services. But the differences in the formalization and use of compliance varied more dramatically. While only 19 per cent of management consulting firms had established written dress codes, 60 per cent of the hotel/restaurant/entertainment groups used written codes.

The data revealed that differences in the use of written codes existed between types of services, and that these were statistically significant at the.05 level. Only 42 per cent of management consulting firms considered dress code compliance in evaluation of their employees, while 80 per cent of employment placement/personnel services considered dress compliance as a factor in performance reviews. The respondents were asked to rank the level of importance of eleven factors when developing a dress code. The scale ranged from "very important," "fairly important," "of little importance," to "no importance," with each given numerical weights of 1, 2, 3, and 4 in corresponding order. Mean scores and the percentages responding to each level of importance are reported. Customer expectations, tradition/convention in the profession, and the opinion of the organization's C.E.O. were the three most important factors listed by the respondents in the development of dress codes.

Among those respondents whose organizations employed any type of dress code, chi-square analysis was performed to compare the classifications of the companies to the formality of the dress codes. Though not statistically significant, the study revealed that more of the local/independent service organizations used formal written dress codes, while more of the multi-located firms utilized dress codes which were informally communicated. Over one-third of the respondents indicated that their dress codes had been established within the last 20 years.

Many of the companies had made changes in their dress codes within the last 10 years. Though not statistically significant, it was found that the firms with revised dress codes were more relaxed in requiring a traditional business look. The differences in the degree of requirement for wearing a "traditional business suit" by type of business organization. Of all types of services in the sample, financial services most required business suits, and engineering/computer least. Those organizations classified as personnel services expected the wearing of suits with skirts more often than others, and again the engineering/computer services required the traditional suit with skirt to the least degree.

Most of the respondents indicated that dress is important in marketing services and that compliance to a dress code is a criterion for employee performance evaluation. While most administrators agreed that dress is a significant factor in their companies' success, few organizations had formal written dress codes; dress codes are more often communicated orally. The results of this study lend support to the premise that dress and appearance of employees could be a salient attribute of the buyer when involved in the purchase process of a professional service. Although the usage of dress codes differed among service organizations, many administrators agreed that dress and appearance are particularly important in making an initial impression and in progressing in a business career. More needs to be known about the actual impact of dress and appearance on the communication process with clients and customers in professional service organizations.

QUALITY IN SMALL- AND MEDIUM-SIZED HOTELS

Total Quality Management can be defined as a satisfaction of social shareholders via implementing effective planning, programmes, policies, and strategies, as well as using human and other assets efficiently and continually within an organization.

This approach will continue to be one of the hot topics among practitioners, academics, and professionals in the new millennium. This presents how a new TQM readiness model can be utilized for providing social shareholders' satisfaction and continuous improvement in small- and medium-sized hotel organizations.

Five-star hotel staffs appear to have better organizational strengths than four-star hotel staffs in North Cyprus. Four-star hotel employees indicate substantial differences in their perceptions concerning TQM readiness elements. An extensive literature review has been conducted.

Issues examined include the following:

- Where to start?
- Is it valuable to bring such a total system?
- Should some parts be imported instead of the whole? and
- Is there any cheap way to bring TQM to small- or medium-sized organizations?

Oakland, the first decision of where to begin can be daunting, referred to as the Total Quality Paralysis problem in quality-management literature. This has been confirmed by other experts and academics who state that small- and medium-sized enterprises generally are less comfortable in bringing TQM into their organizations than large companies are due to limited managerial knowledge, skill, ability, incentives, resources, and time. Only a few studies have been developed on TQM readiness assessment criteria in small- and medium-sized firms. Scholars and others have a common understanding that the more clearly the TQM readiness factors are assessed, the healthier a transition can be achieved to the TQM process. The TQM literature states, "Organizations, which are ready for change in climate, have more opportunity to achieve a successful implementation in a shorter period of time". A common point endorsed in the literature is that there must be a readiness survey before designing, developing, and implementing a TQM programme. This may help to determine TQM factors within an organization and to identify potential problems that may create resistance to TQM and will help to develop a database for future comparisons. Walker and Salameth have stated that only a small percentage of hotels have heard "the siren call of TQM implementations" even in the U.S. It is interesting to note that after 10 years, the literature regarding hotels is still sparse.

Although some viable hotels in limited geographical areas have reported that their TQM performance resulted in profit increased, employee satisfaction, and better usage of economic resources, only a few case studies have been published. As Bloomquist and Breiter indicate, "While those case studies are important in elaboration on the theme of quality management, there remain no reliable statistical data on industry-wide performance credited to quality management."

CHALLENGE FOR HOTEL ORGANIZATIONS

Cyprus is the third-largest island in the Mediterranean. Cyprus has a great historical heritage, conserved environment beauties, and a good climate, and after the war in 1974, the island was divided into north and south parts. No study has been conducted on how TQM can be applied in small- and medium-sized hotel organizations in North Cyprus, which is a major deficiency since tourism is the leading sector. North Cyprus is certainly not the only country where tourism is the most important business sector. The World Tourism Organization statistics, tourism in the world is expected to reach a volume of $US 4 trillion after 2000. This will mean that one out of nine people in the world will be employed in tourism industry in 2010.

The aim of this analysis is to provide a better understanding of how different groups of managers, chiefs, and employees perceive their readiness towards the TQM philosophy in North Cyprus four and five-star hotels. In June 1999, a preliminary investigation was carried out through one-on-one interviews with several assistant general managers, department managers, chiefs, and other lower-level employees from the four- and five-star hotels of North Cyprus. The aim was to design a more realistic TQM readiness model, as well as to prepare a better quantitative questionnaire for the targeted hotels.

The hypotheses of this study are as follows: There is no difference between small-and medium-sized hospitality organizations' hierarchical levels concerning their TQM readiness. There is a difference between small-and medium-sized hospitality organizations' hierarchical levels concerning their TQM readiness. A new model with its first selected eight factors of TQM culture was identified.

These factors are leadership, participation, teamwork, employee satisfaction, empowerment, influence, change, and training. It is important to mention that the assessment factors may not represent all the TQM readiness culture factors. In time, other related factors may be added to this group.

THE ASSUMPTIONS UNDERLYING THE MODEL

The assumptions underlying this model include the following:

- The readiness model factors are iterative; in other words, every organization may use several different preassessment factors, and the rank of these factors also may be different.
- TQM is not a completely new strategic system but rather is a process of developing the current system, opening its way to continuous improvement.

- The readiness model will decrease the total cost, time, and energy of an organization in transforming it into a new TQM culture.

The model involves two important stages. The first stage is to understand and to monitor the present organizational system, especially when dealing with the factors of TQM philosophy and its soft components such as leadership, teamwork, participation, influence, empowerment, and employee satisfaction.

The second stage is the process of examining the gap between upper, middle, and lower layers of personnel in order to prevent possible resistance from different layers at the time of transitioning to a new TQM culture, as well as preparing a database for future assessments. This database may serve as a benchmark where yearly data can be compared with the previous year, necessary precautions can be taken against weaknesses, and the organization can open its way to a continuous improvement process.

Of course, if the necessary proactive precautions can be taken successfully every year, the actual gap among the layers of staff will be narrowed in terms of employee resistance and inefficient use of time, money, and energy. As a result of successful TQM applications, the social shareholders will be more satisfied, and effects of internal challenges will be minimized for the organization.

The data in this study were obtained from four- and five-star hotels. In these hotels, the general manager, usually the owner or a relative who has a very close relationship to the investors, has overall responsibility for all activities. The department managers work under the control of the general managers and report directly to them.

Department chiefs largely serve the role of supervisors, reporting to the department manager. The rationale for selecting four- and five-star hotels is because they attract the majority of tourists in North Cyprus. A total of seven out of 10 hotels were included in the study. There are two hotels that are identified as five-star hotels; the remaining five are four-star hotels. All seven of these five- and four-star hotels were sampled, which provide an overall 100 per cent sampling ratio among five-star hotels and 87 per cent sampling ratio among four-star hotels. This stratified-sampling ratio is very high, and therefore the research is designed to be representative. Stratified sampling has been used in determining the number of employees of four- and five-star hotels. The stratified sampling technique "separates the population into relative homogenous groups".

The hotels employed approximately 550 permanent staff according to statistics gathered from the tourism ministry at the time of the research. The average return rate from the quantitative survey collected from the managers, chiefs, and employees was 73 per cent, 85 per cent, and 39 per cent respectively. Among the 500 questionnaires distributed, 267 were returned, 10 were not completely answered, and 13 were considered biased. Consequently, 23 responses were deleted from the analyses.

The net return rate of 43.8 per cent was quite adequate for the set of questions. A perception survey, a self-administered questionnaire addressed to all managers, chiefs, and employees of the targeted hotels, was prepared in order to collect the necessary readiness data from a more comprehensive perspective.

Respondents were asked to indicate their degree of agreement with each statement on a five-point Likert scale: 1=strongly agree, 2=agree, 3=somewhat agree/disagree, 4=disagree, and 5=strongly disagree. Furthermore, three questions were asked about the ranking of the hotel, type of ownership, and the job position. Items for each subscale were subjected to a reliability assessment. The Cronbach coefficient alpha value for the total scale was 9602, and the subscales were 9092, .8425, .8812, .7177, .6993, .7164, .6976, and.7744 for leadership, team, influence, empowerment, participation, training, change, and satisfaction.

Usually, a reliability coefficient above 0.50 is considered to be a sufficiently high reliability. A factor analysis of the TQM readiness questions in the survey was performed. In order to identify the actual factors in the survey, all questions that did not load cleanly on one factor were dropped from further analysis, which left 61 questions. The frequency and one-way analysis of variance were calculated as a second statistictical technique. Levin and Rubin, ANOVA tests are used for determining the significance of the differences among more than two sample means.

The critical mean scores of the TQM readiness survey for the four- and five-star hotel mangers, chiefs, and staff. A one-way ANOVA analysis is used to explore whether there is a significant difference in the perceptions among upper-, middle-, and lower-level employees of the hotels. In terms of highest and lowest scores, it has been observed that there is little consistency in perceptions among the three staff levels. Results for five-star hotels indicate that employees have significantly higher scores on seven items: teamwork, leadership, and influence.

For those seven items, employees had the highest mean scores. Considering all 61 questions, four-star hotel employees are less positive than five-star hotel employees. They have significantly higher scores on 32 items. For those 32 items, all staff has different scores on each item. Interestingly, the managers have higher mean scores than chiefs and employees on eight items, which are mainly dealt with through satisfaction, empowerment, participation, and leadership.

The chiefs gave negative scores to change, empowerment, teamwork, and participation factors through six questions. Four-star hotels had aggregate means for the 61 items indicated by managers, chiefs, and employees. Both managers and chiefs expressed a moderate level of TQM readiness, while employees exhibited a low level of TQM readiness. However, in five-star hotels, the aggregate means for the same items were managers, chiefs and staff, where all expressed a moderate level of TQM readiness.

Therefore, the null hypothesis was rejected, and the alternative hypothesis was accepted. North Cyprus is a suitable island for tourism because of its undeveloped industry, rich historical and cultural heritage, natural beauty, and relatively unspoiled environment. The various governments that have come to power all have stated that tourism is the primary sector in achieving economic development. The aim of this research was to find out how different groups of managers, chiefs, and employees of four- and five-star hotels in North Cyprus perceive their readiness towards the TQM philosophy With this study it is possible to point out to the owners arid managers the weak and strong aspects of the TQM soft side components they are practicing, and it also provides an opportunity to remove the resistance and conflicts that arise because of perception differences about this philosophy Some researchers point out that in many cases, TQM has been applied without any readiness research and has thus resulted in failure.

As Weeks, "The perceptions of managers, chiefs, and employees are crucial because individuals act as if their beliefs or perceptions are real." Social shareholders are defined by the author as interested or chain parties who are in the same business arena and are a part of the same business life in a free market economic system such as customers, owners, employees, suppliers, government, municipality, and so forth. Two of the five-star hotels are in the same complex and therefore are considered as one hotel. Two hotels have been excluded from the research due to extraordinary reasons.

COMPETITIVE ADVANTAGE

This offers an in-depth treatment of conversion franchising, where new franchisees are added to a franchised system by recruiting existing independent entrepreneurs or competitors' franchisees. The first part of the paper examines conversion franchising as a source of competitive advantage. This discussion leads to the articulation off our propositions. The second part of the paper looks at the empirical results of our study of 72 North American franchisors.

Seventy-two per cent of these firms use conversion franchising in their domestic markets, and 26 per cent use conversions in international locales. The propositions relating to a franchisor's decision to use conversions based on increased levels of experience, economic resources, and to a lesser extent skills! knowledge, all were supported. These results lend support to the literature indicating that resources and skills serve as sources of competitive advantage. Implications for research and practice are discussed. Franchising is emerging as a preferred method of doing business throughout the global economy.

A recent study by the International Franchise Association estimated that, by early in the new millennium, nearly 50 per cent of every U.S. consumer dollar would have been spent in franchised locations. Business franchising has spread rapidly to most continents during the past decade. Given the widespread use of franchising, how can firms leverage better this method of doing business? Some firms have gained increased advantage by adding mobility to their franchised operation by bringing their products/services to the customer where and when they demand them.

But increasingly, firms are turning to conversion franchising as a way of enhancing growth and of gaining competitive advantage in multiple markets. Conversion franchising occurs when a franchisor adds new franchisees to the system by recruiting existing independent businesses or competitors' franchisees.

The purpose of this paper is to examine closely this emerging phenomenon by drawing on relevant literature and by reporting the results of an exploratory study of conversion franchising. Before discussing some of the competitive advantages that can accrue from employing conversion franchising, it first is instructive to review some of the advantages of traditional franchising. Franchising's longevity and success also may be due to the fact that, organizationally, it represents a collaborative alliance.

The alliance depends on the cooperation of two entrepreneurs in order to be successful. Further, these partners depend on cooperation among a network of entrepreneurs to advance common methods and goals, like the sharing of information on innovations that potentially could benefit all franchise partners.Franchising traditionally has offered many competitive advantages over independently formed and operated businesses. The franchisor has access to capital at lower risk; cost sharing with the franchisee; rapid market penetration at a relatively lower cost than establishing one's own distribution system; economies of scale; a motivated workforce of indigenous entrepreneurs; and reduced monitoring and control costs. The franchisee gets an opportunity to enter a business at less cost with a proven product or service and brand name. Additionally, the franchisee frequently receives management assistance in the areas of business location, facilities design, operating procedures, purchasing, and marketing.

These advantages have been born out by a superior survival rate for franchising over independent ventures. Next, we turn to a discussion of conversion franchising and its competitive advantages. Conversion franchising occurs when a franchisor adds new franchisees to the system by recruiting independent businesses, chains, and/or franchisees from other franchised systems. Conversion franchising offers additional advantages to those discussed under traditional franchising. The use of conversion franchising appears to be expanding in recent years, as several industries have experienced changing environmental conditions that often have combined to favour this form of franchising.

The environmental conditions fostering conversions include economic, market, competitive, and technological changes. A contracting economy can mean tight credit policies, making it difficult to raise funds for new projects. During one such period, 3.7 per cent of the domestic hotels converted to a new brand affiliation. A restricted real estate market has led many fast food franchisors to convert existing urban locations to their system rather than to devel op new sites. Saturated markets and increased competition coupled with the growing consumer demand for rejuvenated brand names have generated conversions in the real estate and hospitality industries.

Independents have converted to ReMax and ERA, while Holiday Inn has converted some Ramada Inns and vice versa. Keeping abreast of changing technology has forced firms to seek conversions with systems on the cutting edge of technology, such as Century 21 and Coldwell Banker in Real Estate or Marriott's reservation system in the lodging industry. Resource-based models of organization indicate that established know-how serves as a basis for competitive advantage. Experienced franchisors have developed such managerial capabilities.

Moreover, experienced firms often operate in more competitive arenas, in turn forcing them to try innovative strategies such as conversions. Experienced franchisors have learned to share their know-how with franchisees and have established a record of strong performance, in part because they have taken the time to build brand equity and economies of scale in purchasing, advertising, and distribution, all of which are attractive to independent businesses. Thus, we suggest the following proposition: Proposition 1: The decision to use conversion franchising is associated positively with the experience of the franchisor.

Once a business has converted to a new franchise, is the conversion likely to lead to sustainable competitive advantage? Possible answers to this question are examined in the ensuing discussion. Using the framework of competitive advantage from the field of strategic management is consistent with the view expressed by Castrogiovanni and Justis that researchers need to consider findings from outside the franchising field to assess their generalizability to franchisors.

Competitive advantage is concerned with developing a value-creating strategy by uniquely combining bundles of valuable firm resources and skills to yield positional advantages that result in positive outcomes. Firm resources include both tangible and intangible assets. Firm skills include organizational, technical, and market knowledge, among others.

Aaker argues that a retail location superior to the competition's can act as a key asset, leading to competitive advantage. Barney suggests that a valuable location can act as an imperfectly imitable physical capital resource for the firm, while Day and Wensley see location as a tangible resource that can enable a firm to exercise its capabilities, leading to positional advantage. An existing location may be the only space available on a crowded playing field. This is particularly true in the restaurant, retail, and hotel industries, where location is a key element. Franchisors can acquire location resources in tight real estate markets by converting independents or chains that possess strategic locations.

A strong brand name may be regarded as a superior resource or as a key asset, leading to competitive advantage for today's firms. Consumers in every industry are increasingly brand conscious. At the core of the franchising concept is the bundling of a brand or a trade name with a good or service to sell to entrepreneurs in return for fees or royalties. The need to maintain brand equity motivates franchisors to grow their systems in order to develop promotion economies and, therefore, to spread promotion costs over more units. Converting independents to a franchise system allows for rapid growth and increased name recognition.

For example, in the hotel industry converting members of other chains has been shown to lead to increased occupancy rates. Thus, conversions permit firms to reposition themselves under a new brand to enhance their competitive position. Human resources are critical to the proper execution of any strategy Franchising taps into entrepreneurs who sign on as franchisees to manage individual business units. Sen provides an extended discussion of the franchisee as a source of managerial talent. While entrepreneurs may be motivated to do well, they often are inexperienced and require considerable training on the part of the franchisor.

Using inexperienced franchisees poses a risk of adverse selection, that is, the franchisee misrepresents his/her abilities to the franchisor. Conversion franchising enables the franchisor to bring in experienced franchisees who already have managed a similar business in the industry, either as an independent or as a franchisee for a competitor, thereby reducing the risk of adverse selection. Experienced managers are more likely to enhance a repositioned unit's performance than one with less industry experience. Furthermore, such an experienced franchisee requires less training support. An existing customer base is a major resource that independents and members of other chains possess that can be internalized by the franchisor upon conversion. Since converts can resume business rapidly with existing customers, royalty streams also can begin flowing quickly to the franchisor.

Of course, an additional benefit is that a competitor now has been co-opted into the system instead of working against it. We suggest the following: Proposition 2: The franchisor's decision to use conversion franchising is associated with the potential resource advantages provided by conversions. It has just been argued that conversion franchising brings together key resources of the franchisor and franchisee that have a high potential for improving the competitive positioning of each alliance member.

We now will examine important skills that can play a role in creating competitive advantage. As a cooperative alliance, conversion franchising facilitates the sharing and enhancement of skills to improve the competitive position of both the convert and the franchisor in expanding markets. Skills or capabilities are those attributes that enable the firm to coordinate and to exploit its resources. At the core of the firm's capabilities are its knowledge base from which the skills originate. Thus, we now examine the role knowledge of markets, technology, and organization plays as key sources of competitive advantage provided by a firm's skills.

When a franchisor enters a new market, he or she does so with a limited knowledge of local market conditions and consumer preferences. Since cultures, consumer behaviour, and marketing methods are often different in various markets, franchised systems may need to be adapted to fit local requirements better.

Feltenstein argues that firms need to think globally but to act locally and that much of the variability in sales, service, costs, and margins is determined by local market knowledge. Experience in growing the business provides enhanced knowledge for franchisors in areas such as market and site selection. Acquiring experienced converts helps leverage the advantage of such experience. Moreover, converting independents or other chain members who have been operating in the local market for some time allows the franchisor to internalize these skills into the franchise system. Newly allied members also can aid the franchisor in maneuvering around local rules and regulations that otherwise could slow down or could block a venture. Since conversions typically are of firms operating in the same type or in closely related businesses, converts bring their technical knowledge and expertise to the partnership.

Two general types of technical knowledge are especially relevant in the case of conversions: industry and franchising knowledge. Knowledge relevant to the industry in terms of competitors, substitutes, methods of distribution, and general industry practices are critical to determining competitive advantage. A convert brings new perspective on industry knowledge to the franchisor, broadening the latter's knowledge base and vice versa.

Experience in a particular type of franchising is critical to a system's competitive advantage. The franchise concept is developed on what is believed to be a successful set of practices, and then knowledge bundles are replicated for franchisees. Independents who convert may obtain the immediate advantages of competing with a proven franchise concept. Converts who are previous franchisees presumably have switched because they perceive the new franchisor to have a superior franchise concept.

Such franchise-experienced converts, however, also may provide additional knowledge from their prior franchising experience to enhance the concept of their new franchisor, thereby providing advantages for the entire system. Converts' technical skills are enhanced by the franchisor through extensive training of new members through operating manuals and procedures, and through technical guidance and support. For example, PIP Printing, a leader in the quick-printing industry, offers its franchisees training workshops. The technical skills of the franchisee are enhanced further by the introduction of sophisticated computer systems. In real estate,

20 per cent of the firms in the U.S. are organized as a franchise. New franchisees in this industry gain access to nationwide databases of existing housing stock. Franchising enables a firm to harness the efforts of entrepreneurs while reducing the costs of monitoring a large multiunit organization. Thus, organizational skills revolve around monitoring to prevent franchisees who either may under invest in their units or may shirk on product quality because these actions affect the entire franchise system.

The scale or size of the system contributes to improved organizational coordination. Increased size of the firm enhances monitoring capabilities of the franchisor by reducing the lower per unit costs of monitoring. Conversions enable a franchisor to expand more quickly, thereby strengthening the organizational monitoring skills of the franchisor. Another way to control opportunism is through the payment of fees to the franchisor; this provides financial incentive not to behave opportunistically because the franchisor risks forfeiting the fee if the franchisor suspends the relationship.

Monitoring capability also can be enhanced by learning how best to control the franchisee's behaviour over time. Thus, the longer the franchisor has been offering franchises, the greater the likelihood of improved monitoring skills. Independents can gain other improved organizational efficiencies, such as increased purchasing power, joint or pooled advertising, and other benefits of similar economies of scale, by joining a franchise system. We offer the following proposition: Proposition 3: The franchisor's decision to use conversion franchising is associated with the potential skill advantages provided by conversions.

The literature on competitive advantages stresses those factors that facilitate the development of competitive advantage. However, traditional strategic management theory also notes that the acquisition of skills and resources may also be seen as threats or as challenges confronting the firm when undertaking a new strategy. Anecdotal evidence from franchise experience suggests that certain problems may be encountered when making conversions. Some of the resource-related challenges posed by conversions include the added time it takes to implement a programme or to socialize or to retrain converts. Newly acquired entrepreneurs may be experienced but may be unwilling to work as part of a team or to readily adopt new business methods, thus diluting the advantages of a conversion.

Market, technical, and organizational capabilities may be threatened because of the need to adopt new rules or methods to accommodate a new local market or to attract a convert to join. In short, the franchise concept and standard contract may be changed for opportunistic rather than strategic reasons in order to attract and retain new converts. The reality of the existence of such threats or barriers suggests the following: Proposition 4: The franchisor's decision to use conversion franchising will he associated negatively with the perceived existence of threats posed by the conversion.

The purpose of this empirical part is to provide a description of the current nature and extent of the use of conversion franchising among North American franchisors; and to provide an initial examination of the propositions relating to the factors behind the decision to use conversion franchising by franchisors. A random sample stratified by size and industry of 250 North American franchisors were selected for the study from the Franchise Annual. The top manager of each firm was sent a cover letter and a two-page questionnaire concerning their use of conversion franchising; one follow-up mailing was sent three weeks later.

Seventy-eight firms responded. Six decided not to participate because of mergers, company policy, etc.; 72 firms returned useable questionnaires for a 29 per cent response rate. This compares favourably with other surveys of franchise companies that have reported similar return rates. The profile of franchisors in our sample reveals a good distribution of firms across eight broad industry sectors. The firms are large, averaging 746 total units and having an average of 23 years experience in franchising. The majority of responding managers hold sufficiently high level positions in their organizations to be considered knowledgeable about their firm's franchise strategies. A comparison of respondent firms to a random sample of 40 non respondents in terms of industry, size, and age revealed no significant differences. This should reduce concerns of response bias in our sample. The survey instrument consisted of 10 questions. After defining conversion franchising, the first question asked the respondents to indicate their agreement concerning 18 characteristics of conversion franchising.

These characteristics represented the advantages and barriers of conversion franchising. Responses were made on a Likert-type scale ranging from 1 = not at all to 5 = highly descriptive of your experience. Other questions asked whether the firm used conversion franchising and explored the extent and reasons for doing so. The last three questions explored the use of conversions in international markets. We describe the variables used to explore the four propositions. The decision to convert was assessed by the following survey question: Has your firm used conversion franchising now or in the past?

A simple yes/no response was recorded. This is the categorical dependent variable for investigating the propositions. The remaining variables serve as the independent variables. Franchisor experience was expressed as the number of years the firm had been in business. These were combined further into two factors using principle components analysis with varimax rotation; these factors explain 50 per cent of the variance in conversion advantages. One factor represents "market/location skills" and is comprised of 4 items and has an eigenvalue of 1.58 and a reliability of =.60. The second factor represents "economic resources" and is comprised of five items and has an eigen-value of 2.87 and a reliability of varies =.73.

Two items did not load on any factor. A third item was dropped from the market factor due to reliability problems. These latter three items were not included in any tests of the propositions. Other sources of competitive advantages based on skills were drawn from the Franchise Annual. Technical advantages included seven dummy variables representing eight industry sectors. Franchising knowledge was assessed by the number of years the firm had been franchising. The organizational skills assessed were monitored through scale and financial bonding. Scale was measured by the number of franchised units possessed and financial bonding was measured using the initial franchising fee charged by the franchisor. Competitive barriers/threats were assessed strictly with subjective measures drawn from the eighteen conversion franchising characteristics described earlier. Seven of the items represented potential barriers or threats.

These were reduced to two factors using principle components analysis. The factors explain 49 per cent of the variance in conversion barriers. One factor was labeled "changes" because of the adjustments to existing procedures required by conv ersions. This factor was comprised of three items and has an eigenvalue of 1.52 and a reliability of infinity =.50. The second barrier was labeled "effort" because of the extra effort required by the franchisor to make conversions and was comprised of four items and possesses and eigenvalue of 1.89 and a reliability of infinity =.60 The nature and extent of conversion franchising is described using descriptive statistics. The exploration of the propositions was analysed using discriminant analysis.

The decision to convert represents a nominal dependent variable. The analysis derives a linear combination of independent variables that will discriminate best between the firms that use conversion franchising and the nonusers. The analysis determines whether the competitive advantages and barriers posed by conversion franchising account for a significant variance in the decision to convert. In addition, this method of analysis determines both the predictive accuracy of the independent variables and their relative importance in explaining the decision to convert.

Seventy-two per cent of the firms surveyed use conversion franchising in their domestic markets. Almost half began using conversions prior to 1987; the remaining firms have started using conversions since that time. Among the firms using conversions, an average of 26 per cent of their units are conversions. In responding to an openended question as to why businesses converted to their franchise, our respondents identified eight major reasons. The most frequently cited reasons were to acquire a brand name, which represents one of the major competitive resources conversions can provide businesses.

Awareness, identity, and recognition on a national or global level were cited as the chief benefits of branding. Franchisor characteristics and operating results were tied for second as the most frequently cited reasons for conversion. Key franchisor characteristics included proprietary products and quality of operation and system. Operating performance benefits of conversions included better pricing, leading to increased sales and profitability.

Support services such as technology and research and development, as well as training, each were tied for third in importance for conversions. These represent technological and organizational skills frequently mentioned as advantages of joining a good franchise system. Cost savings and other marketing benefits represented the fourth and fifth major reasons why franchisors believe that businesses convert to their system.

These reasons appear to be congruent with the expected competitive advantages of conversion franchising discussed previously. One of the difficulties in using conversions is that franchisors may have to make adjustments to their normal franchise plans in order to attract well-run businesses to convert. However, less than 25 per cent of the franchisors using conversions needed to make any changes to their normal conversion franchise plan.

Most changes made to attract converts included reduced fees; added training; reduced royalties; covered remodeling costs; additional capital; longer contracts; and other. Thus, a variety of changes are made by a minority of franchisors in order to attract businesses to convert to their system. The majority of franchisors who are currently using conversions to grow plan to continue using them in the future. Thirty-one per cent plan to increase their use of conversions; 25 per cent plan to use them at the same rate as in the past. Only two per cent of the franchisors plan to decrease their use of conversions in their domestic markets. These intentions indicate that franchisors are satisfied that conversion franchising delivers distinct advantages over other forms of doing business. The survey also briefly explored the franchisors' use of conversions in international markets.

Twenty-six per cent of the respondents use conversion franchising in international markets. Half of these franchisors began using conversions internationally in 1990 or after, and currently an average 5.8 per cent of their overseas units are conversions. The country markets in which they have the largest number of conversions include Canada, Germany, France, and the U.K.. Importantly, of the franchisors using conversions internationally, 61 per cent intend to increase their future use of conversions internationally.

By way of summary, the descriptive data reveal that a substantial proportion of North American franchisors are using conversion franchising. Businesses were attracted to convert because of numerous competitive advantages associated with conversion franchises. The future of conversions appears to be quite promising, especially in international markets, as the domestic market becomes more saturated.

All four propositions advanced regarding the factors associated with a franchisor's decision to use conversion franchising were examined using discriminant analysis. Since there were only two categories for the dependent variable, a single discriminant function was derived. The function, using competitive advantages and barriers to predict the decision to convert, is meaningful. The function accounts for 55 per cent of the variance in the decision to convert.

The validity of the function is ascertained by how well it predicts the classification of firms between those that use conversion franchises and those who do not. The derived function correctly classified 93 per cent of the firms. This is almost a 33 per cent improvement over chance alone. A statistically significant and valid function also may be interpreted. For interpretation, we use the discriminant loadings from the structure matrix. These loadings are simple correlations between each independent variable and the discriminant function. The loadings can be interpreted similar to factor loadin gs to assess the relative contribution of each independent variable.

The analysis of the discriminant loadings and their ability to discriminate between franchisors who convert and those who do not reveals five variables that significantly explain the decision to convert. Proposition 1, the decision to convert is associated with franchisor experience. Only experienced franchisors with an established reputation and system can use conversions meaningfully. Proposition 1 is supported as "experience," has a relatively high, positive loading, and is also a significant discriminator between franchisors who use conversions and those who do not.

Proposition 2, concerning the resource advantages associated with conversion franchising, is supported. "Economic resources" has a high positive loading, and its mean is also significantly different between the two groups of franchisors. Firms that use conversions perceive that they derive greater competitive resource advantages than firms who do not u se conversions. Proposition 3 concerning the association of "skill/knowledge" advantages of conversion partially is supported. Franchise skills market skills, and industry knowledge all are associated with the decision to convert.

Franchise and market skills have the two highest, positive loadings and are significant discriminators as indicated by tests of mean differences. The retail industry sector has a moderate but negative loading. The negative loading suggests that nonretail industry experience is more relevant in the decision to convert; other industry categories did not have high loadings, however.

The ability of this variable to discriminate between the two groups is marginal. Organizational monitoring skills achieved through scale and bondings had relatively weaker loadings and were not significantly different among the two groups of franchisors, contrary to our proposition. Finally, competitive barriers did not add significant discriminating information to the decision to convert, contrary to Proposition 4. Neither effort nor changes had strong loadings, nor were their means significantly different between the two groups of franchisors. However, the negative sign of the loadings for effort was in the predicted direction.

Overall, our implicit model of franchisor experience and the competitive resources and skill advantages provided by conversion franchising appear to be significant predictors of the decision to use conversions. Although competitive barriers appear to exist, they do not appear to contribute significantly to the decision to convert, at least among this sample of franchisors. Although conversion franchising appears to have been used for some time, its use has accelerated recently. Over half of the firms have started using conversion franchising since 1987.

While conversions appear to be more prevalent in domestic rather than international markets, a greater proportion of firms intend to increase their use of conversions in international versus domestic markets. The descriptive data also seem to support the franchising and strategy literature regarding why firms convert to a franchise system. Resources such as brand identity, franchisor support, and training were among the most frequently cited reasons.

Three of four propositions concerning the factors affecting the decision to use conversion franchising were supported in whole or in part. The most significant discriminant variables explained 69 per cent of the variance accounted for by the discriminant function. Our results confirm that firm experience, economic resources, market skills, franchising knowledge, and selected industry experience all contribute significantly in explaining why franchisors use conversion franchising as part of their growth strategy.

These results support the strategy and marketing literature, indicating that resources and skills serve as sources of competitive advantage. The results also support the franchising literature regarding the various benefits of this form of business organization. Competitive barriers were related negatively to the decision to use conversions but did not have strong loadings, nor did the means of the barriers differ significantly between those firms that use conversions and those that do not. It seems reasonable to assume that franchisors tend to focus more on the advantages rather than on the threats when considering whether or not to use conversion franchising.

The results of this study should be examined in the light of its potential limitations. The sample size may be considered somewhat small, especially when analysing the propositions due to missing data. The results are pertinent only to North American franchisors. However, North American franchisors are the most mature and therefore are the most likely to consider conversions.

Our data reveal that business experience is a significant factor in the decision. Our respondent companies had similar profiles to nonrespondents, minimizing response bias. Our measures of competitive advantages and barriers were drawn mostly from the field rather than the literature; this may reduce their explanatory power. However, both subjective and objective measures of competitive advantages were used to reduce same-source bias.

Slightly more than half of the variance in the decision to convert was accounted for by the variables examined in this study. Thus, these results provide a partial but not a complete picture of the factors affecting a firm's decision to use conversion franchising. With the limitations in mind, we offer some implications for practice and research. North American franchisors considering the use of conversions should possess significant experience in their business to develop both their business concept and a strong identity for their brand.

Having done so, franchisors then have something to offer to businesses seeking to join their franchise system. When investigating potential businesses to convert, franchisors must evaluate carefully the resources needed to attract technically qualified businesses with a good track record in order to gain resource advantages. Conversions may enhance the franchisor's market skills if the new franchisees are located in more distant markets and possess a prime business location. Conversions appear to be more attractive in nonretail sectors such as business and personal services and lodging. However, additional research is warranted to confirm these results. North American businesses seeking to convert to a new or different franchise system are advised to seek a franchise with a proven concept and a strong brand identity in the markets in which they want to expand.

Successful business converts should have a proven track record of financial performance. These potential converts should demonstrate that their management team is well experienced and qualified in their industry; however, they may lack some key resource or skill that the franchisor can provide. This has demonstrated the relevance of employing theories of competitive advantage to guide systematic studies of conversion franchising. Future studies should develop more robust measures of competitive advantages and threats.

Larger samples from other parts of the world also should be included to determine if the factors affecting the decision to use conversion franchising are the same in other national or regional markets. A particularly fruitful avenue for future research suggested by our data is the use of conversion franchising for international expansion.

While a minority of the North American firms currently are using international conversions, the majority of these firms intend to increase the use of conversions for international growth. Studies examining the factors affecting the international conversion decision also would be a valuable addition to the franchising knowledge base.

CATERING AND FOOD SERVICE

Catering is the business of providing food service at a remote site. Mobile catering is the business of selling prepared food from some sort of vehicle. It is a feature of urban culture in many countries. The food service generally encompasses those places, institutions, and companies responsible for any meal eaten away from home. This industry includes restaurants, school and hospital cafeterias, catering operations, and many other formats. The companies that supply foodservice operators are called foodservice distributors. Foodservice hard goods like ovens and refrigerators are often sold by large buying groups.

Some companies manufacture products in both consumer and foodservice versions. The consumer version usually comes in individual-sized packages with elaborate label design for retail sale. The foodservice version is packaged in a much larger industrial size and often lacks the colourful label designs of the consumer version.

Foodservice sales to restaurants and institutions are estimated to be approximately $400 Billion, about equal with consumer sales of foods through grocery outlets. A food cart is a motorless trailer that can be hauled by automobile, bicycle, or hand to the point of sale, often a public sidewalk or park. Carts typically have an onboard heating or refrigeration system to keep the food ready for consumption.

Foods and beverages often served from carts include:

- Halal food such as lamb or chicken over rice, or in a gyro
- Ice cream and other frozen treats
- Coffee, bagels, donuts, Egg sandwichs and other breakfast items

Food Truck is a mobile kitchen, known colliqually in some regions as a "X" Truck, is a mobile venue that sells food. Some, including ice cream trucks, sell mostly frozen or prepackaged food; others are more like restaurants-on-wheels.

Food trucks make frequent appearances at carnivals, construction sites, and other temporary venues where large numbers of people gather. Some college campuses and surrounding areas boast many food trucks with loyal followings; for example, visitors to Harvard University or MIT in Cambridge, Massachusetts or the campus of the University of Pennsylvania in Philadelphia may see some very popular trucks parked outside the main entrances to buildings at lunchtime. At Rutgers University, the Grease Trucks serve "fat sandwiches" that contain an ensemble of ingredients such as steak, cheese, chicken fingers, french fries, mozzarella sticks, jalapeño poppers, and more. In the United Kingdom, these are known as burger vans and can be found on nearly all major trunk roads at the side of the road selling their food. A 1/4lb burger can be purchased for about £2.

Many people prefer to stop at one of these Burger vans when travelling due to the cheap price, rather than stop at a motorway service station where prices can be extremely high. Sometimes also called "maggot wagon," "roach coach," or "gut truck," these rolling restaurants can frequently be found at or near construction sites. An early version of the food truck was the US Army's mobile canteen and before that the old West's chuckwagon.

A mobile kitchen is a modified van with a built-in grill, deep fryer, or other cooking equipment. It offers more flexibility in the menu since the vendor can prepare food to order. A vendor can choose to park the van in one place, as with a cart, or to broaden the business's reach by driving the van to several customer locations. Examples of mobile kitchens include taco trucks on the west coast of the United States, especially Southern California, and fish and chips vans in the United Kingdom.

A concession trailer has preparation equipment like a mobile kitchen, but it cannot move on its own. As such it is suited for events lasting several days, such as funfairs. In addition to being operated as private businesses, mobile catering vehicles are also used after natural disasters to feed people in areas with damaged infrastructure. The Salvation Army has several mobile kitchens that it uses for this purpose. An event caterer serves food with waiting staff at dining tables or sets up a self-serve buffet.

The food may be prepared on site, made completely at the event, or the caterer may choose to bring prepared food and put the finishing touches on once they arrive. The event caterer staff isn't responsible for preparing the food but often help set up the dining area. This service is typically provided at banquets, conventions, and weddings. Any event where all the attenders are provided with food and drinks or sometimes only hors d'oeuvres is often called a catered event. A catering company or specialist is expected to know not just food preparation, but how to make it attractive. Many events require working with the entire theme or colour scheme. Catering companies have moved towards full-service taking charge of not only food preparation but also decorations, such as table settings or lighting.

It's not that food is no longer a focal point, but rather that it is part of a broader mission. Many suggest that catering is about satisfying all the senses. A caterer and his or her staff should be friendly and coorperative because, after all, they are in the food service industry and should follow the motto "the customer is always right". Catering is typically sold on a per-person basis, where adding additional people is a flat price per person.

Keeping the cost of the food and supplies below this is required to make a profit on the catering. With the correct atmosphere, professional event caterers experience can bring clients satisfaction of all the senses in a way that makes an event special and memorable. Of course, beautifully prepared food can appeal to your sense of taste, smell and sight—perhaps even touch, but the decorations and ambiance should play a significant part in the clients enjoyment as well. Industrial catering includes providing food for airline passengers, schools, prisons and other institutional settings. It can include contract management of client foodservice facilities.

Airlines often have divisions or hire third parties to provide food for passengers. Catering is covered by two different groups. "Independent caterers and companies with a catering business on the side" is a phrase that could be combined with the previous sentence.

CATERING TIPS AND TRICKS

CHOOSINGRIGHT CATERING SERVICE

Food is an integral part of any party so one must choose a catering service wisely. But how does one choose the right caterer for an event? It is important to do a lot of research, check references, and often request a sampling to make your final decision. List your catering needs In order for a caterer to provide an accurate estimate for your party or event, you must communicate your needs clearly. Do you have a location for your party/event reserved and is there a kitchen on site? How many guests are coming to your event?

Find out if the potential caterer has a minimum guest requirement. Take into consideration that some of your guests may have special dietary needs and be certain to communicate this with your caterer. A great caterer will be ready for any surprise that may surface, but at what cost to you? Discuss your budget with your caterer and what options are available. Ask yourself, do you prefer a buffet style or a silver-service sit down dinner for your guests?

Be clear about your proposed menu, do you have a theme or style at the event that will be reflected in the cuisine? Your budget may or may not determine how flexible your caterer is to meet your needs. Keep in mind; it is the type of food that often determines the bulk price of the catering job. Find out, and possibly request, if the caterer will provide a detailed contract of service and outline what the payment terms will be. Does the caterer use fresh or frozen food for recipes? Is the produce grown locally? Is it organic? Will any of the dishes be pre-made and then frozen until the party/event? Does anything come from a can?

Does the potential caterer supply decorations, linens, tables and chairs? Very often there will be a brochure catering services supply with examples of past event and table decorations. It is important to be very clear in what your event needs and what the caterer will be supplying. Is a menu board provided for the guests that describes the ingredients of the dishes being served?

Will the catering company provide a wait-staff? What is their required dress code? What is the ratio of servers to guests? A rule of thumb is one server for every 10 guests. Be certain to ask your potential caterer if taxes and gratuities are included in the final bid. What happens to the leftovers? Often, upon request, a catering service will compile a food basket at no additional charge for the host or hostess of the event. Remember, it is critical that you communicate with your potential caterer exactly you want; the result, you get what you want and the caterer can provide an accurate bid for the job as well as the exceptional service your event deserves.

SERVING ALCOHOL AT YOUR EVENT

When one commits to planning an event or party, one must decide whether or not to serve alcohol to the guests. There are a few considerations to keep in mind and discuss with your caterer. Where will your event or party be taking place? It is important to confirm that your event or party site will allow alcohol on its premises. Once you have made certain that you can serve alcohol at your chosen site, ask your caterer if he or she holds a liquor license.

He or she must have a valid liquor license. If he or she does not hold a liquor license, then you must contact a liquor-licensed dealer. Prepare to provide a guest estimate for your caterer to work with. The caterer in turn will supply you with a quote for the number of bartenders that must attend bar and the quantity of ice, glasses, and mixers necessary.

The amount of bartenders depends on the number of guests. Your caterer or licensed liquor dealer will be responsible for setting up the bar. You must now determine what you wish to be served from the bar as well as if you require your guests to pay for alcohol themselves. A cash bar requires the guest to pay for their drinks. Guests tend to consume less alcohol when it isn't free. This is a basic bar with all the works and at no charge to the guests. The open bar includes hard liquor for mixing drinks, wine, beer, and soft drinks.

A limited bar will set boundaries on what will be served and in what moderation. An example of a limited bar is an event in which beer and wine is offered to the guests at no charge and hard liquor is offered at a pre-determined price. Whatever you decide in regards to serving alcohol at your event or party is up to you.

WEDDING CATERING

After watching the happy couple exchange vows and begin their married life together, your guests will be hungry. Many of the guests may have scaled back on eating in order to look good for pictures or just because they were so busy during the day. When you're putting together such a large assortment of people, there are bound to be those that have certain ways or preferences of eating. You may find that there are vegetarians or those that can not eat dairy.

You might have a diabetic in the crowd or some other health restriction. You should certainly try to have options for any sort of eating arrangement. In the case of those that don't eat meat, you might want to have a cheese lasagne available or other pasta dish. This is becoming widely popular to have two options anyways, so why not offer them?

Another way to cope with varied needs is to serve dinner in a buffet style. This allows each person to pick only what they want or what they can eat. A lot of wedding caterers rely on word of mouth to get their services recognized. If you can, talk to other people that have gotten married in your town to see who they recommend. Of course, you will still want to see them for yourself, but this list can be a great starting point. Another way to find good catering is to talk to the reception hall coordinators.

Many times they will either require the use of a particular caterer or they have a list of those that they recommend. Of course, you will want to schedule an appointment with all of the catering candidates in order to do a taste test of their menu options. At that point, you can pick what you think your guests will enjoy. A good meal is a great way to send your thanks to your guests for coming to your wedding. This is the part that shouldn't be skimped on for any reason.

Of course, that doesn't mean that you can't find moderately priced options. Try your favourite restaurant, for example. If they're able to cater, then you may be able to get a better deal because you're buying food in bulk. Having a friend who is a cook is even better-so long as they don't mind working through the wedding. So you've tasted the offerings of the caterer and you've selected your main menu options. What about drinks? Much like selecting the menu options, you will need to factor in what kinds of drinks everyone would like to drink. The easiest way to take care of this is to offer a full service bar.

In this way, guests can have mixed drinks of all varieties or they can stick to wine and beer. You want to plan this option out carefully as you may end up paying more than you would like. Check with the provider as to how many drinks each guest can have, or can expect from the supply that will be brought. In most cases, there is no limit. A word of advice: Don't ever have a cash bar. Making your guests pay for their drinks when they may also have paid for their outfits and transportation is just a lot to ask.

In terms of wine and beer, tastes and varieties are enormous-how does someone choose? The best advice is to select four to five different kinds of beer with each one having enough to fill everyone's glass. This may surprise you, but sometimes all of your guests will like the same thing and you may want to make sure that they can have it. As for wine, you may want to have at least one of each a red varietal and a white varietal.

This ensures a milder and more acidic selection. A way to make sure that everyone is happy is to find blends of each of these wines. By blends, this means to find a red that includes a merlot, syrah, and pinot noir, while the white might include a chardonnay, reisling, and zinfandel. These can be tricky to find, but they are crowd pleasers. Toasts are just not toasts without a little glass of champagne. It's common sense to make sure that the new couple and their wedding party have the very finest in champagne, while the rest of the guests have another variety.

In many reception halls or catering services, the champagne for the wedding party is provided. Of course, there will also be designated drivers at the wedding, so you will also want to have water, sodas, coffee, and juices available as well. When you're planned it thoroughly, everyone will be well-watered throughout the evening.

HOW TO START A CATERING BUSINESS

The catering industry in the United States is estimated to be worth $5 billion a year. Caterers are hired to perform an assorted number of jobs-everything from cooking to serving, mixing drinks, and whipping up delicious desserts. Functions range from dinner parties that serve a handful of guests to enormous events that serve thousands of guests. Normally a caterer will define their niche, meaning a caterer will choose what type of functions to specialize in as well as their job description.

For example, you may offer the best fondue table for up to 100 guests, perhaps you would rather prepare meals for business catering parties that are held within banker's hours. There really are no limits in regards to catering styles.

Once you have arrived to the idea stage it is great to begin a business catering plan. Be meticulous when you detail how the catering business will be operated, managed and capitalized.

The following checklist can help you organize your ideas into the beginning of a business catering plan:

- What services will your catering business offer? Will you run a full service catering business, corporate catering service, custom event catering service, or a scheduled events catering business?
- Research necessary permits and requirements your local government imposes on a catering business.
- Determine your start up costs of your catering business. Remember to include everything-permit fees, catering equipment, marketing, uniforms, catering supplies etc.
- Construct a budget, forecast and projection.
- How will you finance the start up of your catering business?
- Research liability insurance needed to protect your catering business.
- Where will you house your catering business office and how will you manage your business? Prepare to think about cancellations, payment policies,

consultations, menu-planning as well as samples, contracts and the transportation of food.

- What food suppliers do you intend to work with?
- Will your catering service rent equipment for special requests?
- What will you name your catering business?

  Owning a catering service not only includes cooking but also be prepared to wear many hats such as: accountant, manager, marketer, sales representative, and bill collector. Additional questions to consider when constructing your catering business plan:

  - Is my business idea practical and is it in demand?
  - What is my competition?
  - What is my advantage over existing services?
  - Can I deliver a better quality service?
  - Can I create a demand for my business?
  - What will be my legal structure?
  - How will I compensate myself?

Your answers to these questions will help you create a focused, well-researched catering business plan that can serve as a blueprint for your new catering service. Whatever you choose to specialize in, running a catering business offers creativity, flexibility, and growing opportunities. Maybe you've got the details of the actual wedding ceremony worked out, but what about the reception?

One of the major costs of the wedding reception will definitely be the food, so you'll want to make sure you'll have enough food for everyone without spending too much money. Here are some top ways to cut on your catering bill that will ensure that your guests enjoy your reception-and you save money. Most couples want to order an extra tray or two of hors d'oeuvres in case extra guests show up.

This is fine but you should still make sure that you're not order more appetizers than you actually need; use your discretion based on the guest list. For instance, if you know a number of your guests are vegetarian, you may not need to order as many appetizers with meat. Also, ordering two or three types of hors d'oeuvres will help to reduce your catering bill. If you buy more of the same dish, you can usually save money with most catering companies-different kinds of foods will increase the bill, so it's important to keep it classy but simple at the wedding-even when it comes to food. Caterers will also try to encourage you to spend more than you may need to on the actual meal as well.

You may not need a five course meal if you've already purchased three types of appetizers and a salad, or three extra desserts if you already have a pretty large wedding cake. The time of day that you hold your wedding will give you a good indication of how much food to serve; if you're having the ceremony in the afternoon or early evening, you may want to serve more food.

There are some foods that are always going to be expensive, even if you only order small amounts. So, since you have to order a considerable amount of food, ordering dishes that aren't so costly will help you to keep your catering bill reasonable. Certain seafood, like shrimp, lobster and salmon will definitely make your catering bill higher, so if you have to have them, try to use them as only one of the course choices for dinner, or purchase these fo1ods as appetizers to save on costs. Food stations are a unique way to serve a variety of foods at your wedding reception, and you can be sure that everyone will find something they like to eat. This way, you won't have to worry about people changing their minds about their meal choices once they arrive at the reception. A food station with different types of pasta is usually a hit with most guests, and can be very economical.

You can also include food stations with other types of the ethnic foods, such as Mexican or Indian fare, to celebrate the cultures of the people who will be attending your wedding, or to acknowledge your backgrounds. You may also be able to cut your catering bill by not requesting an elaborate setup for your food stations and tables. Using a single colour for tablecloths, usually white, will cut down on labour costs.

4

Customer Measurement

INTRODUCTION

Every company must be able to satisfy and retain customers. That is the key to its business performance. Your job—as an executive in charge of improving quality, customer satisfaction, or loyalty—may be to enable others to act through training and support. Alternatively, if you're in the quality, customer assessment, or development areas of your company, your job may be to do the work directly—to collect, analyse, or use customer data to improve quality, satisfaction, and retention.

Whether you are an enabler or a doer, customer satisfaction and retention are your responsibility. Providing high-quality products and services builds strong relationships with customers and ensures future revenue streams. Even though you may agree about the importance of customers in driving performance, an important question remains. Does your company align its activities to satisfy and retain customers? Too often the answer is either "no" or "not so well." To help understand the problem, consider how a customer focus has evolved in recent decades.

In the 1970s, quality gurus argued that "quality is free." That is, a tireless pursuit of improvement should not only increase efficiency but also increase customer satisfaction in the process, saving enough on costs and bringing in enough new and repeat business to more than cover any expenditures on quality. This was an underlying concept in the success of many Japanese companies. In the 1980s the experts began to focus more directly on increasing customer satisfaction as an explicit goal. Satisfying and keeping customers, it was argued, is simply less expensive than constantly replacing them. More recently, quality and satisfaction have been viewed as not sufficient by themselves. Companies boast of moving "beyond" quality and satisfaction to focus directly on customer loyalty as the key to profitability.

Yet to argue that quality, or satisfaction, or loyalty is what matters misses the point. These factors form a chain of cause and effect, building on each other so that they cannot be treated separately. They represent a system that must be measured and managed as a whole if you want to maximize results. An example from our teaching experiences underscores the nature of the problem and why companies need to take a systems approach to customer measurement and management. Back in 1993 an executive seminar participant from a Fortune 100 company introduced himself as the "customer satisfaction manager" for his organization.

This prompted one of the authors to ask, "What happened to the quality manager?" The participant replied that quality was passé, and that customer satisfaction had become the hot topic in his organization. In fact, being the quality manager had become the "kiss of death" from a career standpoint—a dead-end job! Five years later, a seminar participant from the same company introduced himself as the "customer loyalty manager" for the organization.

Again the natural question arose, "What happened to the customer satisfaction manager?" "Oh, him?" It turned out that the satisfaction manager was now the one with the dead-end job. Many business organizations are beginning to recognize the need to avoid this "Book of the Month Club" mentality and to view customers from a systems perspective.

They want explicit linkages that extend from internal processes to customer perceptions to customer satisfaction to loyalty—and ultimately to bottom-line performance. The framework in this book will give executives hard numbers and not just persuasive theories to show that the connection is real and that improving satisfaction and loyalty really does improve profits. And those on the front lines—the quality engineers and service providers—will get specific guidance on what to improve and how to improve it to get the optimal response from customers. This book will show you how to create an integrated customer measurement and management system that will help you allocate resources and increase profits.

To create such a system, you must first understand your company's entire system for generating profit, from internal quality through to business performance. A systems approach acts on the basis of collected and interpreted customer data—but then you have to use the data to allocate resources and create change in the system or else you merely waste time and money. With an effective customer measurement and management system, you can build organizational value.

To do so, you will continually pursue three key activities that underlie a customer orientation: (1) gather customer information, (2) spread that information throughout the organization, and (3) use the information to maintain, improve, or innovate in products and processes. You need solid information about the concrete product and service attributes or features that customers value, the more abstract consequences and benefits these attributes provide, and ultimately the personal values they serve.

The purpose is to understand what your customers want not only in today's products and services but in tomorrow's as well. When you understand your customers at the various levels that motivate their behaviour, you can see their present needs and predict their future needs as well. To maintain a customer orientation throughout your organization, you need to make sure that customer information gets to everyone who is involved—either directly or indirectly— in improving quality and value and satisfying customers.

This both prepares the entire organization for change and provides benchmarks by which to monitor its performance. Finally, you need to prime the organization to act on the customer information to improve product and service offerings so as to increase satisfaction, loyalty, and profitability. This makes it essential to clarify the links among these three factors and understand how your company delivers a compelling product to its customers. Creating a customer measurement and management system is central to the pursuit of all three of these activities. With such a system in place, you have your customer information in a form that can serve as a basis for both incremental and more revolutionary product and service improvements.

The system also makes it easier to share customer information throughout an organization, enhancing its ability to follow through on that information to make product and process changes. It is essential to view customer measurement from a systems perspective that encompasses multiple areas of measurement and expertise (from engineering and design through market research and strategy to finance and accounting) so that you pick up both concrete and abstract details— both what the customers like and dislike and why they react that way—and develop information that will be genuinely useful.

Now you may well be saying, "But we already do a good job of gathering customer information, spreading it, and acting on the voice of the customer." The question is whether you really adopt the "lens of the customer" in this process or fall into the trap of relying on the "lens of the organization." The lens of the customer shows you your products and services—and the benefits they provide—from your customers' perspective.

You see them as they really are in the marketplace, rather than the different and potentially misleading picture you're likely to get from the lens of your own organization. For example, if you run a convenience store chain you may be inclined to view the chain's stores as providing customers with people (service), products (from soft drinks to gasoline), and operations (such as opening hours), each under the management of a different department or business function. The problem is that customers may not share this perspective. Customers view products and services from the standpoint of the benefits they provide and problems they solve, which may not align well with individual business process areas. In this case, customers are looking for safety, convenience, and cleanliness, which are benefits that are not uniquely provided by specific business process areas. Rather, they cut across the people, products, and operating policies of the stores. Aside from providing a more accurate picture of the drivers of satisfaction and loyalty, adopting the lens of the customer has other advantages. It blurs functional boundaries and provides a common basis and language for communication.

The forging of concrete links from area to area within a company is also a key to effective implementation. When an organization reaches a consensus on the importance of customer benefits that are not defined along functional or business process lines, it finds it much easier to engage in the cross-functional activities required to truly innovate and implement change. We emphasize the word *framework* here. Our aim is to show just what links and models are possible.The actual elements and links in any model vary tremendously from company to company and context to context.

After describing the framework, as suggested, show this point using two very different cases in which companies (Volvo and Sears) have developed models to become more customer focused. The framework includes four general areas: internal quality, external quality and satisfaction, customer loyalty and retention, and financial performance. *Internal quality* encompasses various production and maintenance processes.

In the case of a manufactured product, it includes everything from manufacturing processes to the physical characteristics and attributes that describe the product. In a service and retailing context, it includes the service offer, the physical surroundings, and the satisfaction of employees and the resulting service quality they provide. External quality and satisfaction encompasses what customers see in the purchase and consumption experience: the attributes and benefits that products and services provide and the costs they impose, and the conclusions the customers draw about the company. In the area of customer loyalty and retention, *loyalty* is a customer's intention or predisposition to buy, while *retention* is the behaviour itself (as when a customer returns to a restaurant, comes back to buy the same brand of car, or purchases another financial instrument from the same institution). Although as suggested, use the term *loyalty* at times to encompass both intended loyalty and actual retention, it is important to understand the distinction. When actual retention information is available, it proves extremely valuable in sorting out the drivers of financial performance.

When it is unavailable, as it often is, you can use loyalty measures as a proxy for retention. Quality, satisfaction, and loyalty ultimately affect financial performance, both directly and indirectly. The framework shows this point and highlights the possibility that there may be a tension between direct and indirect effects. Consider first the impact of internal quality. Producing a high-quality product or service at an attractive price indirectly affects financial performance through its effect on external customer perceptions of the purchase-consumption experience. But internal quality may also have a direct effect on costs and revenues.

The "quality is free" argument, improvements in internal quality can increase productivity and lower internal costs and thus directly increase profitability. Recent research suggests, however, that this link is likely to be more positive for products and less positive or even negative for services. Why the difference? Services are produced and delivered at a time and place that is typically dictated by the customer. Thus improving service quality often requires an increase in personnel and operating or contact hours, which raises operating costs.

The external quality, value, and customer satisfaction component of the framework also has both direct and indirect effects on costs and revenues. Indirectly, a positive overall experience predisposes customers to stay loyal towards a product, service, or provider, which generates future sales. Satisfaction thus contributes to financial performance through its effect on loyalty and retention. But satisfaction also has direct effects, independent of loyalty. The cost of maintaining a customer account—or fixing a product—is a direct function of how happy the customer is. Satisfied customers are less likely to demand expensive product repairs or replacements or to invoke service guarantees. Also—even outside the world of TV commercials—people do talk about the products and services they buy, and your company's entry into that stream of word-of-mouth publicity is through perceived quality and satisfaction rather than through loyalty. Satisfaction is *news*—something to talk about—while loyalty is a background state that goes without saying unless something happens to damage it.

The direct effects of loyalty and retention on performance include revenues from repeat purchases, reduction in costs of finding new customers (to replace lost customers), and revenues generated through cross-selling. Another direct effect is the price premium that loyal customers often pay. Because loyal customers are not actively shopping for alternatives, they tend to be insulated from price incentives and offers such as coupons, price cuts, and free merchandise. The recent turnaround at Volvo Car Company provides a good example of how a durable goods manufacturer views the links described in our framework.

In 1991, Volvo was performing poorly in the global automotive market. It ranked as low as twenty-sixth out of thirty-four brands in the J. D. Power Initial Quality Study in the United States, and sales and profitability were suffering. In its comeback effort, Volvo began to develop a customer orientation from a total quality management foundation. Formerly, Volvo had emphasized changing internal quality to improve productivity and reduce costs.

Its management realised, however, that just focusing on internal quality was insufficient. Internal improvements had to matter to the customers before they could create improved external quality, customer satisfaction, and loyalty. Volvo's approach is just one example of the variety of tailored models that are consistent with the framework. Like Volvo, Sears has attempted to radically transform itself into a more customer-focused organization. But since Sears is a retailer that competes primarily on service, its model has evolved quite differently. Internal quality at Sears is primarily about its people and the service they provide. The Sears model draws directly on a service-profit chain that links internal quality (including employee satisfaction and loyalty) to service quality, and the satisfaction generated by service quality to loyalty and financial performance. In developing its model, Sears has discovered both direct effects of satisfaction on financial performance and indirect effects through loyalty, which is consistent with our framework.

A quantitative employee-customer-profit model at Sears has helped the company to establish very specific links that have enabled it to improve financial performance. The model shows, for example, that a 5-point improvement in employee attitudes (on a 0 to 100 scale) drives a 1.3-point improvement in customer satisfaction, which in turn drives a 0.5 per cent improvement in revenue growth. The Volvo and Sears models share a common logic, but each model is uniquely tailored to the organization's own situation. Both models link internal quality through to profitability.

At the same time, each reflects the nature of a specific company, its customers and offerings, and the contexts involved. When you look at your own company, you will see that the same logic will work for you when you develop a similar understanding of your own customers and what you can offer them. The best measurement system can only provide information— it can't make decisions for you. People make decisions, whether it is the convenience store executive who sets corporate priorities, the front-line service manager who translates these priorities into policies and procedures, or the service worker who translates policies and procedures into concrete actions.

At all three levels, decision makers are much more likely to choose to do something that will help the store chain succeed if they understand what matters to customers and how the job at hand can enhance that value. The process of moving from information to decisions draws heavily on *importance-performance analysis*. The most cost-effective areas of product and service performance to improve are those that are important to customers *and* on which, at the same time, the company is performing poorly. Executives and managers must identify these priority areas of high importance and low performance. As an output of this selection process, they can categorize and display the drivers of satisfaction and loyalty using a strategic satisfaction matrix.

The matrix identifies four categories of performance drivers with different market action implications. Again, the aspects to improve first are those where impact or importance is high and performance is weak. This focuses resources and quality improvement efforts likely to have the greatest impact on satisfaction and thus on loyalty and profitability. Those aspects where performance and impact are both high reflect a firm's competitive advantage.

It is essential to maintain if not improve performance on these drivers. When impact and performance are both weak, on the other hand, there is no need to waste resources on improvement. More interesting is the low impact–strong performance category. This may be an area where resources have been wasted in the past because the benefits and attributes are not important to customers. Alternatively, this category may contain drivers of satisfaction that customers see as basic and necessary—so much a part of the product or service that they ignore it as long as it's there when they want it, like electric power or water on tap.

Although such drivers are important in an absolute sense, they have little to no impact on satisfaction because there is little variance in their performance. The danger is that a reduction in performance quality would increase the impact on satisfaction (this danger is often referred to as a "slippery slope"). Another possibility here is to find a new target market segment for the product or service.

For example, if the quality of an electrical system is so constant that it has no impact on satisfaction in one application, the system might be used in applications where minor fluctuations in this quality are more important and therefore likely to have a real impact on satisfaction. There is also a danger that something in this category may become important in the future. For example, few customers considered "environmental friendliness" to be an important factor until recently, but more and more people are beginning to pay attention to this aspect of the goods and services they buy. In a growing variety of fields, companies that predicted the importance of this area and prepared their business accordingly clearly have an advantage over those that did not. The circular nature of the process reflects the continuous nature of a customer orientation.

Customer needs, competitive offerings, and business technologies change constantly, so customer focus is an ideal of constant growth rather than static achievement. The cycle in is thus a continuous process of planning, researching, analysing, deciding, implementing, and learning. This includes identifying the system's purpose or goals within a more balanced set of corporate performance measures (including financial goals, employee satisfaction goals, process improvement goals, knowledge and learning goals, and so forth). The key customer and market segmentation issues upon which the system is based, including the distinction between internal and external customers.

Conducting interviews and focus groups and observing customers provides you with the lens through which customers view products and services. This lens is the basis for your quality-satisfactionloyalty modeling. It discusses ways to develop and administer surveys that assess the attributes and benefits your products and services provide and the overall levels of customer satisfaction and loyalty that result. The goal is to customise the measurement of quality, value, satisfaction, and loyalty for a particular customer segment, company, and context.

Again, the purpose is to identify both the relative importance and performance of key satisfaction and loyalty drivers. It provides guidelines for identifying the area or areas where importance is high and performance is low, which offer the most potential return on quality improvement efforts. We develop a statistical approach to help you estimate your system or model linking quality to loyalty and financial performance. We also provide concrete examples. As emphasized earlier, management must take part in categorizing the output of a customer analysis into a strategic satisfaction matrix. Just where boundaries are set between highversus low-impact drivers and strong versus weak performance depends on a variety of factors, including what you can achieve in the time available, your cost structure, and your overall strategy. Interpreting model outputs also requires appropriate bench for evaluating both performance and importance.

Who should collect your customer data, analyse it, and use it to set priorities and allocate resources? It often seems logical to delegate the satisfaction and loyalty measurement operation to outside research firms and consultants. This is especially true early in the process of becoming a customer-oriented organization, because outside specialists offer specific skills related to collecting and analysing customer data that you do not have. Unfortunately, if you delegate the system, your company does not take ownership of it, and you and your people may fail to learn or acquire the skills necessary to measure and manage customer data on your own.

The consultant's bills, heavy as they are likely to be, are only a small part of the cost of handing off a customer information system. Bear in mind that when customer information is the key to strategy, it should reside within the company. Your best teachers about what is right and wrong with your products and services are your own customers. Direct contact with customers and customer data is a critical part of learning what it takes to satisfy customer needs.

No matter how good the consultants are, they will always function as filters. An important part of establishing a customer orientation as a core competency is creating, over time, internal specialists to measure, model, and manage quality, satisfaction, and loyalty. Early in the process, external experts are apt to be a necessity. They can provide the interviewing, surveying, data warehousing, statistical analysis, and interpretation skills that you may lack or not yet want (or be able) to invest in. Over time, however, continued reliance on external specialists becomes costly and also fails to develop customer measurement and management as a core competency. Internalization of the process allows you to adapt to changing market needs and competitive environments in a cost-effective fashion. More important, your organization accepts ownership of the process and the data—and the decisions that emerge. This is not to say that all parts of the process should be brought in-house in all cases.

You may not want to try to run a survey that involves computer-aided telephone interviews or a Web-based system with highly specialized personnel (such as trained interviewers) and potential economies of scale. Even in the most customer-savvy organization, it may be best to outsource certain parts of the process. At the same time, a truly customer-oriented firm should own rather than rent the ability to observe and to talk to customers, formalize survey instruments, analyse and interpret customer data, and use the output to make resource allocation decisions.

Over the last three decades business organizations have evolved from a focus on quality to a focus on customer satisfaction, and onward to a focus on loyalty as a means of creating value. A customer measurement and management system views each of these areas as an indispensable link in a chain of causes and effects that runs from internal quality through to profitability. The goal of this book is to help you and your organization create an integrated customer measurement and management system for making effective resource allocation decisions and increasing profitability. In the process of building a system, organizations develop internal specialists capable of gathering, analysing, and interpreting customer data.

Truly customer-oriented companies should, over time, add these skills to their core competencies. A systems approach to customer measurement and management also requires that you tailor the system to your unique purpose, customers, and contexts. As an illustration, Volvo's model incorporates the positive effects of improving internal quality on both productivity and customer perceptions of quality, satisfaction, and loyalty. In contrast, a major retailer such as Sears incorporates the central role that satisfied employees play in delivering quality and value to customers. These measurement systems and models are not substitutes for decision making. Rather, they provide the information you need to make resource allocation decisions and manage the process.

The system provides information on how the company and its competitors are performing in different areas and how important the areas are to customers. When combined with cost and strategy considerations, the system allows both enablers and doers to create organizational value through a continuous focus on customers. To maximize the value generated by the system, make sure your company's own staff perform the bulk of the work of collecting and interpreting customer data, so that you get the full benefit of the insights generated by the effort.

Before you dive in and start conducting customer interviews or surveys, you must know how your measurement system will be used. Since a customer orientation builds on internal quality, we'll start with a brief overview of quality management and its role in driving company strategy and customer measures. We'll then discuss two related approaches to translating strategy into action: policy deployment and balanced performance measures.

Then we'll focus on the process of getting started on developing a customer measurement and management system—or improving an existing one—which involves taking a look at the breadth and depth of the proposed system and the role of market segmentation in it. In our customer satisfaction framework, internal quality is the first in the chain of events that drives financial performance.

It's important not to underestimate the role of *total quality management* (or TQM, also known as *company-wide quality management*, CWQM, and as *total quality control*, TQC)—nor to exaggerate it. For longterm survival, businesses have been forced to improve their abilities to change and innovate. But internal quality management is not in itself sufficient to assure success. Internal quality improvements must be linked to improvements in external quality, satisfaction, loyalty, and financial performance. And the links must be established in an environment of constantly evolving customer preferences, markets, competitors, and technologies. The broad principles and methods of quality management apply directly to the development of a customer measurement system.

The concept of quality should unify all of a company's activities. After all, only your customers can ultimately define quality for you! In the end, it doesn't matter how well the production system works, how well marketing functions are performed, or how good the company's strategy is. If no one buys, there will be no revenues.

Quality experts emphasize three basic strategies for successful quality management: use reference models or benchmarks, set priorities for quality improvement, and focus your resources. Do not try to do things completely on your own. Instead, make use of reference models or benchmarks when they're available. Benchmarking is particularly important in developing a customer measurement and management system. Process benchmarking—finding out how things are done— works as well in developing a customer measurement and management system as in any other area of business.

When you can manage it, arrange visits to firms with strong reputations to gauge their practices and learn what they are doing, see how they are doing it, and understand what is possible. Devote some time to reverse engineering their products as well. And don't limit the benchmarking to competitors—in a general area such as customer measurement, you'll find individuals or organizations in many fields who excel in areas that you are interested in improving.

Benchmarking on their processes can help you to learn how to conduct better customer interviews, develop and administer more effective surveys, and analyse customer data in more productive ways—and they're likely to be much more willing to share information with you if you're not trying to sell the same offering to the same customers. For *output* or *performance benchmarking,* you will measure your product or service against direct or indirect competitors on various dimensions such as internal or technical quality, external or perceived quality and value, and overall customer satisfaction, loyalty, and retention. The external benchmarks will help you interpret your findings regarding your own customers and decide just where to devote your resources to get the most mileage from your improvement efforts.

SET PRIORITIES FOR QUALITY IMPROVEMENT

The second basic strategy of quality management is the universal law of priorities. In a quality context, it is often said that 20 per cent of parts, processes, or people account for 80 per cent of quality problems (often called the *Pareto principle*). Each customer and each market will react differently to the various drivers of satisfaction and loyalty, so one of your primary goals in customer measurement is to identify the drivers that are most important to improve.

You need to find out where the impact on customers is high and your current performance is poor. Your goal should be to set priorities and *optimize* rather than *maximize* your quality and satisfaction improvement efforts.

FOCUS YOUR RESOURCES

Once you have chosen the area or areas to change, the third basic strategy of quality management is to concentrate your resources to maximal effect. The goal is to create a company-wide focus on the things that matter most for performance and survival. This is one of the most important yet also most often neglected aspects of quality management. Increasingly, managers face a common problem in that their customer measurement systems point out specific needs for improvement, but their organizations don't respond.

The manager knows what area or areas to attack, but has difficulty getting anyone to do anything about it. This is where the lens of the customer shows its usefulness. Once the concept spreads through an organization the independent actions of each individual and department are much more likely to fit into the overall improvement effort.

TWO WAYS TO TRANSLATE STRATEGY INTO ACTION

Since no amount of information will do you any good if no one will act on it, creating an environment where resources get focused on quality management is in many ways the key element of the process. One basic approach to this problem, called *policy deployment,* has proven very effective where a company has a clear priority regarding what policy to deploy. A variation known as *balanced performance measures* allows a company to determine and deploy a balanced mix of quality improvements.

Policy deployment, or hoshin planning *(hoshin kanri)* as it is sometimes called, is a powerful quality management process that converts a company's strategy into operational change and effectively moves different units within the company in the same direction.

Customer policy deployment, in particular, aims to move the entire organization to focus more on customers in order to increase their satisfaction and loyalty.

Policy deployment includes four major steps:

1. *Mission and Vision:* Clearly state the organization's philosophy, mission, and vision (also called the *president's diagnosis*).
2. *Goals:* Understand exactly where the organization is today and where it wants to be in the short, medium, and long term with regard to specific criteria or goals.
3. *Communication Strategy:* Communicate the mission, vision, and goals throughout the organization.
4. *Priority Setting and Implementation:* Set priorities, align the incentives, and implement quality improvement projects accordingly (using project management).

Making customers a priority became a strategy for Volvo's survival in the intensely competitive global automotive industry.

Back in 1991, the question was how to create a customer orientation in a traditionally engineering-driven company. Volvo quickly realised that policy deployment was a natural means of building on its quality management foundations to move the company from an engineering focus to a customer focus. Here is a summary of how Volvo implemented the four major phases of policy deployment:

- *Volvo's Mission and Vision:* "To be the world's most desired and successful premium car brand."
- *Volvo's Goals:* "To be number 5 in customer satisfaction (according to the J. D. Power IQS study) in 1995 and number 3 in 1997."
- *Volvo's Communication Strategy:* Stop keeping secrets about customer complaints; give employees an open information system and a broad view of the customer value-added process that encompasses the vehicle sales and service experience throughout the life of the vehicle.
- *Volvo's Priority Setting and Implementation:* Use quality teams to focus on the two hundred highest-priority areas (out of two thousand possibilities identified in an initial review), and reward team members based on the degree to which Volvo met its corporate goals as well as on the degree to which the team met its own goals.

Once mission statements work their way through various levels of management, they often end up reading like the Boy Scouts' oath. Companies want to be all things to all people. In contrast, Volvo's vision was specifically to be the most desired successful specialty car brand.

While abstract and forward-looking, the vision nonetheless pointed to a particular segment of the automotive market in which Volvo wanted to excel. Quantitatively, Volvo's goal was defined in terms of placement in a specific independent survey—to be number 5 in its industry by 1995 and number 3 by 1997.

Although any measurement system has its strengths and weaknesses, by defining customer satisfaction using the J. D. Power IQS study, Volvo effectively defined where it was (twenty-sixth out of thirty-four makes) and where it wanted to be at different points in time. Volvo effectively aligned its mission and vision to concrete measures and goals. Volvo's next step was communication. Stellan Flodin, the senior vice president in charge of quality, and Jan-Olof Nilsson, senior vice president of Business Area 900, led the effort to create a communication process and culture of openness across the company. Volvo abandoned its hush-hush approach to quality and customer data in favour of a more open system in which information was made available to anyone who could influence customer satisfaction.

This was critically important at Volvo because its employees perceived their company as doing quite well. Internally, they had been improving products and processes from year to year all along. But externally, relative quality was falling and the company was losing ground to competitors. This decline was a well-kept secret until Volvo decided to change policy and speak freely about its problems.

Many of the problems reported in the IQS studies involved customers' experiences with sales and service, so it was essential that Volvo encompass the entire value-added chain (from production to delivery and dealer service) in its policy deployment process. Over a period of about two years, the company created an environment in which individuals from very different value-adding areas worked together to solve a variety of customer problems. Reported quality problems came to be viewed as opportunities to learn and improve rather than as negative reflections on any particular area, team, or individual.

As noted, Volvo's customer data revealed over two thousand areas in which quality improvements might be made. The final stage of the process, project management, set priorities and put quality teams to work improving approximately two hundred of the most glaring problem areas. On the Volvo 850, for example, customer data revealed that the manual transmission alone generated a surprising number of complaints (about twenty per hundred vehicles). For example, many customers said the manual gear box was too stiff, and people of below average height added that the stick shift was too far away and difficult to reach in some gears. A project team was therefore deployed to improve the quality of the transmission. Additional customer surveys allowed the team to translate customer perceptions into design and part changes that, when introduced, decreased the incidence of complaints by over 50 per cent. A key to making all this happen, however, was that Volvo aligned the project teams' and individuals' goals with overall policy goals.

Team members were compensated based on whether their teams met project goals (such as reducing transmission problems per hundred cars from twenty to ten to five over time) and whether Volvo met its overall corporate goals such as reducing overall problems per hundred cars to reach the number 5 position by 1995 and the number 3 position by 1997. The policy deployment process that Sears is using to create a customer focus is similar to the process at Volvo. The main difference is that, whereas Volvo built on its knowledge of quality management to implement policy deployment from the top down, Sears is using the development of its employee-customerprofit chain to drive the deployment process from the bottom up.

The process has been more implicit than explicit. Retail-service companies have not gone through the same quality management revolution and training as manufacturing companies such as Volvo. But once Sears's employee-customerprofit chain was developed, it became an important tool to drive change in the company's mission, vision, goals, and communication. Everyone from senior managers to store employees had to be taught the logic of the model and its implications, including how the company's competitive environment had changed.

The company held town hall meetings and used learning maps to help employees grasp the logic behind the model so that they, in turn, could apply it at the store level. In the end, the deployment process has helped build a leadership model that incorporates the various aspects of the employee-customer-profit chain. The leadership model is to make Sears a compelling place to work, shop, and invest. Yet the deployment process has progressed more slowly at Sears than at Volvo. The process at Sears has been more data driven, working from the bottom up. Only after the employee-customer-profit chain was developed did Sears executives confront many of the challenges in deploying policy, from a lack of buy-in among top executives to communication problems among their retail employees. And arguably, Volvo has been more successful at implementing its customer orientation and turning the corner on profitability. After some initial success, financial performance at Sears remains weak. These results aren't surprising, and they provide a useful warning to those in service industries.

Product companies tend to have a history of quality management when they begin to implement customer policy deployment, and this gives them a strong head start. Few service companies have gone through the same quality revolution, although there are important exceptions. Disney, Fidelity Investments, and USAA, for example, have long-standing commitments to quality management and its principles.

Disney has used policy deployment in the development of its theme parks for many years. But most service firms simply did not get the wake-up call that hit manufacturing firms in the 1970s and 1980s, when they were confronted with competitors producing higher-quality products in less time and at lower cost. If you manage or work in a service industry such as telecommunication, insurance, or banking, very likely your company is now experiencing or will soon experience the same type of global competition and cost pressures as your counterparts in the manufacturing world. Technology such as the Internet now provides a basis for delivering cost-effective global service.

The warning from product companies is clear. If you hope to continue to prosper, establish a culture that emphasizes quality as your foundation for using customer information to drive organizational change. Balanced performance measures or BPMs share many of the principles of policy deployment. But whereas policy deployment has always been an explicit means of translating strategy into action, BPMs were initially developed as a way of balancing the needs of multiple stakeholders in an organization. Rather than focusing mainly on customers, BPMs recognize that a customer focus must be balanced against the needs of other stakeholders, such as owners, employees, and suppliers. A popular approach to developing BPMs is the balanced scorecard. Companies use the balanced scorecard to assess their performance and strategy in a highly integrated fashion.

The scorecard's four main components are the company's financial perspective, the customer perspective, the internal business process perspective, and the learning and innovation perspective. The *customer perspective* includes those customer measures that are most important for the company to improve, such as targets for customer satisfaction or account penetration. The *financial perspective* includes targets the company sets with respect to both financial (market value) and accounting (revenue and profit) measures.

The *internal perspective* includes internal quality and business process measures, such as the number of hours the company spends talking with customers about current or future projects, or the level of employee satisfaction. The *innovation and learning perspective* include goals and measures for investments in training and new product or service development. For each perspective, goals and measures are developed and drilled down to operational levels for teams and individuals ("personal scorecards"). As balanced performance measurement systems evolved through the 1990s, their relationship to policy deployment has become clear.

For example, in more recent versions of the balanced scorecard, a company's vision and strategy drive a management process that includes strategy feedback and learning, clarifying and translating the vision and strategy, communicating and linking rewards to performance measures, and planning and setting targets. These stages obviously parallel the four main steps in policy deployment described earlier. Yet important differences remain. Whereas a full policy deployment moves an organization in a completely new direction, such as focusing more explicitly on customers, BPMs balance various stakeholders' needs. In this sense, BPMs are a weak form of policy deployment. They more or less presume that the organization is headed in the right direction and align its activities accordingly. A balanced scorecard approach keeps an organization on course through an integrated management and budgeting process. BPMs also lack any guiding framework or model of the drivers of financial performance. The approach focuses generally on synergies among the various perspectives or stakeholder needs.

It is important that you build your measurement system on an evolving understanding of the drivers of financial performance that is tailored to your company and competitive environment, as Volvo and Sears did. Although this book's focus is primarily on the customer perspective, balanced performance measures do serve as a reminder that the measurement and management process described here can be applied to other stakeholders as well. In the Sears model, for example, employee attitudes and beliefs are critically important in driving employee behaviour.

The processes and tools described in this book for developing the lens of the customer can certainly be applied to develop the lens of the employee, supplier, or equity stakeholder as a basis for developing and administering surveys, analysing data, and setting priorities for improvement. When you embark on a strategy of customer-driven quality improvement, questions will arise about how to set up a system to collect the data you need to work with. Many of these questions can be broadly categorized as relating either to *system breadth*— the range of internal and external customers and market segments that you want to measure— or to *system depth*—the level of detail and nature of the information that you gather.

Companies typically serve a range of very different customers both inside and outside the organization. Internal customers may be in the same physical location, as when marketing and finance are customers of information services, or in different locations, as when manufacturing plants are customers of the home office. External customers range from wholesalers and retailers to end users. The customer chain shows three levels of customers: plant customers, retailing customers, and end users. We have kept this example simple to make the relationships easy to see on paper; in practice any given organization or network is likely to have a much larger number of customer levels, as any individual might be considered someone else's customer. And it isn't enough to track exchanges of funds for goods or services, as even external customers don't necessarily pay to assume that role—regulatory agencies are customers for reports, for example, and people downstream (literally or metaphorically) from traditional end users are the ones likely to be customers for ecological and recycling efforts.

To determine just which customers should be your primary measurement and management focus. What links in the customer chain drive your financial performance? Where are the links from quality to satisfaction to loyalty and profitability the strongest? Those are the places where you're likely to get the most mileage out of any investment in improved quality. Even without a detailed measurement system, you probably have some knowledge or understanding of where to start looking.

Think about the nature of the competition and customer choice at each level. The logic of a customer orientation (the idea that quality, satisfaction, and loyalty drive profitability) is based on two critical assumptions. First, the customer is relatively free to choose products and services. This assumption holds for most industries in the developed world today—customers face a dizzying variety of brands of cars, soap, phone service, and most necessities and luxuries, and if one alternative doesn't satisfy there's always another to try. This assumption doesn't always hold true, however—when customers face significant switching costs in moving from one provider to another, or there is only one supplier available, they are essentially hostages.

That is, when it's expensive or difficult to find another supplier, only a very dissatisfied customer will switch to a competitor. Airline customers are often held hostage to the hub-and-spoke system of air travel, where flying on other than the hub airline imposes significant costs in terms of time and convenience. However, no company can count on keeping its customers hostage indefinitely. In the gas and electric supply business, for example, many customers still have few options to choose from—but recent deregulation means that the situation is changing rapidly, and customer satisfaction and loyalty are likely to become drivers of profitability soon. The second important assumption in the logic of a customer orientation is that the important customers are the ones who will generate new business if they're satisfied with their experience—buy replacements for past purchases, buy new offerings, or inspire potential customers to try the company's wares.

Investments to satisfy more transient or one-time customers may not generate future revenues or cost savings. The benefits of increasing satisfaction are thus greatest at the level in the customer chain where your customers have both a choice and a potential to reward you with future revenues at lower costs. Related to the notion of customer choice is the relative *push* versus *pull* of your products and services through the customer chain.

Consider a service provider such as Fidelity, which places investment instruments through a variety of independent retailers. In one region, the end users—the individual investors— may have strong brand attitudes and perceptions that have been created over a long period of time through experience, advertising, and word of mouth. In this case, the most important customer in the chain is probably the end user who goes to a retailer (whether an agency or a Web site) in search of a particular offering.

The choice in this case resides primarily with end users who pull the product through the chain. Although all customers are important at some level, relatively speaking, the satisfaction of the retailer is not as critical in this case as the satisfaction of the end user. To satisfy and retain their own customers, the retailers need to make the Fidelity offerings available to them. Elsewhere, investors may be much more likely to follow the advice of the retailer about which brand to purchase. The retailer may be more established and trusted in the end user's mind than any individual brand. If investors are more likely to defer their choice to a trusted retailer, Fidelity is in a position of pushing the product or service through the chain.

In this case, the most important thing to measure and manage may be the satisfaction of the retailer and its willingness to push the brand on to the end user. The same logic applies regardless of the product or service—if the offering is seen as interchangeable at the end-user level, you have to give the retailer a reason to favour your brand over others.

At each level in the customer chain, the market segmentation scheme is the key element in your strategic market plan to build a customer measurement system. Market segmentation is the process of identifying and targeting unique populations or *segments* of customers and developing tailored marketing strategies to meet the individual segment needs.

To identify and target segments, take the following steps:

1. Group customers into segments based on customer needs, benefits sought, or personal values served.
2. Identify or describe the segments according to their behaviours, lifestyles, or demographics.
3. Evaluate the attractiveness of each segment in terms of, for example, profit potential, risk, capacity utilization, and core competencies required to serve the segment.
4. Determine strategically which segments to target and pursue and, as a result, which segments to measure, analyse, and manage separately.

These steps bring you to a framework for just which customers to measure, analyse, and monitor. Because the drivers of satisfaction and loyalty may be very different from segment to segment, be wary of averaging across segments. Averages can be deceiving. If customer data are aggregated too highly, they provide a profile of an average customer who simply does not exist. If the segments are different enough, they will require separate survey development and analysis.

Even when the same survey is applicable to more than one group of customers, be sure to analyse importance and performance levels separately for each group.

SEGMENTATION IN A HOTEL CHAIN

Consider, for example, the needs of business customers and vacation customers at "Wolverine Inns" a fictitious name for a major mid-priced hotel chain we worked with recently. The chain recently segmented its franchisees according to which segment of customers they are most likely to serve, based on the idea that downtown properties cater more to the business customer segment and leisure-area properties cater more to the vacation customer segment. The matrices are used to set priorities for quality improvement.

The company's satisfaction and loyalty survey covers eight general quality areas or customer benefits (reservation process, staff, facilities, grounds, bathroom, room, breakfast, and perceived value) and each area is rated on a variety of attributes. For the moment, just look at the impact and performance aspects of the eight types of benefit. Later as suggested, take up the issue of setting priorities among the attributes that provide each benefit, such as the friendliness, helpfulness, efficiency, and grooming and appearance of the hotel staff. The vertical axes show how each type of property performs on each of the eight benefits using a weighted average of customers' attribute ratings (on a scale where 1 is poor and 5 is excellent).

Both downtown and leisure-area properties, for example, perform very well on the quality of the reservations process. The horizontal axes show the relative importance of each benefit as revealed by its statistical impact on overall satisfaction. For example, the impact score of.75 for quality of the room for the downtown properties shows that as room quality increases by 10 per cent, satisfaction increases by 7.5 per cent (10 per cent ×.75). (This example is based on standardized scale values.) The results reveal vast differences in the drivers of satisfaction across the two property types. Business customers who frequent downtown Wolverine Inn locations look for the hotel to simply provide a clean and comfortable room. They use the hotel for a place to get a good night's sleep and have little interest in its other services. In contrast, a much wider variety of factors drive satisfaction for the vacation customers who frequent the chain's leisure-area properties. The quality of the room is secondary to the quality of service and advice that the staff provides.

The quality of the grounds, bathroom, and breakfast are also more important for the vacation customer. As hotel manager at any given property, you would certainly want to know impact and performance levels for your target customers. Assuming the described results for individual hotels, the downtown manager would see improving the quality of the rooms as the greatest priority, given its high impact and currently moderate performance.

In contrast, the manager of the leisure-area property would see improving the quality of the staff as relatively more important. Neither manager would have much incentive to do anything about perceived value—the customers' view of the price they are paying for the experience—even though it is far and away the lowest performance area in both cases, because the survey results show that neither group of customers cares much about it. Lowering prices would be costly for the hotel and would make it more difficult to sustain improvements in areas that matter to the customers, so it's best to avoid this step unless the hotel has an incentive to change its customer base to one that regards the current price level as a barrier rather than a minor irritant.

After deciding which customer levels to include in the measurement system and what customers or market segments to include, the next step is to ask what level of generality or detail about the lens of the customer the system should contain. Customer satisfaction is a complex matter, made up of the way the customer perceives the concrete attributes of a product, the benefits the customer derives from those attributes, and the personal values that the product supports. All these elements reside with the customer and are beyond the company's direct control, so we refer to them as *external quality factors*. Measurement systems vary in the amount of detail they provide about external factors such as these. For example, macro-level measurement systems such as the American Customer Satisfaction Index (ACSI) only include very general differences in external perceptions of overall quality and value as drivers of satisfaction and loyalty.

Quality is itself measured using customer ratings of the levels of customisation and reliability provided, while value is measured using customer perceptions of the price or prices paid for the quality received. The purpose of measurement systems such as the ACSI is, however, to provide quality, value, satisfaction, and loyalty benchmarks across a very wide range of firms, industry groupings (including products, services, retailers, and government and public agencies), and even countries. Such broad-based comparisons require a measurement system that emphasizes generality and comparability as opposed to depth and detail.

If your goal is to improve or radically reinvent goods and services, you'll need a more detailed and comprehensive information system. It should include information on the range of concrete attributes and abstract benefits that might drive satisfaction and require improvement. The convenience store example and discuss perceived convenience, merchandise quality, and safety as just three of the benefits that directly affect customer satisfaction.

As suggested, discuss how to develop these more detailed or in-depth measurement systems for the purpose of measuring and managing customer data for a particular product or service and market segment. Remember that the information in the measurement system is designed to leverage either incremental (evolutionary) or innovative (revolutionary) activities, or both.

For example, when Volvo discovered that its customers found its manual transmissions difficult to shift (an attribute-level problem), it translated the problem into one of changing certain parts that immediately reduced complaints. In contrast, when product or service designers are pursuing major innovations, they shift upward from the attribute level to more abstract customer benefits and personal values as input to the design process. Developing a fuel cell or electric vehicle, for example, requires matching the benefits and consequences that the new technology provides (such as zero emissions and moderate performance) with the benefits and values that are important to target customers (such as a willingness to trade off vehicle performance for environmental impact). Product or service design is then a process of developing a whole new configuration of product and service attributes to better serve customer needs.

We are often asked when to engage in revolutionary innovation rather than more evolutionary continuous improvement. The key, of course, is to avoid focusing on one to the exclusion of the other, but rather to balance both activities. Masaaki Imai, who was instrumental in developing the *kaizen* or continuous improvement process, emphasizes the importance of maintaining a balance among three activities: maintaining the quality of existing products, services, or processes; achieving kaizen or continuous improvement; and achieving innovation.

The temptation, Imai argues, is to focus only on innovation as a means of making rapid changes and leapfrogging the competition. This ignores the long-term benefits that continuous improvement brings to a company. When all three activities are balanced, the result is a formidable competitive advantage. Disney is a great example of an organization that consistently manages to balance all three activities. The regular development of new characters for use in movies, television shows, and theme parks is a constant source of innovation.

At the same time, Disney works to maintain or keep improving every stage of its customers' experience. The combination has created a legendary service organization that is built on a quality foundation *and* reinvents itself on a regular basis. Measuring quality, customer satisfaction, and loyalty should be an ongoing, repetitive process. It is difficult, however, to make general recommendations about just how frequently to measure. The frequency varies from company to company and depends on the audience, the stability or volatility of the product or service, and the nature of the market. For instance, if you have relatively few customers it may not be desirable to survey them too often. Needless to say, your customers should never feel that the process is burdensome.

And once you do a survey and set some priorities, be sure to implement the changes before you launch another survey. Otherwise, your customers will ask the obvious question: "Why should I bother filling out this survey when you didn't pay any attention to the last one?" A product's life cycle also affects the frequency of measurement. You need frequent contact with customers early on, when the market is evolving and changes to the product or service can have a great impact on a company's success. Consider the battle between Ericsson and Nokia in the cellular phone market. The early adopters of cellular phones were business people.

They simply wanted a reliable phone, which gave Ericsson the edge. But Ericsson did not keep up with the evolution of customer needs in the market and emergence of new market segments that demanded more features and design improvements. This allowed Nokia to achieve a greater advantage as the market evolved. Later in a product's life cycle, customers are much harder to attract, more valuable to keep, and more costly to lose, so again you want close and frequent customer contacts. And, of course, it is always important to listen carefully to customers when the threat of competition has increased.

The general point is that contact with customers should become more frequent during certain critical stages of the product life cycle and market dynamics. Keeping these contingencies in mind, we recommend a customer satisfaction survey at least yearly. More frequent surveys are likely to have little effect on your improvement efforts when the product and the market are stable. If competition is really active and is moving quickly in a market, it may be necessary to carry out more frequent studies—perhaps even on a quarterly basis. But make sure you have enough resources to process and implement the findings, or the efforts are wasted. It is often a good compromise to measure every six months in times of change. Finally, remember that there's a difference between customer measures and surveys as the basis of a measurement and management system and more informal surveys or methods designed to take a quick pulse or to identify problems as they occur.

The latter methods typically focus on the most recent episode or transaction with a customer (such as the latest stay at the hotel or visit to the bookstore), and are often loosely structured (an informal interview by the manager or an open-ended "opinion" card). Their value towards allocating resources and deciding strategy is limited. At the same time, they may be a valuable source of information for service managers or front-line service personnel to catch and resolve certain classes of problems as they occur.

Providing external quality and customer satisfaction depends directly on the quality of your company's internal processes, operating policies, strategies, and plans. Whether your company provides products or services (or both), quality management provides a solid foundation for developing and deploying strategy and measuring quality through the lens of the customer. You will see the three basic strategies of quality management. As suggested, describe the use of reference models or benchmarks to interpret and analyse customer data. As suggested, show you how to optimize rather than maximize customer satisfaction and loyalty by setting priorities for quality improvement.

Finally, as suggested, describe ways to maximize use of available resources to implement the change. Policy deployment and its variants, including balanced performance measures, are important tools for creating a more universal and consistent focus. These approaches provide companies with a means of translating their customer strategies into action. Just where to begin building the system requires decisions regarding which customers to include, or system breadth, and how much detail to provide, or system depth. You want to include the kinds of customers that drive business performance. To do this, you will need to ask "which of our internal or external customers are both a source of future profits and have a choice about where they take their business?" To drive profitability, produce and deliver high-quality products and services to satisfy and retain these customers.

When including customers in the measurement system, remember that customers do not all value the same things and behave in the same way. Build your customer measurement systems on an understanding of how your customer base at any given level (such as retail or end-user) is segmented. Segmentation is a process of identifying individuals or populations of customers with unique needs and wants. By paying attention to segment differences you will avoid the pitfall of setting priorities based on "average" customers who don't exist. In your planning process, also consider just how much detail you will need to measure and how you will use your measurement system.

At a general level, macro-level customer measurement systems provide for broad-based comparisons and benchmarking but give only general guidance about what companies should improve (such as product or service quality or value). In this book, the focus is on measurement systems that are more specific to the company or segment; they provide detailed information regarding concrete product or service attributes as well as information about more abstract consequences and benefits.

By continually improving the concrete attributes of existing offerings and finding completely new ways to provide customer benefits, you can leverage your customer data to create a truly exemplary level of performance and competitive advantage. To link internal quality to profitability, you have to find out how customers see the products and services they purchase and consume. Your first step will be to develop a model of how customers view your firm's products, services, and activities—the "lens of the customer" that will guide the rest of your efforts. As discussed earlier, people inside an organization too often develop customer surveys from their own perspective, or how they believe customers view their products and services. The result is a survey or measurement instrument that embodies the lens of the organization rather than the lens of the customer. You'll often see airline surveys organized in this fashion, for example, full of questions broken out by organizational activity (check-in, preflight service, food and beverage, flight crews, and cabin environment).

A survey that aligns question areas with organizational responsibility in this fashion does have the advantage of producing recommendations that are fairly straightforward to implement. If the survey results and prioritysetting process indicate that flight crews are most in need of improvement, then the responsibility for making improvements within the organization is clear. Unfortunately, this type of survey may warp or entirely miss issues that cross organizational boundaries, as when flight crews get blamed for being short-tempered about carry-on baggage that should never have been allowed into the cabin in the first place.

Customers tend to form opinions regarding such benefits as service, convenience, and safety that cut across the functional areas of an organization. It is essential, therefore, that the measurement system be based squarely on the lens of the customer. In addition, having a survey instrument that better captures the customers' perception of the company makes the data easier to analyse. We are able to explain more variation in key customer evaluations and behaviours, such as satisfaction and loyalty, when the questionnaire is based on the customers' view.

For an airline, such a questionnaire might address a whole range of activities from seat reservations through boarding to baggage claim under the heading of convenience, and everything from the gate lobby staff to the seat cushions under the heading of comfort. The concrete attributes of a product or service and the abstract benefits it generates occupy different levels in the customers' lens.

This distinction is very useful but may take some getting used to. The rectangular objects at the left-hand side represent the concrete aspects or dimensions on which customers can readily report performance via survey measures (such as whether a sales staff keeps its appointments and returns telephone calls and e-mail messages). The circular objects to the right of the attributes represent the relatively abstract or *latent* variables that capture the benefits or consequences that the attributes provide or, at an even more abstract level, the personal values that they serve. For simplicity, as suggested, refer to all the abstract drivers of satisfaction and loyalty as *benefits*.

As in a traditional marketing perspective, the customer satisfaction model embodies the view that products and services compete primarily on the benefits they provide or the needs they fulfill. The concrete attributes of the product or service are only the means to these more abstract ends. Letters, e-mail messages, and faxes all, for example, provide the benefit of communication. You can thus view benefits as the primary drivers of satisfaction in the lens. Notice, however, that benefits may be measured using different numbers of concrete attributes.

Satisfaction in the model is defined as a customer's overall evaluation of the purchase and consumption experience with a product, service, or provider. This definition is quite different from transaction-specific definitions of satisfaction that capture a customer's immediate reaction to a particular episode or experience. Why discard the immediate response in favour of a more cumulative or overall definition of satisfaction? Although it seems more remote, the latter turns out to be more directly tied to customers' repurchase intentions and behaviour.

Customers' repurchase decisions are affected by their entire purchase and consumption history with a company or brand, not just the last trip to the restaurant or last shipment from a supplier. Although we list loyalty, broadly defined, as the desired outcome of satisfaction, there are other constructs we could have shown there as well. Customer satisfaction may also lead to an enhanced reputation and greater brand equity for the company, which will in turn attract additional customers who are disposed to develop loyalty of their own.

The also see overall satisfaction and loyalty in circles, treating them as abstract constructs that can be measured in concrete terms. Overall satisfaction is reflected in different concrete satisfaction measures, which might include a satisfaction scale, how the product or service performs overall versus customer expectations, performance versus an ideal product or service in the category, and performance versus "best in class" competitors.

Similarly, loyalty may be measured using a variety of behavioural intentions (ratings of the likelihood that customers will return, will purchase other products and services from the company, or will speak positively of their experience to others) or actual behaviours (such as whether customers do return, how often they return and how much they purchase when they do, and whether they bring or refer additional customers). Note the dotted arrow that runs from an attribute-benefit cluster directly to customer loyalty.

This captures the possibility that customers' intentions or decisions to repurchase are affected directly by certain benefits. In a recent study of satisfaction with hair care providers, for example, we found that the quality of the haircut, the relationship with the stylist, and the atmosphere of the salon all affect loyalty via overall satisfaction. However, the timeliness and ease of scheduling an appointment have direct effects on loyalty in addition to their effects on satisfaction. Price can also affect loyalty directly— customers are likely to weigh price or value much more when evaluating loyalty than when evaluating satisfaction.

"I love his work, but I can't afford to go back every month" You can't develop the lens of the customer by sitting around and reflecting on how customers view the world. Instead, you need in-depth, qualitative research to show you the issues from the customers' own perspective. Keep in mind that the goal of conducting qualitative research (such as interviews and focus groups) is not to immediately set priorities for quality improvement— it is to identify a comprehensive range of issues (benefits and attributes) that potentially drive satisfaction, loyalty, and profitability. The customer sample that you use at this stage of the research should represent a good cross-section or range of customers from the population or target market of interest, but it need not be truly random as you're not looking for statistical validity at this point. The lens or model that results from this qualitative research provides the foundation for more systematic survey research, which in turn becomes the primary basis for setting priorities when you get to that stage of the process.

Marketing books offer a wide choice of qualitative methods that you can use to identify product and service attributes and the customer benefits they provide—one-on-one interviews, group interviews or focus groups, protocol methods (having customers "think out loud" while using or evaluating a product or service), and a variety of observation techniques. Here, we focus on one qualitative technique that is particularly well suited to the development of a customer model or lens: the *critical incident technique* (CIT). The CIT can be used to identify satisfaction drivers for a range of internal and external customers.

It typically involves an interview in which individuals or groups of customers are asked to provide a list of the things that they like and dislike about the product, service, or company in question. Bob Hayes, an expert on the CIT approach, "A critical incident is a specific example of the service or product that describes either *positive* or *negative* performance. A positive example is a characteristic of the service or product that the customer would like to see every time he or she receives that service or product. A negative example is a characteristic of the service or product that would make the customer question the quality of the company." The critical incidents themselves should be as specific as possible in describing a single feature of the customer's purchase and consumption experience.

Hayes argues that a good critical incident should cover a single behaviour or characteristic, and should either describe the service provider in behavioural terms or describe the service or product using specific adjectives. One retailer noted positively that "the range (variety) of products is good"—

pointing to a particular characteristic of the tires (the available range) using a specific adjective (good). Another retailer noted negatively that "regional representatives arrive too seldom" — pointing to a specific behaviour of the local salesperson (waiting too long between visits). If the critical incidents are too general, the interviewer needs to ask additional questions to clarify what the customer really has in mind. For each specific incident, it is also useful to ask the customer for comments on the significance and consequences of the incident.

Such questions will elicit valuable information for the next stage of the process, categorizing the incidents into attributes and benefit groupings. When encouraged to elaborate, for example, the retailer who praised the product range pointed out that carrying a range of tire products allowed him to offer "a tire for almost every customer that walks into my store." The one who said the regional representative arrived too seldom said that "he should come every month ...just to see how things are going." Overall, the CIT process involves a number of steps that are helpful to describe using an activity-based flowchart.

Step 1 is to compile and assess whatever relevant secondary research or knowledge pertaining to the lens of the customer already exists within the company. (One should avoid, of course, any biases from the lens of the organization.) Perhaps similar studies have been conducted in slightly different research contexts that shed light on how customers view the product or service. Step 2 is to make initial visits to different customers early in the process. We have found this important for two reasons. First, the visits will provide firsthand observations of the

QUALITY-SATISFACTION

You'll usually need several sources of data to establish all the links from quality through to profits. Consider the experience at Sears and Volvo. Sears uses one survey to measure internal quality in the form of employee perceptions and attitudes and a second survey to measure external quality and satisfaction from the customers' perspective. Information from both sources is then combined with financial performance information for individual stores to trace the links in the employee-customer-profit chain. Volvo tracks internal quality with engineering-based measures of vehicle performance, and uses customer surveys to track external quality.

Now we focus on ways to develop and administer the survey that measures customer perceptions of quality, satisfaction, and loyalty. The lens of the customer will serve as a blueprint for your survey, identifying the attributes to include and the order they should appear. To make the survey results useful, however, you will also need to specify and include measures of satisfaction and loyalty so as to be able to combine the individual customer responses into a meaningful pattern of causes and effects.

Step 1: The Preliminaries

As in any other activity, if you don't know what you want to get out of customer measurement, it's going to be hard to tell if you've found it. So before you develop the survey itself, you need to figure out what information is required—which is a function of what you're planning to do with it—as well as how to segment your customer base, what survey method or methods to use, and how to sample the population.

What Information Is Required?

Start by restating in simple terms what you want your customer survey to tell you, and what you plan to do about it. This might be as generic as "We want to know what our customers want so we can give them more of it—and what they don't want, so we can avoid including it, " or it might be tailored to your particular business.

Then look back at the lens of the customer and list the attributes and benefits it identifies as having the potential to drive customer satisfaction and loyalty. Then list some direct questions about customer satisfaction and loyalty. From a statistical standpoint, these are the primary dependent variables that the model is to explain based on customer perceptions of attribute and benefit performance. Make sure that the things you're asking about are at least partially under your control, so the results will be meaningful and useful. There is no point in finding out that your customers are uniformly unhappy that every day they get a day older, unless you're in the business of providing some way to preserve youth and prolong life. So consider just how the results will affect areas and individuals in your organization and what actions you may need to take based on the results.

How to Segment Survey Respondents?

The next step is to figure out which market segments to include in the survey—and just how to classify respondents into those segments. The choice of segments should be based on their importance in your strategic market plans. Beyond the choice of key segments (such as "daily" and "weekly" convenience store customers), another important question related to segmentation and sampling is whether to include current, past, or potential customers in the research. Companies are often content to focus only on current customers.

Unfortunately, if current customers are systematically different from those you've lost or those you would like to pursue in the future, your results from a currentcustomer survey could be misleading or incomplete. Market segment classifications may be based on information collected prior to the survey. Existing research may already have determined which customers are classified into which segments.

If survey respondents can be identified and classified into segments beforehand, then it is perhaps unnecessary to have segment-related information in the survey itself. Otherwise it will be critical to include information in the survey that allows you to sort or select customers by segment. The sorting or selection criteria may be direct or indirect.

THE INDIRECT APPROACH

Using the indirect approach, you might include descriptive items in the survey such as demographic variables (age, sex, income level, education level, ethnic background), geographic variables (city, country, or geographic area), and experience-related variables (frequency of purchase or consumption of the product or service, confidence in evaluating the product or service, and so on).

These measures would then be analysed *after* the surveys are administered to develop distinct clusters or groups of customers that differ on the variables of interest (such as male versus female or frequent versus infrequent convenience store customers). This approach is indirect in the sense that the descriptive measures are only proxies for identifying more needs-based segments. A disadvantage of this approach is that it can lead to the inclusion of so many descriptive variables that the survey becomes long and cumbersome.

An advantage of the approach is that it provides a database that can be used to develop and identify new segments. This allows you to *cut,* or sort the data, in various anticipated and unanticipated ways. Descriptive variables are typically collected near the end of the survey. If a customer feels sensitive about answering particular questions (such as age, income, or education level), encountering such questions up front may bias the responses to the whole questionnaire or lead the customer to give up on it entirely.

THE DIRECT APPROACH

Using the direct approach, you provide an existing segmentation within which customers place themselves in a needs-based segment. Often companies have some existing knowledge of the major segments or populations in their customer base. If simple descriptions of each of the different segments can be included in the survey, customers can indicate directly which segment they most identify with. For the convenience store survey, for example, independent research conducted prior to the survey helped us define five major segment profiles. We then used the profiles to develop descriptive statements for each segment:

- *Segment 1:* I tend to visit a convenience store several times a day for snacks as well as meals.

- *Segment 2:* I am a parent who occasionally goes to a convenience store mainly to buy fill-in items, emergency items, or things for the kids.
- *Segment 3:* I visit a convenience store daily to buy one or two items such as a soda, coffee, cigarettes, or candy.
- *Segment 4:* I go to a convenience store once or twice a week to buy a snack, soda, or coffee.
- *Segment 5:* I shop at a convenience store less than once a week, mainly to buy snacks and party items or items for a trip.

In the resulting convenience store survey, we asked survey respondents to indicate which of these statements best described their behaviour. The primary advantage of this approach is that it is based directly on an existing segmentation scheme. This greatly simplifies the analysis of the survey data. The responses are simply sorted according to their segment identification and analysed.

The disadvantage of using existing segment profiles is that it assumes that the profiles provide an accurate description of the underlying segments. If the nature of the segments changes between the segmentation study and the quality-satisfaction-loyalty survey, the results of the latter will be skewed in unpredictable ways. We recommend using a hybrid of the direct and indirect segmentation approaches when possible. Using existing segment profiles simplifies subsequent analysis and bases the analysis squarely on a segmentation scheme. But it is helpful to include some additional descriptive questions. The convenience store questionnaire, for example, augments the segment-level questions with a small number of demographic questions used in U.S. census questionnaires.

The hybrid approach allows for some exploratory analysis using the demographic variables to sort or cluster respondents into new segments. The demographics also provide descriptive details of the segment profiles, such as whether "daily" convenience store customers tend to be male, female, older, younger, and so on. Prior to developing the survey, you also need to decide just how to communicate with customers and administer the survey. The choice of survey methods has important implications for the nature of the questions and scales involved. There are various approaches, the more common being one-on-one interview surveys, telephone surveys, Web-based surveys, and written surveys. Each method has its strengths and weaknesses.

The choice of methods should depend on the context. One-on-one interviews are well suited to business-to-business applications, where the population of customers is relatively well defined (such as those customers who purchase a certain type of chemical or part). Conducting personal interviews is a good way to increase response rates; it shows customers that you are deeply interested in their opinions. This is important if your organization has a reasonably small number of key customers that you want to take special care of. A disadvantage of one-on-one interviews is that they can become difficult to manage when the sample of respondents is large.

Problems also arise when the individual conducting a survey interview has a vested interest in the results of the survey, as when the salespeople's bonus system is tied to the data that they collect from customers. Anyone who has purchased or leased a new automobile in the last few years might remember the pleas from salespeople to "give me 10s on the survey—my bonus depends on it!" It is crucial to maintain independence and objectivity in these cases through the use of a third party within the company (such as a manager or a salesperson who does not serve that customer) or an independent data collection agency to conduct the actual interviews.

Telephone surveys, particularly those using a computeraided telephone interview or CATI system, are particularly well suited to end-user products and services where representative samples of consumers are needed from a large population. The advantages of telephone interviews include their relatively low cost per completed interview and the control the interviewer has over who is responding to the survey (compared, for example, to written or mail surveys). A human interviewer can clarify any misunderstandings or problems that a respondent may have in answering a survey question. And when they encounter respondents who are simply not able or willing to respond to the survey, trained interviewers can quickly say thank you and terminate the interview. The disadvantage of the telephone interview approach is that interviewers may generate unpredictable effects of their own.

They must be carefully trained, as the way questions are stated is likely to have an impact on how customers respond. Through the use of randomization techniques (such as random-digit dialing), telephone interviewing typically yields more representative samples of customers in a population than you get with other methods. Using this approach, time zones and area codes can be systematically sampled. The American Customer Satisfaction Index survey, a large national survey, uses this approach to obtain valid cross-sections of U.S. consumers.

The survey samples are checked against census data using demographic profiles to ensure that they are properly balanced with respect to age, sex, income and education levels, and ethnic background. Internet-based surveys are growing in importance as the population of Web users becomes more representative of specific customer groups. Web surveys offer significant advantages in that data can be collected, transferred, and updated continuously online. And unlike CATI survey participants, Web respondents have a written version of the survey available on the computer screen to help keep the questions and scales clearly in mind—and they all see exactly the same questions, which eliminates the danger of interviewer bias.

Web surveys have already become the preferred method of data collection in those industries where Web samples are representative of the customer base (as for certain financial services and online retail operations). Yet many customer populations continue to contain large percentages of individuals from lower income and education categories that do not have direct access to the Web (such as convenience store and mass merchandise retailer customers). This situation is likely to change in the near future. Infrastructure changes, such as the diffusion of broadband cable, will broaden the population of Web users in the years to come. Even now, creative solutions can be used to give more customers Web access for the purpose of conducting a survey. For example, a kiosk system can be placed in a location that all customers could access (such as a convenience store or an employee lounge). A crosssection of customers could be encouraged to use the kiosk using personal communication or incentives (such as store coupons).

Easy-to-read touch-screen displays can be used to collect, transfer, and even analyse the data on-line. Another alternative is to use printed versions of the survey that can be handed out or mailed to customers and later scanned and processed on-line. Written surveys, particularly mail surveys, remain a popular approach to data collection. An advantage of written surveys is their relative low cost *per targeted respondent,* or survey sent. Written surveys can be mailed or distributed efficiently to a relatively large number of customers.

The problem is that response rates tend to be low for this approach. Because of the low yield, direct mail often proves more expensive than telephone or Webbased surveys and the respondents are not as representative of the customer population. The quality of the survey data also suffers in that, compared to phone or interview surveys, written surveys offer less control over the interview itself. Written surveys may be passed along for others (subordinates or other family members) to fill out and there is no easy way to clear up misunderstandings or ensure that the respondent is responding carefully to the questions.

One solution to the weaknesses inherent in any one method of data collection is to combine elements of more than one approach. For example, one-on-one or small group interviews can be used to explain the purpose of the survey and motivate participation. To ensure anonymity, written surveys could then be left with the respondents to fill out and return after the interview. Another successful approach in retail contexts is to use store intercepts in combination with written, telephone, or Web surveys. The store intercepts are used to explain the survey and motivate participants to participate in it, while the follow-up survey (in writing, by phone, or by Web page) allows respondents to participate at their convenience.

Sampling is the process of selecting respondents or customers from a population for inclusion in the survey. Naturally, then, sampling starts with the customer population or populations of interest. Your market segmentation scheme and the specific segments that you have decided to include in the research largely define your customer population.

The wide variety of techniques for sampling from customer populations fall into three General categories:

1. Census samples
2. Judgment samples
3. Statistical samples

Census samples involve gathering information from every possible member of a population, such as all of an organization's customers—or all customers in a given segment. Census samples are perfectly representative because the sample and the population are one and the same. Census samples are feasible primarily when the population size is relatively small (such as potential purchasers of jumbo jet engines or highly specialized industrial tools). If you define your population as all customers who have recently recorded transactions, your own records can supply a census sample of current customers.

When the population of customers is too large for a census sample, judgment or statistical samples are called for. Judgment samples involve—as you would expect—using your judgment to decide who should and should not be included. One common method of judgment sampling is to take a list customers and pick people well dispersed with respect to age, sex, income, education, and so on.

The drawback is that the inclusion of respondents in the sample is at the discretion of the researcher. This makes it difficult to generalize any results to the population at large. At the same time, this approach is useful when the goal is simply to identify potentially important issues, as when conducting qualitative research. For example, that the primary goal of using the CIT (critical incident technique) method is to find out what attributes and benefits to include in a more systematic survey. Statistical sampling involves using statistical probability to determine a sample.

Hayes tells us that the primary differences between judgment and statistical sampling are that statistical sampling involves the use of random selection to include cases or respondents in the sample, the ability to statistically determine an appropriate sample size, and the ability to determine how representative the sample is of the population. Thus statistical sampling allows for greater generalization of the study results to the population as a whole.

Examples of statistical sampling methods include random-digit dialing of customers (as through CATI systems) and systematic sampling from a customer list (start at a random point and then pick customers at set intervals, say, every tenth or hundredth name, until you have the number you need for your sample). Respondents in the ACSI survey, for example, are selected using random-digit dialing. Naturally, the choice of a sampling method or methods is a function of both the size and accessibility of the customer population or populations of interest and the purpose of the research.

Once you've cleared away the preliminary survey questions, the next issue that you face in developing the survey is just how to measure benefit and attribute performance and importance. With respect to performance, the survey results should provide reliable and sensitive measures of customer benefits, customer satisfaction, and loyalty. When measuring importance, you must choose between direct customer measures of importance (using, for example, scales or other rating tasks) and derived importance or impact measures based on statistical analysis. There are two important factors to consider when you measure perceived customer benefits, customer satisfaction, and loyalty. First is the abstract nature of the constructs involved. Customers do not obtain satisfaction directly from the concrete attributes and features that describe product and service offerings. Rather, satisfaction and loyalty are a function of the benefits and consequences that the attributes provide. These benefits (such as convenience, safety, and service quality), being abstract or latent constructs, cannot be observed or measured directly using single survey items and scales.

The same is true for such overall evaluations as customer satisfaction and loyalty. Abstract or latent variables are reflected in a variety of concrete measures. Benefits are reflected in the attribute ratings that make up the benefit, satisfaction is reflected in a variety of overall performance ratings, and loyalty in a variety of behavioural intentions. The best way to empirically measure these latent variables is to use multiple concrete *proxies,* or survey measures.

For example, qualitative research shows that a convenience store customer's perception of convenience is reflected in ratings of store location, hours of operation, speed and efficiency of employees, and the availability of parking. A latent variable can be measured using a weighted average or *index* of these survey measures. The convenience index of a convenience store thus becomes a weighted average of a customer's ratings of store location, hours of operation, speed and efficiency of employees, and the availability of parking. Overall satisfaction becomes a weighted average of a customer's ratings on such measures as satisfaction, overall performance versus expectations, and overall performance versus a "best in class" competitor.

The second factor to consider when measuring perceived customer benefits, customer satisfaction, and loyalty is the distribution of the data as it relates to your need for *sensitive measures*—measures that can differentiate among fairly small differences in the underlying conditions. This is an ongoing problem in customer surveys because perceptions of quality and satisfaction almost never fall on a normal distribution. That is, there are typically no bell-shaped curves in the data. In a competitive economy, only those competitors with relatively high quality and satisfaction ratings tend to survive.

As we know this results in quality and satisfaction data that is strongly *skewed* (where most of the responses are bunched near the high end of the quality and satisfaction scale and the tail of the distribution trails off towards the low end of the scale). The measurement challenge is to be able to distinguish among customers that are crowded together at the high end of the scale.

To show the problem, consider what happens if you use a very insensitive measure of satisfaction. When asked yes-or-no questions (say, Are you satisfied?), the overwhelming majority of customers answer yes. In a recent study of airline passengers we found 95 per cent of customers responding yes when asked to evaluate their satisfaction on a yes-no scale. Unfortunately, yes-or-no questions give you no way to distinguish among customers that range from moderately to very satisfied.

The sensitivity of the scale improves when you move to a 5-point scale (where 1 = poor performance or very dissatisfied and 5 = excellent performance or very satisfied). Research on quality and satisfaction scales suggests that using a 10-point scale is better still. Going beyond 10-point scales, however, is not beneficial as respondents have trouble using all the scale points. Most sensitive of all is the use of multiple 10-point scale questions to form an index.

Consider that any given survey measure is composed of two sources of variation, that which is supposed to be measured (what statisticians call the "true score") and that which is not meant to be measured (the "error"). The *true score* is what the various items in an index have in common, while the *error* is more a function of the biases or problems inherent in individual survey questions.

By averaging the measures into a single index, you can increase the amount of true score and reduce the overall error variance (relative to an individual survey measure or question) as error from the individual questions is canceled out. As a result, in statistical analysis and modeling, when you use indices in place of single item measures, you explain more of the variation in satisfaction and loyalty, and the relationships involving quality, satisfaction, and loyalty are stronger. In state-of-the-art quality and satisfaction modeling, the use of indexing to measure abstract or latent variables has become the norm. Consider a simple example of the value that indices bring to an analysis. When you assess the financial health of your company, you know that any one marketing, accounting, or finance measure (customer retention, return on investment, return on capital employed, stock price) is an imperfect reflection of overall state of the company.

Taken together, however, the measures provide a more accurate picture of financial health than is possible using any single measure. The next step is to decide whether to use direct or derived measures of attribute and benefit importance. Many satisfaction measurement systems rely heavily on the "gap" model, in which the measure of what needs improvement in quality or satisfaction is the difference between customers' direct ratings of attribute importance and direct ratings of performance (performance minus importance).

There are three kinds of direct measures commonly used in marketing research:

- *Direct scale ratings:* Respondents rate the importance of a product or service's attributes on a scale ranging, for example, from "not at all important" to "very important."
- *Point allocation methods:* Respondents distribute importance "points" (say 100 points) among a given set of attributes where the proportion of points allocated to an attribute indicates its importance.
- *Paired comparison ratings:* Respondents rate the relative importance of attribute pairs.

Paired comparison ratings can place tremendous burdens on respondents because of the number of attribute pairs involved. They have also been heavily criticized for producing arbitrary measures of importance.Direct scale ratings are considered more accurate (less biased) than point allocations and easier for respondents to provide than either point allocations or paired comparison ratings. These factors make direct scale ratings the more popular choice, so the remainder of this discussion will focus on this method of assessing customer responses. The primary advantage of direct importance scale ratings and the gap model is their ease of implementation. They require minimal analysis (plotting averages and taking difference scores) and can be easily understood at various levels in an organization, from front-line service personnel to CEOs.

Yet there are several problems associated with using direct measures. The method assumes that customers understand what you mean by "important" and also that they know just what attributes are important to them—and are willing to tell you about it. In the end, we find that asking customers directly to rate the impact that an attribute has on their satisfaction and loyalty is an extremely difficult task. Direct importance measures often result in socially acceptable or status quo answers and poor discrimination.

Using direct scale ratings, for example, respondents have a difficult time differentiating among those attributes that are most important to them. We have rarely found significant differences in importance among the top-rated fifteen to twenty attributes in a survey. Research also shows that the importance measures or weights that people report and those that they use when making a decision often differ dramatically. The insight that direct ratings provide drops off as the number of attributes increases.

We show both the strengths and weaknesses of the gap model using a study in which we examined the drivers of satisfaction for a pharmacy. Approximately a hundred customers evaluated twenty-nine attributes of a retail pharmacy.The mean values of rated attribute importance are ordered from least to most important and plotted question by question (where 1 = not at all important and 10 = very important).

The corresponding attribute performance measures are also plotted (where 1 = poor performance and 10 = excellent performance). The key attributes to improve are those where the "gap" (performance minus importance) is lowest. On the positive side, gap models are relatively easy to implement, analyse, and explain. The analysis simply involves plotting the two dimensions, importance and performance, and examining their differences. This often makes gap models a good option for companies that are just beginning to develop a customer orientation. The models identify the "low-hanging fruit"—the obvious gaps that need to be closed—and get the company into the habit of monitoring customers.

The prioritysetting logic is also the same as for the strategic satisfaction matrix. Attributes on which both importance and performance are rated high are core competencies, while attributes with high importance and low performance need improvement. However, a major problem with the approach is that customers rate most everything as important. The conclusion is that the company needs to improve most of the items with low performance ratings, and it's hard to tell which ones would make the most difference to results.

Basically, importance scales are effective at highlighting the *least* important attributes but ineffective at highlighting the *most* important attributes. The direct importance ratings are simply not diagnostic. It is primarily the *performance* measures that drive the priority-setting process. Another problem with direct importance measures and the gap model is that the survey has a tendency to grow. Because the approach requires at least two ratings for each attribute, the survey becomes nearly twice as long as a survey where importance measures are derived by other (statistical) means. One question is required to rate an attribute's performance and another to rate its importance.

Direct importance ratings may be the only option when the customer population (or the sample size) is too small or ease of implementation is an overriding concern. Where feasible, however, it is much more economical to take the statistical approach and add good dependent variables, such as satisfaction and loyalty, for use in a regression analysis. Importance measures do not need to be measured directly. They can be derived statistically from attribute performance ratings and ratings of overall satisfaction. Because statistical estimations are more objective and less biased, they are often superior to direct customer ratings. Statistical analysis provides estimates of importance as the impact that one variable has on another. Customers indicate how they perceive a product or service to perform on a number of attributes as well as their overall satisfaction and loyalty. Variation in performance and satisfaction across customers allows the researcher to estimate (using regression or regression-based statistical techniques) the impact that different aspects of quality and value have on satisfaction and loyalty.

Statistically determined importance ratings can avoid many of the problems that you encounter with direct importance ratings. But the quality of the statistical estimates can vary significantly. *The important question is whether or not the estimation builds on the lens of the customer!* The lens should be viewed as a blueprint for both survey development *and* analysis. A major problem facing regression-based estimates of impact or importance centres on the correlation among the drivers of satisfaction.

If attribute ratings are too highly correlated, that is, if changes in one rating tend to follow changes in another without regard to outside factors—what statisticians refer to as lacking sufficient *independence*—the statistical estimates of impact may be poor. The lens of the customer, which is based on thorough analysis of qualitative research, shows just which attributes go together in the customer's mind. By combining multiple attribute ratings together into benefit indices, the lens provides a means of reducing correlation among the satisfaction drivers; it increases their independence.

The result is a set of benefit and attribute importance weights that are superior to those that can be collected directly from customers. Once you go through the background analysis outlined thus far, you'll be in a position to develop a survey instrument you can use with confidence.

The process described here follows the flowchart which we have found useful in developing and administering our own quality-satisfactionloyalty surveys. The primary purpose of the opening statement is to persuade your targeted respondents to take part in the survey. There are three main messages that can be communicated in an opening statement to help maximize the response rate:

- Emphasize the importance of the topic or problem area to respondents.
- Emphasize that the primary purpose of the research is to better understand the problem.
- Emphasize that the organization or entity conducting the research will use the results to improve the situation.

In the convenience store survey, the emphasis in the opening statements is on the latter two points. The statements point out that the survey is meant to understand what quality areas are important to convenience store customers and that the results will be used to guide quality improvement efforts. The opening statements may also include screener questions needed to identify customers.

The convenience store survey screens respondents to include those individuals who have visited a convenience store within the last three months. The screener in the survey also provides an explanation that convenience stores do not include grocery store chains, drug or discount stores, or mass merchandisers. If asked, the interviewer explicitly defines a convenience store as "typically a small franchised market that is open long hours."

These explanations and definitions were added as a result of pretesting and revising the survey. Once respondents have been screened and agree to participate, their first task is to evaluate attribute performance levels. In some cases the ratings may only apply to the product, service, or retailer of interest (say, stores in the Seven-Eleven chain). In other cases the ratings may apply to multiple competitors (say, Seven-Eleven, Quik Stop, and other widely known chains).

Before providing the information, the survey must instruct respondents on how to perform the task. This includes who or what is being rated and how to use the scales. The types of scales and their explanation depend partly on the method used to collect the data. If, for example, it is important to explain multiple anchors on the scale (such as what a 1, 2, 3, 4, or 5 actually means in the context of the survey), it is easier to do this in a written or Web-based survey where respondents can refer to the written anchors. It is more difficult to do so in a telephone survey. Because the respondent has no written list to refer to, the emphasis is typically on keeping only the two endpoints in mind.

In the convenience store survey, for example, it is explained that a rating of 1 means poor performance and a rating of 10 means excellent performance. Keep in mind that the choice of scales and the need to label scale points depends on the researcher's approach to measurement. Given the abstract nature of the constructs and the need for sensitive measures, we strongly advocate using indices to measure customer benefits, customer satisfaction, and loyalty. The use of indices gets you away from very concrete, individual scales where each point on the scale is ascribed some meaning. Indices resemble temperature scales—they just show that the reported value is higher or lower than some benchmark.

The meaning you attach to the index levels is based on how a product or service performs against competitors and over time. By deemphasizing concrete scale points in favour of more sensitive indices, you have less need to ascribe meaning to anything more than the end points. We recommend using 10-point scales, where 1 is poor and 10 is excellent, to evaluate performance across data collection methods.

The next parts of the survey present all of the attributes the lens of the customer research recommended for evaluation. The lens of the customer provides a blueprint as to how the attributes are organized— how they go together in a customer's mind.

The survey should leverage this lens and present the attributes in clusters defined by the benefit categories (quality of the service, product offerings, store layout, and so on). Particular to the convenience store survey is the inclusion of two questions at the beginning of this part to assess customer perceptions of store reputation. Satisfaction is the customer's overall evaluation of his or her experiences with a product or service provider. In your subsequent analysis, it will be a major dependent variable that you will explain using your measures of attribute and benefit performance. Satisfaction is a latent variable that will be manifested in a variety of more concrete performance ratings.

As we have said, it is critical to combine multiple measures of satisfaction in a satisfaction index. In addition to a simple rating of satisfaction, other measures include evaluations of overall product or service performance against different benchmarks. You might ask customers to evaluate performance versus their expectations, versus an ideal product or service provider in the category, or versus a "best in class" competitor. Notice that we do not advocate using any one of these as a proxy for satisfaction.

Rather, satisfaction as a latent or abstract construct is what all of the various evaluations have in common. The measures simply represent different benchmarks that customers use to evaluate performance and from which an index can be constructed. The convenience store survey has respondents evaluate performance using three different questions. The first asks them to express overall satisfaction, the second asks for an evaluation of performance versus expectations, and the third seeks an evaluation of performance versus an ideal product or service in the category.

These questions were modeled directly on those used in the ACSI survey, which have been shown to provide a very reliable and sensitive measure of satisfaction. An added benefit of using the ACSI questions is that it allowed us to benchmark the survey results for convenience stores against other industries and firms included in the ACSI survey. Whereas satisfaction measures apply more or less universally across industries and contexts, loyalty measures do not.

The desired outcomes of satisfaction are highly specific to the nature of the business, product, and service involved. Volvo, for example, has specified a range of desired customer outcomes, from the repeat purchase of a Volvo vehicle to the purchase of Volvo financing, Volvo insurance, the purchase and use of a Volvo gas card, and the spread of positive word-ofmouth advertising. If your customers are retailers who turn around and sell your product to end users, loyalty may take the form of the *push*—the sales effort they make on your behalf. If your product is a once-in-a-lifetime purchase (a piece of jewelry or a collector's item), loyalty may involve the customer's willingness to buy other products or services from you (cross-selling) and to tell other potential customers about your offerings.

In an industrial context, the level of satisfaction may have little effect on whether a customer buys at least some of your products and services. At the same time, it may have a great effect on just how *much* they buy (account penetration). Another desired outcome may include the trust that customers place in you and their resulting commitment to maintaining a relationship.

Our point is simply that, whereas satisfaction measures are more or less universal, loyalty measures must be customised. In the convenience store survey, the desired outcomes for the store chains and franchisees are rather straightforward. They include enhancing the customers' likelihood of visiting the store again in the future and their likelihood of recommending the store to others. The measures used in the Råtorp Tire Company survey were quite different. As in the convenience store survey, they included the likelihood that the customer (in this case a retailer) would continue to purchase, but they also included whether the proportion of products ordered from the manufacturer would likely increase or decrease in the future (account penetration) and the degree to which the retailer would recommend the manufacturer's products to its customers (push).

Descriptive questions (including market segment profiles and demographic questions) are typically added near the end of the survey. As noted earlier, the main reason for this placement is that the questions, being more personal in nature, are apt to lead a respondent to terminate the survey if asked early on. Once the interviewer has developed some rapport with the respondent and the interview has the momentum provided by answering the performance, satisfaction, and loyalty questions, descriptive information is often easier to get. The primary purpose of the descriptive questions is to group customers by characteristics such as age and income level for later analysis, so as to track their representativeness and discover possible new segments. The convenience store survey contains both a direct question regarding segmentation and a group of indirect demographic questions that can be used to segment or describe customers.

As noted earlier, the primary benefit of having respondents selfselect into preexisting segments is the ease of subsequent analysis. The drawback is that it presumes that the segments do not change or evolve significantly over time. A golden rule of survey research is to conduct one or more tests before you put any survey into the field. The primary purpose of preliminary testing is to identify and resolve whatever problems respondents might have in answering the questions. Pretesting tells you whether the survey is able to collect the desired information, and where you need to reword questions to make them simpler and easier to understand. If the pretest is weak and major revisions are required, the revised survey should be tested again before being put into the field. Pretesting is not just the domain of those who administer the survey; it can raise questions of strategic relevance to top management as well.

Another rule we like to follow is to involve both those directly involved in the survey process and those who will use the information to make resource allocation decisions. In pretesting the convenience store survey, for example, we learned several lessons. One was that many people were unclear as to just what a convenience store was in the first place. Does it include gas stations that sell some other merchandise?

Grocery store chains that sell gasoline? This led to the inclusion of more specific screening questions and definitions that the interviewer could use as needed. Pretesting also raised questions about what benchmarks the customer should use to evaluate the competitiveness of a convenience store's prices.

Should the benchmarks be limited to other convenience stores, or should they include other stores that sell similar merchandise (such as grocery stores for bread, milk, and soft drinks). Based on top management input, it was decided to let customers compare prices to other stores at which they may buy similar merchandise.

The reason was that executives at the various chains were very interested in the gap between perceived and actual price differences between convenience stores and other types of stores. Whereas convenience stores are often perceived as having relatively high prices, actual price differences are often small or nonexistent. Just how the survey is arranged and conducted is largely a function of the method of contact. Telephone surveys often involve random-digit dialing or random selection from a customer list.

The interviewer makes a pitch for participation and, if the time is not convenient, can arrange for a better time to call back. Before collecting survey data in a one-on-one interview, the respondent is usually called and an explicit appointment is made. Store intercepts are also a valuable tool for selling the survey—persuading people to take part in later administration either by phone, Web, or mail. Web surveys may use an e-mail message to introduce and gain interest in the survey and then instruct the respondent on how to access the survey.

Customers may also self-select to participate in surveys that are available on a company's Web site. Just who administers the survey is a function of both the sheer number of respondents and the need for objectivity. We suggest that people within the sponsoring company administer the survey themselves as long as the number of respondents is not too large and administrators can remain objective. A truly customer-oriented company should not routinely leave the job of collecting customer data to outsiders. But for a large-sample survey, it will be more cost-effective to use a professional data collection firm. If the interviewer's compensation is a function of customer responses (the number of "10s" on the survey), the objectivity of the responses and resulting data will be compromised. If a more objective interviewer cannot be found within the company, it would again be best to use a third party to collect the data. The development of a quality-satisfaction-loyalty survey builds directly on the lens of the customer. Survey development should not be a process in which people from different parts of a company sit around and decide what they would like to see on the survey.

Rather, the lens of the customer provides a blueprint for deciding which attributes to include and the benefit categories to use for organizing them. Even before developing a survey it is important to understand what populations or market segments to survey, what data collection method or methods to use, and how to sample from the target populations. In leveraging the lens of the customer, the construction of a quality-satisfaction-loyalty survey should follow certain guidelines. Benefits, satisfaction, and loyalty are abstract constructs that cannot be measured directly using any one concrete survey item.

They are best measured using an index of multiple measures or proxies. Indices also provide for more sensitive measures than single survey items, so they can explain more of the variation in satisfaction and loyalty and are better at identifying important satisfaction drivers. The importance that customers place on attributes and benefits has traditionally been determined by two different approaches: direct measures of importance and those derived from statistical analysis. Among the different direct measures, direct scales (ratings from "not important" to "very important") are often preferred. They are straightforward to collect and as good as or better than other direct approaches (such as point allocation or paired comparisons).

Yet, when done properly, statistically derived measures of importance are better than direct measures at objectively capturing the impact attributes and benefits have on satisfaction and loyalty. It is important for statistical analyses to leverage the lens of the customer when grouping variables for analysis. Otherwise, even the most rigorous statistical estimates may be a poor reflection of reality. With the lens of the customer in mind and the data collection methods chosen, you can complete the survey instrument in a systematic way. First, assess attribute performance by benefit category. After that, obtain overall evaluations of satisfaction. Then select loyalty measures and customise them to fit the product, service, or context.

To some, loyalty is simply a matter of whether a customer comes back to buy the same product or use the same service. To others, loyalty is a matter of how much more customers will buy (account penetration) or what else they will buy (cross-selling). After adding descriptive questions to help identify market segments, pretest the survey to identify any unforeseen problems. Arranging and conducting the survey yields the data that serves as input to the next phase of the process. W hen it comes to analysing your customer survey data, you have a lot of options.

We recommend a variation on *principal-components regression (PCR)* that is relatively simple to use and provides as much detailed information as you need to make quality improvement decisions. It combines two statistical methods: principal-components analysis and regression analysis. *Principal-components analysis* is a data reduction tool that shows what any group of survey measures have in common, so you can develop the benefit, satisfaction, and loyalty indices. *Regression analysis* relates these indices to each other and lets you determine the benefit, satisfaction, and loyalty impact scores.

We present a flowchart to show the necessary steps used to apply PCR to the lens of the customer. To support our recommendation. We begin by describing just what information you can and should be obtaining from your analysis. After describing our data analysis method, illustrating the links with examples from Volvo and a major hotel chain. These financial links, which highlight the payoff from investments suggested by customer measurement, will help you inspire people to make real quality improvements based on the information the survey process develops. When you analyse satisfaction and loyalty data, you're really looking for answers to two relatively simple questions. Where does your company need to improve quality or value to increase satisfaction and loyalty? And once satisfaction and loyalty are improved, what are the payoffs? The basic assumptions are that improved quality leads to increased satisfaction, which in turn makes customers more loyal, and that you get more profit from loyal customers than from those who don't care where they get the product or service you're selling. Now, how do you quantify the links?

The prerequisite is that your measurement system should provide sensitive *and* reliable measures. Your goal is to provide managers with truly diagnostic information—with levers they can push to improve quality and satisfaction. You don't want results that suggest that everything (or nothing) is important, or results that show differences (as among competitors) or changes (over time) that are not valid and meaningful. In other words, you want a system that produces results you can trust. Finally, you want to be able to predict what happens when satisfaction increases.

How likely are customers to come back and how much more revenue or profit will they generate? To make your measurement system a reality, you will need to analyse your survey data to produce multiple levels of information in the system. The circles labeled "satisfaction" and "loyalty" are the key to understanding your customers' overall consumption experience. Best measured using indices made up of multiple concrete measures, these abstract constructs are important in benchmarking performance versus competitors and tracking performance over time.

These benefit-level indices are the heart of the lens of the customer. They provide an overall view of how you are performing in quality areas as defined by your customers. But because these indices are abstract, they cannot be acted upon directly. Action requires moving down to the level of the underlying concrete attributes. Attribute values are obtained directly from the quality-satisfaction-loyalty survey ratings. For the benefits and attributes, 1 is poor performance and 10 is excellent performance. But setting priorities requires you to measure impact as well, that is, the extent to which a change in an attribute will lead to a change in satisfaction, loyalty, and other desired customer outcomes. As there are attribute and benefit levels of performance, so there are also attribute and benefit levels of impact. The benefit-level impacts, indicate how much impact each benefit has on customer satisfaction. It is helpful to focus initially on these benefit-level impacts to gain an understanding of the consumption experience. Looking at the attribute or question level impacts will help you relate your improvement efforts to the everyday activities of the company that have the highest payoff.

Attribute impacts are more the focus of continuous improvement efforts, while benefit impacts are the focus of innovation efforts—attempts to find completely new ways to deliver the benefits that customers value. A benefit-level impact of 0.5 shows that a 1-unit change in that benefit index is associated with a 0.5-unit increase in the satisfaction index. Once you have impact information at every level of the model, you can quantify the change that improving an attribute or benefit would make in loyalty (and subsequent profitability, once this data is added to the model). The impact of changing an input to the model (an attribute) on the output of the model (loyalty or profitability) is simply the product of all impacts in the chain of causes and effects.

(Where there is more than one path or chain of cause-and-effect relationships, it would be the sum of the different impact chains.) If you are familiar with traditional PCR, you will see that our approach to principal-components regression has some unique features. Traditional PCR factor-analyses all the attribute ratings simultaneously to produce a set of independent components or factors. It ignores benefit clusters of the type we recommend you develop using qualitative research to create the lens of the customer.

The problem is that the approach is too data driven; the factor analysis dictates the lens. In contrast, our approach uses the benefit groupings or clusters in the lens as a theory or model to structure the PCR analysis. This approach provides the technical sophistication and diagnostic information that your analysis requires. The main alternative to using our version of PCR is *partial least squares* (PLS). Both our PCR approach and PLS use the lens of the customer as a guide to structure the analysis. PCR is a two-step approach in which the benefit, satisfaction, and loyalty indices are first estimated using a series of principal-components analyses.

The researcher then uses these indices or latent variables in a series of regression models to estimate a causal chain of events (as from quality through to financial performance). PLS performs both of these steps for the researcher. It estimates an entire causal chain or model using an iterative estimation procedure that integrates aspects of principal-components analysis and multiple regression. Researchers in the areas of quality, marketing, and consumer research regard PLS as the state of the art in customer satisfaction modeling.

The disadvantage of PLS is that it requires special software and training, and the software is neither user-friendly nor easy to find. If you have mastered PLS, by all means use it. At a conceptual level, our flowchart and procedure for evaluating the quality of your analysis still applies. Otherwise, we recommend that you use PCR, which is straightforward to do using easily available and user-friendly software packages. Comparing the two approaches we find a 0.99 correlation in estimated benefit-level impacts and a 0.98 correlation in estimated attribute-level impacts. In other words, the results are virtually identical.

The following parts describe how to analyse a customer satisfaction model using our PCR method. The sole purpose of analysis is to make sense out of the data you collect. This part includes a step-by-step guide to analysing data sets that you can use if you're in charge of performing or managing the data analysis. Even if you're remote from the actual research and your responsibility is to create an environment where customer data will be developed and used, the guide will still be useful as it will demystify the process and, as a consequence, make you more constructively critical when evaluating the output of an analysis. The first major accomplishment will be to create the latent variables for benefits, satisfaction, and loyalty. Then the process will go on to derive the actual values for the impact of one level of the model on the next, and to establish benchmark values for the benefit, satisfaction, and loyalty indices. The combination of impacts and indices will provide the cause-effect chain. Once you've built the lens of the customer for your products or services and seen the valuable information it can help you produce, it's tempting to sit back and ask, "Well, now what do the numbers say we should do?"

But it's not that simple. The critical next phase of the process is to use the information to set priorities for improvement. And don't underestimate the importance of obtaining top management input to your action plans at this point. This may require some persistence. Too often managers view measurement systems, including the quality-satisfaction-loyalty model we present here, as a means of avoiding tough decisions—but "the numbers" don't pay the bills, and they don't make decisions, either.

Managers who are in charge of implementing their company's strategies and hold the authority to budget and who allocate resources to improve quality and satisfaction cannot absent themselves from the process. The numbers simply help managers base their decisions on facts. We first discuss management's role in using the output of the measurement system to set priorities for improvement. We then discuss how to implement the priorities. We bridge the gap between the customer benefits and product or service attributes that need improvement and the internal changes they require.

Setting priorities requires both impact and performance information for the various drivers of satisfaction and loyalty. But to set priorities, you must make some critical decisions regarding just what constitutes high versus low impact and high versus low performance. These decisions require you to consider a number of factors beyond the information in your impact-performance chart, including your strategy and competencies as well as relevant benchmarks, costs, and market dynamics. The basic logic is to categorize the various benefit and attribute drivers of satisfaction into one of the four cells of the matrix, each of which is associated with its own market action implications. Generally, the essential areas to improve are those where impact or importance is high and performance is low. Customers are essentially telling us that we are falling short in these important areas. Improvements to these areas will effectively focus resources where they have the greatest impact on satisfaction and subsequent loyalty and profitability.

This is also the cell in which you are most competitively vulnerable. If competitors do an excellent job in these areas, they will lure your customers away. Those areas that are important to customers and in which your performance is strong represent your core competencies and competitive advantages. It is essential to maintain if not improve performance on these drivers. The implications for the opposite cell, where impact is low and performance is weak, are also clear. Generally, there's no reason to waste resources on improving these areas. The customers, performance here just doesn't matter.

The implications for the remaining cell, in which impact is low yet performance is high, are less straightforward. This may be an area where resources have been wasted in the past because the benefits and attributes are not important to customers. In one recent application, for example, we found that customers at an IKEA furniture store in the United States rated traditional Swedish amenities—a child-care facility and a Swedish bake-shop—very positively. Nonetheless, these amenities had little to no impact on satisfaction and loyalty. From a cost-benefit standpoint, we concluded that having the amenities was not costeffective for the U.S.-based store. Alternatively, benefits and attributes in the low impact-high performance category may contain drivers of satisfaction that customers consider to be basic and necessary.

Customers may find these benefits and attributes everywhere they look and take them for granted. Although important in an absolute sense, these features offer no differentiation because there is little to no variance in their performance across customers and competitors. Airline safety is a classic example here—as long as the planes aren't falling out of the sky, passengers tend to regard one airline as much the same as another. That doesn't mean that any airline can afford to ease off on safety! The same sort of consideration can apply in less dramatic circumstances as well. In the IKEA project, we found that "ease of assembly" was also rated highly and had little impact.

Our conclusion here, however, was to make certain that we assure continued high performance on this benefit. Withdrawing resources and reducing performance would only serve to put us on a "slippery slope" and decrease satisfaction. The area would quickly return to the high impact–low performance category. Another possibility in the high performance–low impact quadrant is to find a new target market segment for the product or service. It may well be possible to find new customers who would especially value these benefit areas (such as customers who would value the child-care and bakery facilities in the IKEA store).

But data analysis does not determine where to draw the cell boundaries. Managers must draw the lines and decide just where the improvement should occur. Again, the impact-performance charts are a primary input to this decision process, but there are several other factors that you need to consider. Your strategic market plan leads you to focus on particular segments of customers to leverage core competencies.

But what if your customer data analysis suggests that you improve in areas that are inconsistent with your basic strengths? Management must decide whether or not the areas that need improvement are those in which core competencies and a competitive advantage can be achieved. If not, you may be pursuing customers you can't please with your strengths, at the risk of alienating customers who currently value your offerings. Perhaps you should reconsider your entire strategic market plan instead. At the same time, the information may be very valuable in deciding on network partners who can help provide customers with the benefits they need. Think back to the convenience store survey, which revealed that safety is the primary driver of satisfaction for customers. In practical terms, safety is not something that a convenience store can completely control, so the implication may be to network and collaborate with those who can have more effect. In some cities, for example, convenience stores provide an area where local law enforcement officers can take a break, make phone calls, and do paperwork.

This win-win solution saves the officers time and creates a greater atmosphere of safety than the stores could provide on their own. It is also critically important to benchmark both impact and performance when using this information to set priorities. In the Råtorp Tire Company case, impact-performance charts are supplied for three main competitors in the market. As the reader quickly finds out, making decisions for Råtorp requires a careful consideration of impact and performance levels for the competitors as well. In an absolute sense, impact may be high and performance low in a given area, suggesting the need to make improvements.

But what if your closest competitor shows even lower performance and higher impact? It may be a mistake to improve that area if there are others that also call for attention. Relatively, it may be a competitive strength, at least in the short run. At the same time, do not ignore the absolute levels of impact and performance. Over the long haul, the absolute levels of performance and impact highlight your vulnerabilities, as well as those of your competitors, and suggest where new competitors may enter or improve to take customers away.

When you tie your model and analysis to increased profit per customer, you then have some idea that the costs typically incurred to improve quality are covered. But in most cases, managers must consider the relative costs of making improvements when deciding which areas to improve. Remember that the goal is to optimize rather than maximize satisfaction and loyalty. If two areas show equally low performance and high impact, managers should ask, "Which is more cost-effective to improve?" One source of cost information is management itself. Another is through the use of tools such as QFD that translate product improvements into internal change and explicitly consider cost information. Finally, consider where your market is headed over time. Just what factors will become more or less important? For personal computers, will processing speed become less of a differential advantage going forward? For convenience stores, will prepared foods become a greater source of differentiation and impact? Both social and technological forecasting are important bases for predicting these market dynamics, but are beyond the scope of our discussion.

The exercise provides the output of a survey and data analysis for Råtorp and its two main competitors. We strongly encourage you to work through the data in the case and set priorities for Råtorp. Based on the data, consider what you expect the competition to do as well. The case will force you to consider several factors, including what Råtorp's strategy should be, how the benchmarks influence interpretation of the results, how the competition is likely to evolve over time (such as the role filled by import brands), and what the improvements might cost.

The case emphasizes that the task of moving from information to decisions is far from trivial. It requires significant reflection and input from managers in a position to set and implement a strategic market plan. Once you have targeted which benefits and attributes to improve, you have to figure out just how to improve them. In effect, you need to build a bridge from your model of customer perceptions and behaviours to your internal metrics, parts, processes, and people. When you do this, you'll soon find that—as with any bridge—the traffic on this one flows both ways.

The framework integrates aspects of two leading approaches to improving quality and satisfaction: *quality function deployment* (QFD) and customer satisfaction modeling. Together, the two approaches show qualitatively different steps in the overall process of translating satisfaction into its means of accomplishment. Our satisfaction models translate overall satisfaction down into the customer benefits that drive satisfaction and into the product and service attributes that provide the benefits. These are the uppermost stages of the framework. The lower stages, taken from QFD, translate these attributes further down into their means of accomplishment or production. It is important to consider what we mean by *translation* in the framework. Consistent with the arrows is a process of moving from the most abstract information of interest to the most concrete.

Customer satisfaction is customers' overall evaluation of their purchase and consumption experience. Moving downstream in the framework from satisfaction to production is, therefore, a process of translating abstract, subjective evaluations into concrete, objective means of accomplishment. In contrast, the process of moving up in the framework from concrete processes and attributes to abstract benefits and overall satisfaction is more of an inductive or *change monitoring* process.

After determining what changes to make, it is important to track the changes back upstream in the process. Did, for example, the changes we made internally have a subsequent effect on customer perceptions and satisfaction? To what degree did our improvements to production processes improve process operations, parts deployment, engineering or design characteristics, and ultimately attribute and benefit performance? The combination of translation and change monitoring forms a two-way traffic that is essential to close the loop on the quality improvement process.

A central point of the framework is that QFD picks up where satisfaction modeling leaves off. The product and service attributes that are the output of the priority-setting process represent the input to QFD. The four houses or phases of QFD thus represent phases four through seven of an overall translation process. The translation is, however, different for pure products than for pure services. For products, targeted attributes must be translated into engineering or design characteristics, parts characteristics, process operations, and finally production requirements. Because services are co-produced by customers and employees at a time and place of the customer's choosing, service production is a different beast. In service applications of QFD, targeted attributes for improvement must be translated into service qualities (for example, hotel arrival), service functions (airport shuttle service), service process designs (number of shuttles, routes, and personnel), and operating policies and procedures (daily schedules and contingency plans). An important implication of the framework is that for a given product or service, there are at least seven conceptually distinct stages in the overall translation and change monitoring process.

It highlights the difficulties and challenges that we face even after a satisfaction model is analysed and priorities are set. Our goal here is not to exhaustively discuss the implementation phases, but rather to introduce you to QFD as one tool that has helped thousands of companies around the world to link their customer data to product and service improvements. A thorough treatment of how tools such as QFD are used to implement product-driven product and process changes is beyond the scope of this book.

It is, in fact, the subject of our next book in the UMBS Management Series. The work is usually documented in a series of matrices. Its primary benefits are reduced design costs and development time. Other benefits include improving communication and cohesion within a product development or improvement team and solidifying design decisions early in the development cycle. Generally there are two variants of the QFD methodology.

The first is the four-phase system captured and presented in more detail later. In this approach, QFD starts with an input list of customer-desired attributes. These attributes are often ordered hierarchically to handle the large number required to describe a product (such as an automobile door system). At a higher level of abstraction are the benefit categories similar to those used in our satisfaction model (such as that a door system "operates well").

At a lower level of abstraction are the more concrete attributes (such as that a door system is "easy to close from the outside"). The QFD translation process begins in Phase 1, the "House of Quality, " where attributes are translated into engineering characteristics. In subsequent phases—often called *houses*— engineering targets are translated into parts characteristics; targeted parts characteristics are translated into key process operations; and key process operations are translated into production requirements or work instructions. As mentioned, this system is altered when applied to services.

The second variant of QFD recognizes that the four-phase system that only fulfills a portion of the planning that is needed for a new product. Separate matrix systems are required to incorporate product quality deployment, technology deployment, cost deployment, and reliability deployment throughout the planning, design, trial, manufacturing, and service phases of product development and launch.

5

Operations in Hotel Management

AN OVERVIEW

Operations in hotel management focuses on carefully managing the processes to produce and distribute products and services. Usually, small businesses don't talk about "operations management", but they carry out the activities that management schools typically associate with the phrase "operations management." Major, overall activities often include product creation, development, production and distribution. Related activities include managing purchases, inventory control, quality control, storage, logistics and evaluations.

A great deal of focus is on efficiency and effectiveness of processes. Therefore, operations management often includes substantial measurement and analysis of internal processes. Ultimately, the nature of how operations management is carried out in an organization depends very much on the nature of products or services in the organization. People and industry have moved from the so-called rust belt to the sun belt. The hotel business has been active in reborn and reconstructed central cities.

The explosion of technology and information-based companies has concentrated human endeavour in technological corridors in California, Massachusetts, Washington, Texas, and North Carolina, to name a few such places. It can be safely said that where jobs are and major concentrations of economic activity occur, hotels will follow. It should be noted that the word modern can be loaded with the potential of much misunderstanding. Hotels are changing and will continue to change. As a result, the techniques of management of modern hotels must adapt to changing circumstances.

INFLUENCES

Like many other businesses, hotels have been affected by shifts in emphasis and its children mature, the population of the countries will for many years be older, healthier, and better educated than previous generations. These facts will present new challenges and opportunities to all business managers. *Technology*—in the form of computers, communication, personal devices, and laboursaving mechanical equipment—has had and will have a major effect on the way in which hotels are managed and operated.

The speed with which information is accumulated, stored, manipulated, and transferred is such that today most travellers expect that the hotel rooms they rent will allow them to be as productive as they are in the office or at home. Increasingly, with portable computing, personal data assistants (PDAs), wireless communication, and virtually everything somehow connected to the Internet, hotels must provide services and access that allow guests seamless transition from the business, travel, or home environment to that of the hotel. Increasingly, entertainment must be fused with communication and productive processes.

The concept of market segmentation, or ever-increasingly finely tuned market definitions, will dictate hotel structures and organizations, and management tactics designed to address those market segments have become even more important to the management of hospitality service businesses. With the increased power in the information and data manipulation realm, hotels have available to them ever expanding databases about guests and are creating new products to attract those markets. One of the effects of the aging demographic is the emergence of vacation re- sorts—a modern incarnation of the timeshare properties of several decades ago. Because these are being developed and operated by name hotel companies and are marketed to the affluent, healthy, well-educated population segment, resort managers have had to absorb new managerial realities. The well-documented change in the complexion of the national economy from one that emphasizes goods and, to a lesser extent, natural resources to one that emphasizes services has kindled new ideas about the way in which we manage the design and delivery of these services.

Hotels, restaurants, and travel services are now seen as unique entities that dictate special kinds of managerial techniques and strategies. Changes in people's travel patterns have altered the way we manage our hotel properties. Deregulation of the airlines has driven a change in the way millions of people travel each year, given the huband- spoke design of airline services. Many hotel companies are now locating major hotel properties adjacent to hub air transport facilities, taking advantage of the fact that business travellers may not need to travel to a central business district (CBD) to accomplish their purpose in a given area.

Meetings and conferences can now be scheduled within a five-minute limousine ride from the air terminal, and the business traveller can be headed for his or her next destination before the day is over without having to stay overnight in a CBD hotel. New patterns of investment in hotel facilities have emerged in the last two decades, and more attention is now paid to achieving optimum return on investment. Because people from outside the hotel industry are now participating in its financial structuring, hotel operations are no longer dependent on the vision of a single entrepreneur. Managers now must design tactics and strategies to achieve heretofore unanticipated financial goals.

The same trend has also altered the complexion of management and organization of the modern hotel. This is especially true of publicly owned hotel firms, where Wall Street stock analysts heavily influence stock prices through expectations of quarterly revenues and profits. This puts pressure on hotel companies and their operations managers to perform, on a quarterly basis, in a way contrary to many managers' instincts. Most of the foregoing issues and influences still operate (to a greater or lesser extent) on the organizational structures and strategies of the modern hotel. However, other phenomena of an economic, cultural, and social nature have come to the fore, complicating our view of hotel management. This furthers the argument that the hotel industry is a part of the greater economy and at the mercy of elements often completely out of its control.

The cyclical nature of the U.S. and international economies has recently affected significantly hotels' ability to respond to changing circumstances. In early 1993, for instance, employment growth was stagnant; corporate profits were low; the expansion of the gross national product (GNP) was only a marginal percentage above previous years; and travel in most segments was down due to corporate restructuring, downsizing, or reorganizing. Vast layoffs in the hundreds of thousands had been announced every month. While fuel prices continued to be relatively stable, consumer spending patterns and high employment growth had not materialized, particularly in light of corporate layoffs and the ongoing nervousness of consumers about whether or not their financial wherewithal was safe. Unemployment was at an all-time low; the Dow Jones Industrial Average was between 10,000 and 11,000; hotel occupancies had stabilized nationally in excess of 70 per cent; and the federal government was running a surplus for the first time in the memory of most. Then what happened? The terrorist attacks in New York and Washington, D.C., in 2001 changed the face of all business and travel, immediately and probably for the foreseeable future as well. Major airlines are in bankruptcy; hotels are struggling to achieve profitable occupancies; business travel is down; the high-tech stock market bubble burst; the country is at war in a number of locations; security has made travel more difficult, if not actually annoying; and people are nervous.

Join this with an imbalance of trade, the outsourcing of jobs, and the largest federal deficits in history, and the face of the economy is challenging. This translates directly not only to business travel but personal and recreational travel as well.

Finding ways to operate profitably in such an environment is the job of the next generation of hotel operators. Among the predictions made was that cultural diversity will play a role in the management and organizational structure of the modern hotel in the United States. As surely as living patterns, economic cycles, and market segmentation have influenced the hotel industry, so will the change in ethnicity of the workforce. The cultural backgrounds that an increasingly diversified workforce will bring to hotel operations may be seen as a problem or a challenge—or both.

To most operators, it will be seen as an opportunity to demonstrate to an increasingly diverse clientele that hotel companies are committed to hiring and training a workforce structure that mirrors society. See no reason to change that prediction now; if anything, acculturation of the hospitality business will accelerate. The legal and regulatory environments are increasingly important to all business managers, and hotel operators are no exception. Increasingly, operators must be aware of and alert to realms of risk that can engender lawsuits against them.

Several objects and essays in this edition highlight these threats to hotels and their guests. It should be noted that present-day security concerns also have significantly affected the ways in which hotels are operated. Awareness of the risk environment and the regulatory realm are factors that affect a hotel's ability to compete in the early part of the twenty-first century. This is also used to explore ideas that are new to the management process, and that—who knows?—may never completely catch on.

Rather than focus exclusively on the operations of the major chains, the readings here are from the perspectives of operators, leaders, and experts such as regional operators, major industry consultants, and independent branded hotels. John Dew, formerly president of Inn Ventures, a regional hotel management and development company that has built and operated many Marriott products, in addition to a proprietary hotel product, provides an insider's view of the steps needed to bring a hotel from conception to construction and operation.

This unique view of hotel operations connects the concept of hotel development with the realities of day-to-day operation. It should help aspiring managers understand how the intricacies of the development process may influence the marketing and management of the hotel. Peter Cass offers the reader insights, heretofore unavailable in books of this nature, into independently branded hotels that associate to provide market strength. He makes the case that the future success of independent hotels is linked to their ability to find ways to maintain their independence while sustaining competitive advantage in the luxury segment.

Because new construction of hotels diminished greatly after 9/11 but firms still needed to grow, rebranding existing properties generated a lot of growth activity. Rebranding is a complicated process that must be accomplished within critical time frames to coincide with marketing, financial, and operational variables. Today's economic circumstances are different, and business has changed its focus to opening new major projects. His piece serves as a useful companion to that of John Dew, and the two should be read together, with an eye towards comparing Dew's smaller project focus and Dupar's large projects. Perhaps proving the axiom that "everything old is new again," the concept of health and wellness spas as a hotel and resort product has enjoyed a resurgence. Once the province of high-end hotels and resorts, the idea of being pampered in a spa has been added to the service mix in many more modest hotels and resorts.

While the big-name spas at five-star properties still set the standard for pampering and pricing, the comfort of personal service in less lavish spas seems to appeal to the modern traveller as well. Peter Anderson's overview of the spa industry provides insights into this fascinating service product. E.M. Statler's contributions to the modern hotel business are legendary in that he is generally credited with founding and operating the first commercial hotel concept that recognized the realities of the early business traveller at the beginning of the twentieth century. They also highlight other major forces in the development of the modern hotel business.

THE DEVELOPMENT COMPANY

The developer is the entrepreneur, the risk taker, who originates the idea for the hotel. Depending on the business structure selected, the developer often puts his or her personal wealth at risk when engaging in a hotel project. The developer, along with a small staff of people, networks with commercial real estate agents on the lookout for a suitable hotel site. Depending on the type of hotel to be developed, a site of at least two to four acres is required (for comparison, an acre is roughly the size of a football field).

This property must be zoned by the city for a hotel, be visible from a freeway or major street arterial, and have city approval for such construction activities as curb cuts, lefthand turn lanes, and delivery truck access. Commercial realtors offer sites for the developer's consideration that include maps, aerial photos, and proof of hotel zoning. Sometimes the developer views potential sites by driving around the neighbourhood within five miles of the site or touring multiple sites by helicopter, noting where the potential guests live and work and where potential competing hotels are located.

The price per square foot of the land is considered. The higher the cost of land, the higher the rates the hotel will need to charge. Is the price too high for the average daily rate (ADR) in this particular market? Is it too low? Or is it acceptable? This is determined when the hotel financial pro forma budget document is created.

AUTHORITARIAN ORGANISATION

From the point of view of results, the effectiveness of the organisation is determined by the way work is organised and by the way people work with or against each other. The way in which people co-operate with each other, with the leadership and with the community, indeed the extent of their commitment to their organisation, depend on the style of management.

So here we look at different styles of management, on their impact on people, on the way in which people work together and on results. Just think of the many supplies and services required daily to enable a large city like London to survive. Food has to be produced, harvested, stored and transported. Waste products have to be collected and treated or dispersed. Electricity has to be generated and distributed, transport has to be provided. Houses have to be built. Streets have to be cleaned and maintained, the district has to be policed. And all these and much more for millions of people, daily.

In our modern, industrialised, technological and highly competitive international environment it is essential that many experts from different areas of activity and different levels of society coming from different backgrounds work together to successfully achieve the completion of large projects such as exploring space, or the building of large oil gathering and refining installations. Many experts have to work together to provide our daily needs, to enable us to have good and satisfying lives. Discord in one area can inconvenience many people and it is essential that people co-operate with each other freely and effectively.

Experience shows that the larger the organisation the more difficult it is to achieve the necessary degree of co-operation and that larger organisations are usually much less effective than smaller ones as people are working against each other instead of co-operating. As suggested, see that improving the style of management can by itself increase the effectiveness of operating, improve results obtained and the way in which resources are being used, by about 20-30%. The gains to be made by improving the style of management are thus very considerable not only from the point of view of a better return to the shareholders and to the community but also from the point of view of greater contentment and satisfaction felt by employees.

CONSIDER THE FOLLOWING TWO STORIES THE FIRST IS ABOUT A HOTEL SERVANT

When a very senior civil servant retired to his country cottage, he caused a stir in the village. Every morning one of the local boys would call and disappear for a minute or so into his cottage. They persuaded the boy to reveal what was going on: "I am paid to knock on his bedroom door and shout a few words and then he shouts a few words". He finally told them what these words were. He said: "I shouts 'The Secretary of State wishes to see you', and he shouts back 'To hell with the Secretary of State'." The second story is about a man who is working as a foreman in the garage of a Municipal Forestry Commission. The garage wasn't efficient but since he started working for them things run much more smoothly. If a spare part is needed but cannot be obtained, if anything goes wrong, he is the one who sorts things out in his own quiet and effective way.

For example, when the garage was told that it would take some six months for a new radiator to be delivered to them, he simply telephoned the factory to confirm this disturbing news. The radiator was delivered beautifully wrapped the next day by special messenger. You probably know the name of this foreman. It is Alexander Dubcek, the man who led his country in a bid for freedom in 1968. This is what he was doing a few years ago. What he gets from those with whom he comes into contact is not just esteem and respect but also co-operation and as a result 'things run much more smoothly'. Compare this with the attitude to his work of the retired civil servant whose idea of blissful retirement is to be able to shout every morning 'To hell with the boss'.

This kind of frustration with management and workplace indicates internal conflict and struggle, indicates considerable lack of identification with the organisation and its objectives. People live and work together. Important is that the way in which they feel about their place of work, and the way in which they co-operate, depends on controllable factors, depends on the style of management.

Those who live with you, work with you, or work for you will think about living and working with you in either one way or the other. Certain is that the way in which they react depends on the way in which you behave, depends on your style of management, depends on the factors which as suggested, now explore. Kings ruled by 'divine' right and they enforced obedience through, in the end, the death penalty.

Under private ownership, authority is derived from ownership of the means of production and the penalty for disobedience is dismissal. In each case authority is centred at the top. It is the owners who delegate authority to the chief executive, and it is immaterial whether the owners are shareholders as in some countries, or the state in countries such as Russia. In authoritarian organisations it is orders which are passed down from above and the manager's role is to pass orders down the 'chain of command'.

He is usually not expected to make decisions and so carries little responsibility. He does order and may compel the worker to carry out the tasks demanded from him, to produce. Those who run society on such lines find that the working population does not willingly work for the benefit of only its rulers and then they attempt to compel the working population to work. The stick is unemployment and the compelling force is the fear of the economic consequences of unemployment, is the threat of need. They will then do all they can to make the stick more effective.

The higher the level of unemployment and the greater the need of the working population, the greater is the fear of dismissal and the more effective is the stick. Hence it is those who believe in an authoritarian kind of organisation who advocate that the level of unemployment should be kept above a certain minimum level or that it should be increased, and who want to reduce social security spending. To them it appears as if people do not want to work, as if conditions have to be created which force the working population to do as told, by depressing their standard of living and the quality of their lives so that they become more dependent on the employer.

Examples of this attitude towards unemployment are the following newspaper headlines:

(a) Big fall in unemployment and record spending threaten economic trouble.

(b) Sharp fall in jobless a sign of overheating.

Authoritarian organisations are effective in an emergency and perhaps the best known authoritarian organisations are the armed forces. However, enterprises organised on authoritarian lines have many problems. Orders are passed down and mistakes readily result in critical appraisal and dismissal. Hence people avoid making decisions so that matters to be decided are either passed up for the decisions to be made at a higher level, or decisions are made by committees as it is more difficult to dismiss all the members of a committee for jointly making a wrong decision.

There are likely to be many such committees. People survive by becoming expert at passing the buck. Empire building takes place, this being one way of increasing job security. Blame is passed to someone else, empires are built at someone else's expense; people work against each other and we see conflict instead of co-operation. Senior management tends to be overworked, staff turnover tends to be high and workers restrict effort.

The kind of difficulties which arise are perhaps best showd by some examples:

1. On one of the scheduled flights from Moscow to the Soviet Far East only half the seats had been taken up so Aeroflot cancelled the flight and told the passengers to wait. They waited in the packed terminal all that night and indeed all the next day when they were told that their flight would now be leaving. Trying to join their flight they found that they had to pay an extra 25% of their fare as a fine for missing the first flight.
2. Nigeria ordered 20 million tons of cement worth £650 million to be delivered during 1975. By the middle of October there were already 250 ships queuing to discharge their cement cargoes. A further 100 cement-laden ships were due the following week. Some of these would have to wait for more than two years to dock. Only 4 million tons of the 20 million tons ordered had been delivered and in addition there were 150 general cargo ships queuing to discharge their cargoes.

   By the end of December, 2,500 Greek seamen aboard 150 freighters had been "trapped" for more than seven months while waiting for permission to dock and unload. All seamen who had been stuck for more than four months were being flown home for Christmas by their employers.

The Nigerian government then announced a draft decree enabling them to charge owners £7,000 for every day an unauthorised vessel spent in Nigerian waters.

Normally the docks could handle less than one and a half million tons of cement per year and a basic cause of the congestion would appear to be lack of co-operation, contact and teamwork between different ministries and departments.

3. Gerald Smith when leader of the American delegation to the SALT negotiations in Vienna which aimed to limit nuclear weapons, submitted remarkable Russian tables and drawings which compared the number and size of American and Russian inter-continental rockets and shelters for housing them. He was apparently submitting information prepared by Russian military intelligence themselves.

   In a counter-statement the leader of the Soviet delegation, Vladimir Seminiov, made a new evaluation but was openly corrected by his military deputy, Colonel General Ogarkov. After this meeting, Ogarkov took one of the American delegates to the side and whispered to him. He said there was no occasion whatsoever for the Americans to divulge their knowledge of Soviet military data in front of civilians of the Soviet delegation as these matters is exclusively the concern of Soviet military officials.

4. Israel earns much foreign currency from tourist traffic, but it was reported that the Ministry of Tourism continued to receive complaints from Israelis and foreign tourists regarding the inadequacy of sanitary conditions and other facilities at Ben-Gurion airport.

   The Ministry spokesman also pointed out that the

airport was under the exclusive jurisdiction of the Ministry of Transport, to which all complaints should be referred. A clear case of passing the buck which appears to disregard the interests of those using the airport. Just what is the job of a Ministry of Tourism?

These are only a few examples of the kind of wasteful way in which large units run on authoritarian lines muddle on through crisis after crisis. They cease to be able to learn from past mistakes, the same mistakes are made again and again. The reason some of them are still in existence is because their competitors are just as ineffective, are just as incapable of moving forward in any real sense.

Crisis succeeds crisis in badly managed as well as in authoritarian organisations. This may be due to bad management but in an extremely authoritarian organisation crises are often almost artificially created by managers so as to obtain co-operation. If I go to Jim and say "I want you to sweep the floor of this hotel three times within the next half-hour, or else!" he is not going to like this one little bit. He will go through the motions but the office will be badly swept and the next half-hour will appear to him to be an eternity of drudgery, boredom and frustration.

If on the other hand I can say "We are in real trouble, some very nasty stuff has been spilled and it is important for all who work here that the floor be swept thoroughly three times and quickly, say within thirty minutes anyway. I wonder if we've got someone who could do it?", then he is likely to volunteer for the job. It will be done extremely well, it will get done within the half-hour and probably with five or ten minutes to spare. If afterwards go to him and say "Well done, we are all grateful" he will be left with the feeling of having spent half an hour most usefully serving the community, having done a very worthwhile job indeed.

In other words, people try to help each other and in an authoritarian organisation crisis may succeed crisis as this is one way of getting work done. However, one can cry wolf once too often and in an authoritarian organisation 'This must be done today' is succeeded by 'Do this now' which is succeeded by "We are in a mess, drop all else and do this now". In such circumstances people soon learn that crises are the routine rather than the exception and cease to care. Centralised decision making is quick and decisions can be implemented quickly but it generally fails to utilise the potential of the employees. Larger organisations also generally fail to perform as well as they should because of internal conflict, because of confrontation, lack of co-operation and lack of teamwork. Having now looked in some detail at the kind of organisation we find at one end of the scale, namely the authoritarian organisation, we can now look at the other end of the scale, at a completely participative organisation.

Following this as suggested, look at the large number of organisations which are somewhere in between. The story is told that when a new manager was appointed to a hotel in America he walked into a weave room the day he arrived, walked directly over to the agent. The agent nodded and then waved his hand. The workers, intently watching this gesture, shut down every loom in the room immediately. The agent turned to the manager and said, "All right, go ahead and run it." This story with great clarity makes the point that there is another authority besides the manager's.

The workers' representative has authority and exercised it. The question arises, where does his right to command come from and how did he use his power to exact obedience? The shop steward is elected so that his authority stems from those who elected him and who work in factory and office. The source of his authority is the consent of the managed to be managed. The method of power is the withdrawal of that consent which is in effect the withdrawal of one's labour, for example by going on strike.

Employees participate when they agree to allow themselves to be organised by an employer, and organisation which is based on consent of those being organised is participative. In a participative organisation people accept responsibility for work to be done, accept that it is their job to carry out a part of the company's activities and that they will be held accountable for the quality of their work. The manager's job is to back his subordinate by removing obstacles from the subordinate's path, the subordinate asking for such assistance as the need arises. The manager co-ordinates the work of the group which he manages with that of the higher group in which he is a subordinate. As work may be a source of satisfaction or of frustration, dependent on controllable conditions, the extent to which subordinates derive satisfaction from their work also depends on their own manager's and on the organisation's general style of management.

People who derive satisfaction from their work will like doing it and do it to the best of their ability; if work is a source of frustration, they will restrict effort and the work is likely to be done badly. An organisation built on this basis is participative, and this means that participation through decision making, including setting of targets, takes place at all levels of the organisation.

DEGREE OF PARTICIPATION

Large employers are often paternalistic, and employees company oriented, sometimes staying with their employer throughout their working life. Since their employees are economically tied to the company, dependent on it for services such as housing, medical or educational, this does not mean that these companies use a participative style of management. In Japan and similar countries the compelling force is the fear of 'losing face'. In Russia and in China the workers are not allowed to strike in any real sense and thus have no authority and orders are passed down from the top.

Protest is forbidden and to demonstrate takes a highly developed sense of social responsibility and very considerable courage. It is seen that the Russian and Chinese systems of government and organisation are authoritarian systems in which their people work as directed. We have described here in outline two systems of organisation which can be regarded as forming either end of a scale. The position of any organisation on this scale depends in each case on the balance between the two kinds of authority, that is depends on the degree of participation in decision making which is practised.

One can place on this scale any system of running a company or of governing a country, by considering for example whether and to what extent decisions are being made at the various levels or whether people merely follow orders, or whether and to what extent people are free to withdraw their labour, are free to strike, to what extent authority is centred at the top, or where the balance of power lies between management and worker.

The position where an organisation is placed thus depends on the balance of authority between ruler and ruled, between owner and worker, between the establishment and the population. We can now develop this scale and place a number of organisations on it over the complete range from one end to the other.

If we were to do this for individual companies then this would require a detailed knowledge in each case of the style of management and of company effectiveness. So what as suggested, now do in the next is to look at the more generally known balance of authority in different countries and place them on our scale.

STYLE OF OPERATION MANAGEMENT

We are now looking at the way different countries are managed, doing so country by country. The style of management of government in different countries can also be anywhere on the scale, from fully authoritarian (dictatorship) at one end of the scale to fully participative (policy decided by the people) at the other end. This is a fundamental scale which cuts across artificial and ineffective political divides—dictatorship of the left is dictatorship just like that of the right. Dictatorship is dictatorship no matter whether the organisation or political party is on the left or on the right of the political spectrum.

Under participative government and democracy the government and leadership put into effect the wishes of the people, the policy decided by delegates directly appointed by and directly responsible and accountable to the people. Under authoritarian government or dictatorship the government and its 'experts' tell the people what the government or rulers decide the people have to follow. Here 'directly' means selected by the people and voted for, each person having one vote. This is very different from delegates being selected by or being accountable through an establishment such as a political party's or a Board of Directors. Real struggle is not between political left and right but is a struggle for democracy against dictatorship (authoritarian style of management) in all community organisations and at all levels. Authoritarian attitudes result in confrontation, leadership and co-operation result in economic success. The way in which countries are managed, that is their style of management, of course varies from country to country and changes as time passes. shows the style of management.

The left hand side of the horizontal scale corresponds to the fully authoritarian, while the right hand end corresponds to the fully participative way of managing. The two ends are called 'A' and 'B' respectively, for convenience. What we can now do is to place on the scale some lines corresponding to the style of management adopted in different countries and then to discuss the pattern, following this by a discussion of the effectiveness of different styles of management. In doing so we need to remember that we are not in any way concerned with opinions and feelings and beliefs about whether one country is better than another, whether one method of organisation is better than another, whether one political system is an improvement on another. We are concerned here only with the situation as it is, we are concerned only with objective facts.

Hence we assess the style of management by two factors only, namely on the one hand by the extent to which authority is centred at the top and on the other hand by the extent to which authority is centred at the bottom. Our measure for the extent to which authority is centred on the bottom is the extent to which working people may withdraw their labour, that is the extent to which they are permitted to do so by the laws of the land and the extent to which they are actually able to withdraw their labour. We assess the style of management by these factors only and while at the authoritarian end of the scale there is generally little doubt about the extent to which authority is centred at the top, this factor is more difficult to assess in democratic societies and here we find that the extent to which people are permitted to withdraw their labour and the extent to which they are doing so is a clearer and more definite way of assessing a country's style of management on the scale.

In the democratic countries are found a wide range of companies and organisations ranging from highly if not completely authoritarian to the almost completely participative, ranging from the armed forces at one end to worker-owned and controlled enterprises on the other. However, this does not in any way invalidate the scale or its general validity, nor does it detract from the usefulness of the comparison.

On the contrary, the existence of such widely differing systems makes it even more important that we become aware of the impact of different styles of management on people and on results.

CONTEMPORARY THEORIES IN OPERATION MANAGEMENT

Contemporary theories of operation management tend to account for and help interpret the rapidly changing nature of today's organizational environments. As before in management history, these theories are prevalent in other sciences as well.

CONTINGENCY THEORY

Basically, contingency theory asserts that when managers make a decision, they must take into account all aspects of the current situation and act on those aspects that are key to the situation at hand.

Basically, it's the approach that "it depends." For example, the continuing effort to identify the best leadership or management style might now conclude that the best style depends on the situation. If one is leading troops in the Persian Gulf, an autocratic style is probably best (of course, many might argue here, too). If one is leading a hospital or university, a more participative and facilitative leadership style is probably best.

SYSTEMS THEORY

Systems theory has had a significant effect on management science and understanding organizations. First, let's look at "what is a system?" A system is a collection of part unified to accomplish an overall goal. If one part of the system is removed, the nature of the system is changed as well. For example, a pile of sand is not a system. If one removes a sand particle, you've still got a pile of sand. However, a functioning car is a system. Remove the carburetor and you've no longer got a working car.

A system can be looked at as having inputs, processes, outputs and outcomes. Systems share feedback among each of these four aspects of the systems. Let's look at an organization. Inputs would include resources such as raw materials, money, technologies and people. These inputs go through a process where they're planned, organized, motivated and controlled, ultimately to meet the organization's goals. Outputs would be products or services to a market.

Outcomes would be, *e.g.*, enhanced quality of life or productivity for customers/clients, productivity. Feedback would be information from human resources carrying out the process, customers/clients using the products, etc. Feedback also comes from the larger environment of the organization, *e.g.*, influences from government, society, economics, and technologies. This overall system framework applies to any system, including subsystems (departments, programmes, etc.) in the overall organization.

Systems theory may seem quite basic. Yet, decades of management training and practices in the workplace have not followed this theory. Only recently, with tremendous changes facing organizations and how they operate, have educators and managers come to face this new way of looking at things. This interpretation has brought about a significant change (or paradigm shift) in the way management studies and approaches organizations. The effect of systems theory in management is that writers, educators, consultants, etc. are helping managers to look at the organization from a broader perspective. Systems theory has brought a new perspective for managers to interpret patterns and events in the workplace. They recognize the various parts of the organization, and, in particular, the interrelations of the parts, *e.g.*, the coordination of central administration with its programmes, engineering with manufacturing, supervisors with workers, etc.

This is a major development. In the past, managers typically took one part and focused on that. Then they moved all attention to another part. The problem was that an organization could, *e.g.*, have a wonderful central administration and wonderful set of teachers, but the departments didn't synchronize at all.

CHAOS THEORY

As chaotic and random as world events seem today, they seem as chaotic in organizations, too. Yet for decades, managers have acted on the basis that organizational events can always be controlled. A new theory (or some say "science"), chaos theory, recognizes that events indeed are rarely controlled. Many chaos theorists (as do systems theorists) refer to biological systems when explaining their theory. They suggest that systems naturally go to more complexity, and as they do so, these systems become more volatile (or susceptible to cataclysmic events) and must expend more energy to maintain that complexity.

As they expend more energy, they seek more structure to maintain stability. This trend continues until the system splits, combines with another complex system or falls apart entirely. Sound familiar? This trend is what many see as the trend in life, in organizations and the world in general.

PROBABILITY AND OPERATION

The theory of probability is the branch of mathematics which is most useful in operations research. Nearly all results of operations of hotels involve elements of chance, usually to a large extent, so that only when the results of a number of similar operations are examined does any regularity evidence itself. It is nearly as important to know the degree by which individual operations may differ from some expected average, as it is to know how the average depends on the variables involved. In analysing operational data, which are often meager and fragmentary, it is necessary to be able to estimate how likely it is that the next operations will display characteristics similar to those analysed Probability enters into many analytical problems as well as all the statistical problems.

In many situations the system of causes which lead to particular results is so complex that it is impossible, or at least impracticable, to predict exactly which of a number of possible results will arise from a given cause. If a penny is tossed, it is possible in principle to analyse the forces acting on the penny and the motions they produce, and so to predict whether the penny will come to rest with heads or tails showing; however, no one has ever taken the effort to carry out the analysis. When a gun is fired at a target, it should again be possible to predict exactly where the shell will hit, but the prediction would involve a knowledge of the characteristics of the gun, shell, propellant, and atmosphere far more exact than has yet been obtained.

With a perfect penny, tossed at random, there is no more reason to expect heads than tails to appear. We say then that heads and tails are equally likely to appear. In throwing a symmetrical die the numbers 1, 2, 3, 4, 5, and 0 are equally likely. This notion of equal likelihood is basic to the theory of probability. It does not seem to be possible to give it an exact definition, but we accept it as a self-evident intuitive concept At times we reach the conclusion that results are equally likely from considerations of symmetry. In other cases the conclusion is made on the basis of past experience

THE FEASIBILITY STUDY

When the developer selects a site, a feasibility study is

often commissioned to obtain an analysis of the site by an objective third party. Companies offer hotel feasibility studies for a fee and are experts in a particular market, or developers may use the consulting group of one of the major public accounting firms. The company retained to do the feasibility study can spend up to several months gathering detailed data to see if, in their opinion, it makes economic sense to build the hotel. Their conclusion offers an objective third party opinion as to whether the project is feasible, hence the term feasibility study. Generally, the feasibility study considers, evaluates, and makes recommendations about the project based on the following variables:

The Site

- Proper zoning
- Size in square feet/acres
- Visibility from arterials/freeways
- Traffic counts/patterns
- Accessibility from streets, freeways, airports, train stations, etc.
- Proximity to where potential guests live, travel, or work
- Barriers that discourage competition coming into the market, if any
- How adjacent property and businesses are utilized
- Master area development plans
- Local permitting process and the degree of difficulty for that particular city
- Impact fees charged by the city

The Economy of the Area

- Major employers, government agencies
- Business trends for each employer/agency
- Hotel needs and the demand for each
- Leisure travel demand in the area
- Nearby tourist attractions
- Visitor counts
- Conventions, trade shows, and meetings history

The Hotel Market

- The competitors, both existing and planned
- Historical occupancy of hotels in the area
- Historical average rate
- Proprietary data on area travel

Identification of Which Hotel Market Segment to Serve

- Full service
- Limited service
- Extended stay
- Luxury
- Midprice
- Economy
- Budget

Selection of Appropriate Hotel Design

- High-rise
- Midrise
- Garden apartment style
- Hybrid design

Selection of Appropriate Hotel Brand

- Franchised (Marriott, Sheraton, Hyatt, etc.)
- Licensed (Best Western, Guest Suites, etc.)
- Independent
- Independent with strategic market affiliation (Luxury Hotels of America, Historic Hotels of America, etc.)

Ten-year Projection

- Occupancy projection by year
- ADR by year
- Estimated cash generated for debt
- Estimated cash generated for distribution to investors
- Estimated cash-on-cash return (after-tax income divided by equity invested)
- Overall projected yield
- Projected internal rate of return

- Net present value of the project over each of the next ten years. Once the feasibility study is completed, the developer is prepared to move forward with the project. Often, at this stage of the process, the developer purchases an option on the land to tie it up until the remaining development steps can be completed—and to prevent the competition from purchasing it.

CREATION OF THE OWNERSHIP ENTITY

An ownership entity (note that this is different than and separate from the development company) must be created to hold title to the land—and the hotel, once it's built. Considering the limitation of liability to the investors, tax consequences, estate implications for the investors, and potential requirements of the mortgage lender, a business structure is selected, normally in one of the following forms:

- Limited liability company (LLC)
- Limited partnership (LP)
- S corporation

THE DEVELOPMENT AGREEMENT

The newly formed entity now enters into a development contract with the development company to take the project to completion. The development company charges a fee, approximately 3 per cent of the total project cost, for this service.

The agreement generally covers such variables as:

- Selection of architect/engineers
- Selection and supervision of a general contractor
- Processing all building and occupancy permits
- Raising all the equity money from investors
- Securing a construction mortgage loan
- Selecting a franchise company
- Securing the franchise
- Selecting an interior designer that meets franchise company requirements
- Purchasing all opening furniture, fixtures, equipment

- Selecting a management company to operate the hotel
- Liability for cost overruns.

SELECTING A FRANCHISE

Depending on the type of hotel to be built (based on the feasibility study), the developer recommends a franchise company to the hotel owner. A major consideration is the best franchise brand for the market segment to be served. Each franchise company has differ franchise fees, royalty fees, and marketing/miscellaneous fees as part of its agreement structure with the operating company.

Consideration must also be given to the brands already represented in the target market that may be available for franchise. The franchise company is approached and a franchise is requested, with the feasibility study offered as backup for the request. The next step is for the franchise company to conduct an impact study of the market.

This considers such matters as possible negative impact on existing hotels that carry the franchiser's flag. If the impact is judged to be insignificant, a franchise is usually granted to the ownership entity for a one-time fee of about $400 per room, depending on the franchise selected, with continuing royalty and marketing, usually based on a percentage of hotel revenue.

SELECTING AN ARCHITECT

Because the final product of this process is a building the operator has to run as a hotel, the architect's experience in designing hotels, his or her experience with the prototypical drawings of the franchise selected, the fee, and his or her on-time record must be considered. Architect fees can run up to 5 per cent of the total project cost but are often negotiated down, if the project is big enough.

The firm's experience and record on similar projects are critical. The architect does not have to operate the hotel when it is completed. The developer wants the architect to design a hotel that will be easy to operate and maintain. Major consideration are the quality and reliability record of the general contractor and the firm's use of and relationships with the many subcontractors needed for a project as complex as a hotel. Again, experience in building the hotel type is important. It is hoped that the general contractor has learned from any mistakes made in building similar hotels. The general contractor and architect often bid the project as a team; this helps the developer determine the final cost. Often, up to a 10 per cent contingency cost that allows for unforeseen circumstances is built into the project bidding process.

FINANCING THE PROJECT

The following variables must be determined to qualify for financing:

- The cost of the land
- Design and construction cost of the building
- The cost of furniture, fixtures, equipment, and opening supplies
- Pre-opening marketing and labour costs
- A six-month operating capital cash reserve.

The sum of these constitutes the total cost of the project for purposes of securing financing. With this information, the ten-year operating pro forma budget is updated to reflect actual costs. It's now time to go to the money markets for construction financing. The terms and conditions of a construction loan can vary widely depending on the individual lender.

Important terms that can affect the cost of the loan include:

- Personal guarantees by developers and/or equity partners/investors
- Loan origination fees
- Interest rate
- Required loan-to-value ratio
- Terms of repayment
- A requirement that interest/taxes be held in reserve
- Required debt service coverage ratios
- Length of the construction loan; length and costs of extensions.

These are only a few of the considerations that must be analysed when selecting a lender. The developer, on behalf of the owning entity, then approaches a number of lending institutions. The lending institutions analyse the deal and offer a proposed term sheet that answers all of the borrowers' questions. This allows the borrowers to select the lending institution with which they wish to work. The lender then commissions an appraisal of the project by an independent appraisal company such as Hospitality Valuation Services (HVS). Based on the appraisal, the lender issues a loan commitment for the project that usually offers up to 60 per cent of the project cost. The balance must be raised as equity from investors.

RAISING THE EQUITY INVESTMENT FUNDS

With the bank committed to about 60 per cent of the cost, the remaining 40 per cent must be raised in equity commitments by investors. To pursue these, the developer prepares an offering solicitation document that meets current securities and exchange law.

The nature of this document depends on the type of business entity that was formed. For limited partnerships or limited liability companies, a private placement offering circular and project description is prepared. For S or C corporations, stock offerings are prepared for sale consistent with applicable federal and state securities laws. The developer now contacts money sources that have risk capital available to invest.

These can include:

- Individual investors
- Private asset managers
- Opportunity fund managers
- Venture capital fund managers

These potential investment sources are offered the opportunity to invest in the hotel. Based on their study and evaluation of the reports, documents, they decide whether or not to offer funding to the developer. Once the loan is secured, the equity raised, and the building permit issued by the city, the land purchase option is exercised and the purchase is completed. Then the 12–16- month construction process begins.

If the architect's plans work as intended, if the general contractor has no problems with subcontractors, unions, or permits, if all the furnishings, fixtures, and equipment arrive on time, if the weather cooperates, and if the employment market is such that human resources are sufficient to open a hotel, then congratulations! The hotel will open on time.

SELECTING THE MANAGEMENT COMPANY

Often even before the construction activity commences, the owning entity selects an appropriate management company to manage the pre-opening, marketing and sales, selection and training of the opening staff, preparation of the operating budget, and day-to-day operations once the hotel is opened. Management companies charge 3–5 per cent of revenue for this service. In recent years, management companies have charged 3–4 per cent of revenue and 2–3 per cent of gross operating profit so they can be measured and evaluated on both sales and profitability.

The franchise company may offer to provide management services to franchisees. Marriott International, Inc., for example, manages about 50 per cent of all hotels that carry the Marriott flag under 20-year contracts. Independent management companies manage the remaining hotels under long-term management contracts of up to ten years' duration, often with several five-year renewal options.

This is a largely linear explanation of the complicated process that a developer goes through in order to create a hotel. It has been described in a step-by-step process, but in reality, many of the steps are carried out concurrently to save time (and money). Nevertheless, the hotel development process takes about three years from original conception to first guest. It is important to remember that during the initial stages of the process, the developer can have as much as $1 million (U.S.) or more at risk in the process before a final go/no-go decision is reached.

Only after the project is approved and all financing is in place can the developer start to recover upfront costs and collect development fees. Hotel development with its component parts of hotel feasibility studies, hotel appraisal, hotel real estate finance, and hotel management are all among the career opportunities available to hotel and restaurant administration graduates.

EXTENDED-STAY HOTEL DEVELOPMENT PROJECT

The City Development Commission in a Pacific Northwest community purchased a 1.55- acre parcel of riverfront land in the downtown area. The land was previously contaminated with industrial pollutants that made the parcel unsafe for habitation and construction. The City Development Commission used state, local, and federal grants to have the land decontaminated, created a master plan for the area, and then offered the parcel for sale and development. The City Development Commission issued a request for proposal (RFP) that outlined the asking price of $2,076,240 ($30/sq. ft.) for the land and the design requirements set down by the Commission for a building that would fit the intended look and feel of the area. The RFP was sent to many major hotel companies and commercial real estate brokers, asking prospective buyers to submit a purchase price bid along with a statement of the buyer's development history and ability to develop a hotel of the type envisioned by the Commission.

It listed a closing date by which all bids had to be submitted. An area commercial real estate broker contacted a hotel development and management company with a long history of developing and managing extended-stay hotels in the Pacific Northwest, including a property located in a similar setting to that being offered for sale. The commercial realtor offered to represent the developer in negotiations with the City Development Commission, which would be paying the real estate commission on the sale.

An agreement was reached with the commercial real estate broker to represent the buyer to the seller, and the developer went to work in preparing a proposal. The developer conducted a feasibility study to see all of the conditions in the marketplace that would be encouraging or discouraging to this development project. Studies were conducted to estimate how many room-nights were being sold within a five-mile radius, how many extended-stay room-nights were available in the market, how many hotel rooms existed, and how many were being planned over the following five years. From this, the developer was able to estimate the number of extended-stay room-nights available needed to produce an 82 per cent occupancy with an average daily room rate of $141 when the hotel achieved stabilization three years after opening. That provided the basis for a ten-year revenue estimate.

The developer proposed a nine-floor, 258- suite extended-stay hotel with an indoor pool, spa, and exercise facility, a guest laundry, offices, meeting facilities, and a three-floor parking garage with parking for 193 automobiles, all at a total cost of $38 million, or $147,286 per suite. The $38 million construction budget was broken down as follows: Land 6.0% Construction 66.0% Office Equipment 1.4% Furniture, Fixtures, Equipment 7.4% Architecture/Engineering 2.8% Permits/Fees/ Environmental 2.8% Appraisal/Legal/Tax/Insurance 1.3% Pre-Opening Expenses 1.3% Construction Loan Fee 1.1% Developer Fee 2.8% Construction Interest 2.8% Working Capital 2.1% Contingency 2.2% Total 100% The opening date for the hotel was projected at 27 months from the date of proposal acceptance.

The City Development Commission awarded the project to the developer, and work began. First, an ownership limited liability company (LLC) was formed as the ownership entity that would hold title to the hotel. The LLC, in turn, entered into a development and construction management agreement with the development company to manage the arrangements for financing and construction of the hotel.

The developer, as agent for the ownership LLC, also entered into a hotel management contract with a management company to manage the pre-opening marketing, preopening hiring and training, and the day-to- day operation of the hotel once it was opened. The arrangements called for the management company to be paid 3 per cent of revenue and 2 per cent of the net operating income for management services.

The ownership LLC then contacted a major hotel company and applied for a franchise to allow the development and operation of an extended-stay hotel. A 20-year franchise was granted with a fee of $400 per suite or, $102,800. This was to be followed by a 5 per cent royalty and a 3 per cent advertising fee once the hotel was open and operating.

The developer, acting as agent for the owner, prepared a private placement memorandum document seeking investments from accredited investors. These investors were primarily defined as people with a net worth of $1 million, or those with an income in excess of $200,000 over the previous two years and expecting an income in excess of $200,000 in the current year. (*Note:* Additional entities may also be defined as accredited investors by the Securities and Exchange Commission.)

The private placement memorandum offered $100,000 units of ownership to accredited investors, guaranteeing a 9 per cent priority return on the investment and a combined 50 per cent ownership in the hotel. A group of initial investors retained the other 50 per cent in exchange for putting the project together. This effort was successful in raising 40 per cent of the total cost of the hotel in anticipation that a lender would provide the remaining 60 per cent in the form of a construction loan. In addition to the priority return, investors could expect to participate in any future capital gain realised should the hotel be sold.

The development company, continuing to function as agent for the owner, then sought a commercial bank to provide three year construction financing for the project or 60 per cent, of the $38 million development cost was to be borrowed; only major banks were considered as prospective lenders. The size of the construction loan was above the lending limits of most small regional banks.

After a preconstruction appraisal by a third-party appraisal firm chosen by the lender confirmed the value at $38 million upon completion of construction, and for an origination fee of $400,000, a three-year construction loan was secured. The terms allowed the developer, as agent for the owner, to draw down the loan every 30 days after providing proof that funds had been properly disbursed in the construction process. The loan documents set an interest rate and also required that the ownership LLC seek a permanent mortgage prior to the three-year expiration date on the construction loan. The development company then negotiated with and selected a general contractor with significant hotel construction experience who acted on behalf of the developer, as agent for the owner.

The general contractor then selected design-build subcontractors and an interior designer to select colours, fabrics, furniture, fixtures, and equipment to meet the hotel franchise design requirements. Building permits were applied for, and the building design was presented to the City Development Commission for its approval, along with other groups with a stake in the appearance of the finished building in relation to the area and neighbourhood. With all of these approvals in place, construction commenced, and the hotel opened two years later.

Three years after the hotel opened, the ownership LLC had the obligation to secure permanent financing on the hotel to replace the construction loan. The September 11, 2001, terrorist attacks on the World Trade Centre and the Pentagon slowed travel throughout the United States. As a result, the hotel did not achieve the projected occupancy or average daily rate during the three-year construction loan period. An appraisal that was primarily based on the hotel's trailing 12-month net operating income produced a value about $2 million below the original construction cost.

The bank that had provided the construction loan notified the owners that they did not wish to provide permanent financing under these circumstances. The owners were forced to conduct a search for a new mortgage bank. They were able to find a mortgage, but only after buying down the loan by $2 million to bring the loan-to-value ratio back to 40 per cent equity and a loan at 60 per cent of the appraised. This illustrates the risk that developers face when entering into a hotel project. However, as hotel values historically peak and decline on about a ten-year cycle, the owners look forward to the option of selling the hotel on the next peak, which will allow them to capture the original projected return through capital appreciation. Hotel development and ownership is a high-risk, high reward enterprise. Dramatic changes have affected the hotel industry over the past 30 years.

These changes have had a disproportionately high bearing on the independent hotel owner, who, in the face of increasing pressure from large, well funded chains, struggles to maintain independence and to compete on the basis of distinctive hospitality and character. Several organizations provide independent hotels and resorts with reservations and sales services.

As competition has evolved and intensified, some of these organizations have modified their structure and enhanced their services to meet the changing needs of independent hotels and competitive market dynamics. Today, independent hotels may choose from among more than 20 such organizations delivering varying degrees of competitive advantage and ownership independence.

A NEW MARKET MODEL

In the new millennium, the face of the global hospitality market continues to change at a rate never before seen. Four factors contribute to this rapidly changing environment:

- The broadening and diversification of the global consumer market. Both the demographic and psychographic characteristics of the global consumer market are growing and changing radically.
- The rapid advancement and availability of technology. This includes internal hotel operating systems, revenue management, direct-to-consumer communications and booking technology (Internet), marketing technology (customer databases), and telecommunications and automated sales systems that enable central sales offices to become revenue producers.
- The growth and importance of global brands.

Recognized brand names and brand attributes are important in reaching diverse customer segments and in creating customer loyalty.

- Consolidation of multiple brands under a single global management. The management and leveraging of multiple brands use similar technology platforms and shared sales and marketing infrastructures to consolidate and direct consumer demand. Some established ways of doing business— long-term, high-fee management contracts and franchises, a focus on traditional distribution channels, and traditional hospitality industry marketing techniques—are no longer effective in the new consumer-focused market. More and more hospitality marketing budgets are being directed towards technology enabled customer booking and communication; this shift away from traditional hospitality marketing techniques is expected to evolve over several years and involve millions of U.S. dollars in telecommunication, e-commerce, data warehousing, and one-to-one marketing investment.

The independent hotel or resort and many small branded management companies may not be able to fund this requirement. However, this shift will not affect all independent hotels and resorts simultaneously. The first wave of change will hit the global business and city hotel market. This is primarily because of brand competition and the fact that the business travel distribution network is more structured and driven by multinational corporations desiring lower and more predictable costs.

The second wave will affect the leisure market, and the changes could follow quickly. Leisure travel content, including packaging on the Internet, will increase rapidly as the presently fragmented leisure travel distribution network becomes more unified and efficient through consolidation. The emergence of e-commerce modes in the hospitality industry is not eliminating the intermediary and empowering the individual property, as once thought; instead, it is creating new, more powerful intermediaries. Some of these evolve from the hospitality industry, while others are opportunistic e-commerce companies.

MANAGEMENT COMPANIES AND FRANCHISES

In the 1970s, hotel chains continued to evolve as the need for capital to invest in additional properties restricted growth opportunities. This pressure bolstered the proliferation of the management contract, whereby the chain offers the hotel owner the rights to use its brand name and established facility and service standards as well as trained operations management and reservation and marketing services—for a significant fee, usually a percentage of gross sales. The pressure to grow also fostered the development of the franchise concept and franchise system in North America.

The franchise differs from the management contract in that the owner is responsible for operations, including meeting the franchise standards. The growth of management and franchise contracts has been remarkable, and today, according to a recent study, 75 per cent of the hotel rooms in North America are covered by some form of branded franchise or professional management agreement. These new business structures continued to threaten the traditional independent owner by accelerating the growth of the chains' share of the lodging market.

In response, the marketing/referral organizations formed in the 1960s began to offer a wider range of services. While these additional offerings leveraged linkages to the global distribution systems and led to strong relationships with travel agents, the consumer was largely ignored, and the organizations did little to generate consumer brand awareness. In the United States, strong consumer branded operators are attracting increasing amounts of capital to fund their growth at the expense of unbranded operators.

BRAND DEVELOPMENT

As the consumer market became more diverse and the hospitality product more segmented, branding became increasingly important. By the late 1980s, without a recognized brand affiliation or a close relationship with the lending community, owners/developers found it difficult to obtain permanent financing on a new hotel or resort. Lenders, believing that an established brand provided greater economies of scale and established infrastructure, opted for the lower-risk alternative.

In this brand-driven environment, the independent hotels' distinctive style and character became a competitive advantage, but only if they were able to meet recognized standards. As a result, the need for independent hotels to be associated with a clearly defined, trusted brand became more critical than ever. In the late 1990s, independent hotels, particularly those in Europe, began to face the daunting costs of upgrading their technological infrastructure and facilities to accommodate changing consumer needs.

Such upgrades as new property management systems, highspeed Internet access, two-line phones, inroom faxes, and leisure and health facilities became critical to maintaining competitiveness. When coupled with ever-increasing costs of consumer marketing, these costs put unprecedented strains on independent hotels' finances. As a result, these hotels became increasingly focused on leveraging greater returns from their reservation affiliation.

RESERVATION AFFILIATIONS

The relationship of independent hotels and resorts to reservation affiliations has been long and generally successful. These relationships operated best in a market environment that was stable, somewhat homogeneous in terms of demographic market segmentation, and where travel influencers played a dominant role in transient business, group, and leisure travel. Reservation affiliations are most effective in regional hospitality markets that do not have multiple brand competition and when the goals and objectives of the reservation organization are in alignment with the goals of the independent hotel owners. A contributing element to the attractiveness of reservation affiliations has always been the networking and camaraderie opportunities for the professional management at independent hotels. Reservation affiliations focus on traditional channels of distribution. Access to the Global Distribution Systems (GDS) is no longer a competitive advantage; the GDS is a universal pipeline. The new competitive playing field is proprietary distribution channels leveraged by consumer segmentation, e-commerce technology and partners, and innovative customer management programmes.

In the new technology-driven and consumer- empowered global market, the strength and effectiveness of reservation affiliations are challenged by new market and operating imperatives. The cost to compete against chains will grow exponentially. As competition intensifies, it is probable that local and regional maıket share at independent hotels and resorts will be drawn off by local and regional licensees of strong global brands.

Independent hotels, therefore, need to draw more national and international business to fill occupancy gaps. This requirement runs counter to the established business model and capabilities of reservation affiliations. The average room-night contribution of reservations companies to affiliated independent hotels is less than 5 per cent of available rooms.

At least four emerging factors are challenging the effectiveness of traditional reservation organizations:

1. The growing demographic and psychographic complexity of the global consumer market requires significant new expertise and resources in the area of segmentation and analysis.
2. The emergence of consumer direct-booking Internet technology requires significant new and ongoing investment.
3. The new marketplace requires innovative global brand management together with resources to establish and maintain a brand in the face of intense competition. To be competitive, a brand must attract new development and must therefore be strong enough to convince lenders to commit to permanent

financing. Brand management also includes loyalty programme management and the development of regional and global partners to strengthen and extend the effectiveness of the brand.

4. The corporate objectives and governance policies of traditional reservation organizations are influenced by the need to grow and meet shareholder profit requirements. These goals for growth can be at odds with the goals and expectations of independent hotel and resort members.

The traditional reservation affiliations must change not only their focus but also their structure if they want to succeed in this new competitive world. The traditional reservation organization must be prepared to respond to competitive challenges by expanding resources and skills necessary to increase average room-night contribution to affiliated independent hotels to 15 per cent—an average growth per member hotel of at least 200 per cent over present performance levels. In response to this competitive environment and the need for more cooperative and focused business relationships, a new hospitality business structure is evolving for all scales of hotels: the branded distribution company.

CHARACTERISTICS OF A BRANDED DISTRIBUTION COMPANY

The ideal branded distribution organization is a conventional equity company with ownership shared (in some cases) by the individual hotel owners, who have direct input into the corporation through an elected board of directors. This ownership structure creates a true operating partnership and a sharing of energies towards the common goal of creating value through increased brand awareness and room sales. Corporate profits must be adequate to maintain technical and managerial leadership and to support the shareholders' investment. Unlike a reservations and representation company, a branded distribution corporation owns and builds a branded distribution network asset that, in turn. The sole focus is performance for the affiliated independent hotels and resorts. Joining such an organization is appropriate for independently owned and managed hotels and resorts that want to keep owner control but require effective and low-cost distribution, global consumer brand awareness, and group purchasing benefits without the encumbrances and costs of a traditional hotel chain franchise or management contract. It promises the independent hotel awareness of, and access to, their target consumer and rapidly emerging technology through cooperative ownership.

BENEFITS OF A BRANDED DISTRIBUTION COMPANY

This new business structure is attractive from an owner's or a developer's standpoint for a number of reasons, including:

- *Costs:* First, it requires less up-front cash; second, ongoing fees and reservation commissions are significantly lower than with either a pure franchise or management agreement. For example, a 9 or 10 per cent franchise fee in many cases equals 50 per cent of gross profits.
- *Contract terms:* The terms are typically shorter, easier to negotiate, and allow for substantial owner control over the operation, style, and character of the hotel. As a result, conflicts can be avoided, and the branded distribution contract can be completed and signed in as few as 45 days.
- *Marketing:* It frees hotel management from the daunting and increasingly expensive task of acquiring profitable new customers and allows them to focus their attention and operating skills on the delivery of an exceptional hospitality experience.
- *Common objectives:* Both the owner and the branded distribution company enter into the agreement with the same primary objective: revenue.

The branded distribution company receives no revenue if it does not deliver to the hotel or resort. This shared goal strengthens and energizes the relationship between the two partners. From a branded distribution company's standpoint, this structure allows the brand to expand faster because capital is not used to subsidize additional construction or to support an older business model. Instead, funds are used to build and maintain an uptodate global distribution network and infrastructure composed of telecommunications, e-commerce functions, reservations software, data warehousing capability, and sales and marketing. The efficiency of the operation is assured by a focus that is almost entirely on the most important part of this business relationship— the generation of brand awareness and measurable room-night revenue for each affiliated hotel or resort. Unlike hard flags, which focus primarily on hotel operations and asset management such as the Marriott or the Westin, and reservation affiliations, which focus on professional camaraderie and traditional distribution channels such as the Best Western, the branded distribution company is primarily market focused; its full attention is on customer and travel influencer communication, relationship technology, and revenue streams.

In contrast, asset management, profitability, and operating efficiency are the major concerns of management companies, which tend to be public companies with stockholder expectations that must be met. It is often the case that strategic asset management concerns conflict with day-to-day tactical operating needs. This is evident in Marriott's recent move to separate its ownership and operating divisions, to the benefit of both. The same conflict can arise between the independent owners of a hotel property, who are focused on real estate concerns, and the management company they hire. Such misunderstandings can sour what should be a mutually supportive relationship.

The fact that management contract fees are charged and collected, even when the cash flow is negative, does not create owner confidence in the partner. A franchise relationship can cause a similar conflict and put a financial and operating burden on an owner. In contrast, participation of independent owner/operators as shareholders in a branded distribution company enables them to move beyond these concerns and focus on their operation and the consumer—the source of their revenue and the basis of their success.

Bibliography

Aikens: *Hospital Housekeeping,* Detroit Mich: D.T. Sutton, 2000.

Albert: *Equipment for Cafeterias, Lunch Rooms, Restaurants and Dining Rooms, Kitchen Equipment,* London: Waverly Book Company, 2003.

Ankomah, P.: *Education Tourism: A Strategy to Sustainable Tourism Development,* Philippines: Oxford University Press, 2006.

Baker: *The Query Book for Hotelmen and Caterers,* London: Practical Press, 2003.

Bradley: *Cooking for Profit; Catering and Food Service Management,* USA: American school of Chicago, 2001.

Bryan: *Furnishings and Equipment for Residence Halls,* New York: Teachers College Columbia University, 2006.

Carver: *Practical Catering: A Manual of Applied Dietetics for Schools, Institutions and Families,* London: Methuen Publication, 2000.

Charles, K.: *Progress in Tourism and Hospitality,* New Delhi: Oxford University Press, 2001.

Clarenbach: *Clarenbach's Hotel Accounting,* Chicago: Hotel Monthly Press, 2001.

Dahl, Robert: *The Efficient Maid in Hotels and Clubs,* United States: Stamford Connecticut, 2004.

Earle: *Stage-coach and Tavern Days,* London: Macmillan Publication, 2004.

Elliott: *Tea Room and Cafeteria Management,* Boston: Little Brown and Company, 2001.

Emery: *A Handbook of Industrial and Institutional Catering,* London: Bailliere Tindall and Company, 2003.

Gill: *Business Affairs for Institutional Management,* London: Macmillan Publication, 2004.

Hegarty, J.A.: *Ethics in Tourism and Hospitality Education,* Kolkata: Allied, 2004.

Hoke: *Restaurant Menu Planning,* New York: Harper & brothers Publication, 2003.

Jafari, J.: *Towards a Framework for Tourism Education,* Princeton: Princeton University Press, 1998.

Ketyer, E.: *Tourism Education in Formal Education,* New Delhi: Oxford University Press, 1998.

Lavery, P.: *Tourism Marketing and Management Handbook,* New York, Prentice Hall, 2002.

Moilliet, D.: *Hospitality Research Journal,* London: Macmillan, 2001.

Moscardo, G.: *The Journal of Tourism Studies,* New Delhi: Penguin Books, 2000.

Payne, K.: *Tourism and Hospitality Research,* Guwahati: United Publishers, 1998.

Shea, L. J.: *Journal of Hospitality and Tourism Education,* Kolkata: ICSP Publication, 2001.

Tao, H.: *The Development and Construction of Tourism Personnel,* London: Yale University Press, 2003.

Umbreit, T.: *The Role of Education in the Tourist Industry,* Salt Lake City: University of Utah, 2002.

Vukonic, B.: *Tourism as a Field of Research,* New Delhi: Oxford University Press, 2005.

Walle, A.H.: *Journal of Hospitality and Tourism Education,* New Delhi: Indian Institute of Public Administration, 2000.

Watson, J.: *Developing Tourism Managers,* New Delhi: Government of India Press, 2005.

Index